The Philosophy of Love, Sex,
and Relationships

The Philosophy of Love, Sex, and Relationships

An Introduction

Luke Brunning and Natasha McKeever

polity

First published in 2026 by Polity Press Ltd

Polity Press Ltd
65 Bridge Street
Cambridge CB2 1UR, UK

Polity Press Ltd
111 River Street
Hoboken, NJ 07030, USA

ISBN-13: 978-1-5095-5149-1
ISBN-13: 978-1-5095-5150-7 (pb)

A catalogue record for this book is available from the British Library.

Library of Congress Control Number: 2025933309

Typeset in 10.5 on 12 pt Times New Roman
by Fakenham Prepress Solutions, Fakenham, Norfolk NR21 8NL
Printed and bound in Great Britain by Ashford Colour Ltd

The publisher has used its best endeavours to ensure that the URLs for external websites referred to in this book are correct and active at the time of going to press. However, the publisher has no responsibility for the websites and can make no guarantee that a site will remain live or that the content is or will remain appropriate.

Every effort has been made to trace all copyright holders, but if any have been overlooked the publisher will be pleased to include any necessary credits in any subsequent reprint or edition.

For further information on Polity, visit our website:
politybooks.com

We would like to dedicate this book to Elwyn and Maya, who will be making sense of intimacy and relationships in their own ways in the years to come.

Contents

Acknowledgements

The team at Polity ensured the process of writing, editing, and publishing this book was smooth and supportive. Thank you to Ellen MacDonald-Kramer, Ian Malcolm, Nadine Smoczynski, and Leigh Mueller, as well as two anonymous reviewers who provided very useful feedback on the draft manuscript, and to Pascal Porcheron for commissioning the first version of this project five years ago.

We are grateful to everyone who commented on parts of the draft for us: Robbie Arrell, Danielle Bromwich, Sophie Goddard, Ruby Hornsby, Andy Kirton, Pilar Lopez-Cantero, Shaun Miller, and Margot Witte. Your input improved the book significantly.

We are also very grateful to IDEA: the Ethics Centre, and the School of Philosophy, Religion and History of Science, at the University of Leeds – for being so supportive of our research, and for encouraging and enabling us to set up the Centre for Love, Sex and Relationships. Special thanks here to Julian Dodd, Simon Kirchin, Jamie Dow, Heather Logue, Léa Salje, Graeme Gooday, Boluwatife Ajibola, and Ruby Hornsby. The events, discussions, collaborations, and teaching which this Centre have made possible were a key influence on this book.

Our students have been a constant source of inspiration and creativity. Discussions with you have encouraged us to think deeply and carefully about the topics we write about in this book, and we have tried to put together something that reflects your passions and approach.

Our work has also been shaped by the speakers at a number of events we have attended and organized, including: the 2024 Ethical Dating Online Workshop at the University of Leeds; the MANCEPT workshops we have organized over the past few years at the University of Manchester; the Leeds Love Month 2023 events; and the Society for Applied Philosophy conferences we have attended.

Finally, a special thanks to the Love Reading Group at Leeds. Our Friday chats helped us grapple with recent works in the philosophy of intimacy and – more importantly – are always so fun.

Natasha: Thank you to my family and friends, for all the kindness, warmth, and encouragement. A special thanks to my mum, Jasmine, my sisters, Charlotte and Izzy, and my partner's parents, Sue and Ian, for all your help looking after our daughter Maya over the past few years. Writing this book would have been much more difficult without your support. And finally, thanks to Tom and Maya – for everything.

Luke: although long in the planning, I first drafted my contribution to this book over a few weeks in the summer after my son Elwyn was born. Thank you to all sides of my family – to Laura, Rosie, Gary, Roz, Ali, Ryan, Gill, and Ian – for helping me keep body and mind together to have just enough energy spare to meet our deadline. The kindness and cooking of friends Danielle and David fuelled many of these pages. In everything, my deepest gratitude is to Jenny for your love and encouragement, and for years of wonderful conversations on these topics.

Introduction

Intimacy either matters to you, or it does not.

If it does, you've doubtless wondered how to find, understand, and nurture it. It if does not, you've doubtless wondered how to make sense of your preferences, fend off hostile remarks, and live authentically. Either way, intimacy is unavoidable and made an issue for us, by the people around us, our social institutions, and the state. Socially, we are expected to want relationships, to want sex, and to want them in a certain way. Our intimate interactions are usually among the most joyful, rich, and fulfilling aspects of our lives, but they are also often fraught with difficulty, and can leave us confused, contemplative, or unhappy.

The experiences of asexual people are a good example of how intimacy is made an issue. To some it may seem strange to begin a book about relationships, sex, and intimacy with people who do not experience sexual attraction, but we will see shortly that not only would such a view be mistaken on its own terms, but also attention to the experiences of asexual people forces us to tread carefully when thinking about all forms of intimacy. Even if their experiences are not as fraught as those of sexual minorities, most people will at one time find an aspect of their intimate life does not fit perfectly with social expectations. Perhaps you feel an unfamiliar attraction, or desire someone outside your relationship, or wish a friend could be more central to your life, or struggle with domesticity, or find yourself craving unconventional forms of sex.

'Asexual' is typically taken to describe people who experience little or no sexual attraction to others (Bogaert, 2015). We have an incomplete and emerging picture of how many people identify as asexual. Recent UK census data shows 0.06 per cent of the population registered as asexual, but scholars estimate the number is higher, perhaps between 1 and 6 percent of some populations (Przybylo, 2019, p. 13).

What is clear, however, is that asexual-identifying people seem the least satisfied of all LGBTA (Lesbian, Gay, Bisexual, Transgender, and Asexual/Aromantic/Agender/Allied) groups, in the UK at least (Benoit and Santos, 2023, p. 10). Reasons for this are numerous.

A recent Stonewall report notes lack of social understanding, fear of negative reactions, intrusive personal questions, and the continuous felt need for asexual people to justify themselves to others as key dimensions of this unhappiness (Benoit and Santos, 2023, pp. 10–11). Asexuality is rarely protected under equality legislation (with the current exception of local government in New York and Tasmania) and people can feel uncomfortable in working environments. In the UK, marriage can be voided on grounds of non-consummation, for example, which excludes some heterosexual asexual people who do not have sex from marital protections (interestingly, the consummation clause does not apply to same-sex couples in the UK ['Annul a marriage', no date]). Asexual people also find their orientation shapes the healthcare they receive, and how they engage with health providers, with the medicalization of their experiences being a common concern (Benoit and Santos, 2023, p. 21). What is especially troubling is the finding that, again in the UK at least, asexual people are the most likely of all sexual orientation groups to be recommended to undergo medical or psychological testing (Benoit and Santos, 2023, p. 21). Areas in which asexual people often face unwanted attention include their mental and reproductive health.

Asexuals often suffer 'hermeneutic injustice', which is the injustice of being unable to make sense of their experiences due to a lack of conceptual resources available in the social setting in which they live (Fricker, 2007, p. 155). Unwillingness to listen to asexual people, or attempts to deflect away from talk of identity and orientation towards talk of disorder, or hostility to asexual people organizing under LGBT banners, can all make it harder for asexual people to understand themselves. It is no wonder that the asexual community and campaigns for recognition emerged with some force in the internet age, and that community-led forms of organization and research continue to help asexual people resource themselves with the means of making sense of their lives (Teut, 2019).

Asexuals are also silenced when collective prejudice renders certain forms of speech or action ineffective (Langton, 1993; Mikkola, 2011). Attempts to turn down a sexualized overture or line of questioning on the grounds of asexuality, for example, are often just refused uptake entirely, and asexual people are at risk of physical violence and 'corrective rape' (Lund, 2021; Mollet and Black, 2021).

In recent decades, our collective understanding of asexuality, and other dimensions of human intimacy, has been changed by empirical and theoretical research; indeed, this area is a good example of how progress is possible in our study of human sexuality and intimate life.

Empirical research into sexuality is helping us understand the interactions between attraction, desire, arousal, and sexual activity (Diamond, 2008; Nagoski, 2015). We learn from asexual people that sexuality, the experience of desire, the focusing of the mind in fantasy, reasons for and the enjoyment of sex, are far more complex than lazy caricatures might suggest (Brotto and Yule, 2017; Yule, Brotto, and Gorzalka, 2017). Of particular practical relevance, for instance, is the idea that asexuality is different from (medicalized) disorders of sexual desire or arousal.

Philosophers and social theorists are also deepening our understanding of asexuality. One task is to consider the *implications* of empirical research for our theories of desire, or attraction. In previous work, for example, we argued that many existing philosophical accounts of desire fail to make space for the experiences of asexual people, and so we have reason to reject them (Brunning and McKeever, 2021). Another task is to better understand how sexuality is shaped by social norms, ideals, and institutions. The discomfort many asexual people face, for instance, is evidence of the grip of 'compulsory sexuality' – that is, 'the pervasive cultural assumption ... that everyone is defined by some kind of sexual attraction' (Emens, 2014, p. 306; Gupta, 2015), an assumption that intersects with 'amatonormativity': the idea that everyone is defined by a desire for amorous love, and that amorous love is central to a good life (Brake, 2012).

This research helps us disentangle the conflicting attitudes people have towards asexuality. The otherwise open-minded and progressive relationship commentator Dan Savage expressed the commonly held view that asexuality is a mere lack: 'You know, you've got the gays marching for the right to be cocksucking homosexuals, and then you have the asexuals marching for the right to – not do anything. Which is hilarious. Look, you didn't need to march for that right. You just need to stay home, and not do anything' (cited in Emens, 2014, p. 345).

Other people view asexuality as a strange and interesting predicament – one worthy of probing questions, sexualized interest, overfamiliarity, and attempts to cajole or change people.

Engagement with the asexual community, and new research, helps us appreciate that coming to know that someone is asexual tells us little. Can we infer they do not experience sexual desire or sexual arousal or sexual fantasies, or masturbate, or have partnered sex, or have kinks or fetishes, or enjoy being naked, or make porn, or find people beautiful and beguiling, or want romantic relationships or to have children, to share a home ...? We cannot. All we know is that they experience little or no sexual attraction to others. They might also experience other forms of attraction, such as aesthetic or sensual attraction (Przybylo, 2019, p. 5). Similar lessons apply to the other concepts and labels we use to make sense of sex, intimacy, and relationships. Human experiences of intimacy are complex, and diverse, and we have to guard against underlying assumptions and bias which limit our understanding.

Philosophy can help us to make sense of our intimate desires, interactions, and relationships. The tools of philosophy – analysis of the concepts we use, reflection on our ethical beliefs, and evaluation of our values and social norms, to name but a few – can help us understand why we think as we do, and whether things could be different. Indeed, in much of our perplexity about intimacy and relationships we are already asking philosophical questions, whether we know it or not. Some of our questions are moral questions, e.g. 'Is this kind of sex *wrong*?' Some are political questions, e.g. 'Is it *fair* that some people can access intimacy more easily than others?' Some are ontological questions, concerning the existence of things, e.g. 'What *is* a relationship?' Some are epistemological questions, e.g. 'How do we *know* when we are in love?'

Our aim in this book is not to impose philosophy on intimate life, but to show that our existing ways of reflecting on love, sex, and relationships – whether with friends and family, on social media, or in wider social settings – draw on philosophical ideas and themes. Our role is simply to make those ways of thinking salient, unearth some of our buried assumptions, present you with different ways of looking at what is familiar, and to test arguments with various objections.

We write this book as two philosophers who work primarily on the topics of love, sex, and relationships at the University of Leeds. To connect researchers and catalyse work in this area, we established the Centre for Love, Sex and Relationships (CLSR) in 2022, and it has been pleasing to see how many other philosophers are now starting to explore different facets of intimacy.

Why write a textbook when many good ones exist already? For instance, we love and return to these books:

Halwani, R. (2018). *Philosophy of Love, Sex, and Marriage: An Introduction*

Marino, P. (2019). *Philosophy of Sex and Love: An Opinionated Introduction*
McArthur, N. (2022b). *The Ethics of Sex: An Introduction*

We had several motivations in writing this one. First, we wanted to make it as accessible as possible, so anyone who is interested in the philosophy of love, sex, and relationships can find something of use – not just students and researchers. Second, we have tried to explore topics less central to those other texts, such as the ethics of online dating, flirting, ghosting, and alternative approaches to standard topics such as consent. Third, we have tried to focus on contemporary research as much as possible, giving you a snapshot of what philosophers are working on, right now. If you are interested in sex, love, and relationships, we suggest you read this book as complementing, not replacing, other texts.

We want to be upfront about what we have not covered, whether due to lack of space or lack of expertise. We have said little about the family, a hugely important source of intimate relationships to many people. And although we discuss friendship at various points in the book, we do not provide a detailed analysis of friendship. Among other topics not covered, we have also not included as much as we would like about transgender intimacy, or the intersection of disability and intimacy, or topics such as the state regulation of intimacy through marriage and immigration law, or laws around sex work.

These omissions should not be taken to imply these are unimportant topics, or that sexual and romantic intimacy is more valuable than other forms. Far from it. As a starting point for each of them we recommend:

Baron, T. and Cowley, C. (2024). *Philosophy of the Family: Ethics, Identity and Responsibility*
Vernon, M. (2005). *The Philosophy of Friendship*
Zurn, P., et al. (2024). *Trans Philosophy*
Shakespeare, T., et al. (1996). *The Sexual Politics of Disability*

A brief note on writing together. Although we took the lead on different chapters, the overall views expressed here are mutual unless we indicate otherwise.

The structure of the book is to loosely echo the intended trajectory many of us experience in grappling with intimacy – beginning, as it does, with general confusions around sexuality and attraction, moving to our efforts to find partners, date them, have sex together, fall in love, commit to them, and think about the future.

Chapter 1: Attraction, intimacy, labels

In chapter 1, we consider some of the preoccupations that often grip us before we have our first major relationships. How are we to make sense of what sex and intimacy are, and does it matter whether we have an answer? What, if anything, are sexual orientations? We finish the chapter with a discussion of attraction and types. How do patterns of attraction shape society, can we be responsible for them, how might we change them?

Chapter 2: Finding someone

Chapter 2 explores how we find someone to love, date, or be a sexual partner. We focus on dating apps, since they are widely used, philosophically under-explored, and raise many ethical and social issues. We explore some of these issues, from safety to gamification or authenticity, and consider ways to respond to them. What can apps, the state, and individuals do to make finding someone a better process for everyone?

Chapter 3: Dating

Chapter 3 explores dating, another under-researched area in philosophy. The chapter begins with the question 'What *is* dating?' and a discussion of different ways that we might date, which we call 'compatibility dating' and 'erotic dating'. We move to consider flirting, an activity central to lots of dating. What does it mean to flirt? Can we flirt more or less virtuously? Finally, we look at ways in which we move on from dating, with a focus on 'ghosting' – leaving an interaction or relationship by cutting off communication without explanation. Do we have similar obligations in these cases to cases of ordinary relationship break-ups?

Chapter 4: Intimate ethics

Some of the ethical aspects of sex and intimacy are the focus of chapter 4. We start by asking what consent is and how central it is to intimate ethics. Then we explore some forms of bad but consensual intimacy, and ask how we might remedy them. We finish by exploring the place of sex in a good life, considering the ideas of chastity and sexual integrity, and thinking about intimate ethics in general.

Chapter 5: Romantic love

The term 'romantic love' gets used in different ways, which makes it hard for us to orient ourselves towards the concept. We start chapter 5 by mapping out some of these usages, and by describing how romantic love is typically held to differ from other kinds of love. We then move to consider what *kind* of phenomenon romantic love actually is – a biological response, an emotion, a syndrome? Finally, we ask how we might justify loving one person over another, exploring whether love is arational or rational – and if it is rational, whether it is a response to the properties of the beloved, or the relationship shared with them.

Chapter 6: Romantic relationships

Romantic relationships warrant a chapter of their own. Although relationship diversity is increasingly tolerated, most romantic relationships take the form of a monogamous committed heterosexual couple. But should relationships be monogamous? What are the benefits and harms of both monogamy and nonmonogamy? We grapple with these questions before considering the nature of commitment, and asking whether we can, and should, commit to loving, or to staying with, someone. We finish the chapter by outlining some feminist critiques of romantic relationships, focusing on problematic gender norms around dating and marriage, and gendered inequalities in relationships.

Chapter 7: The future of intimacy

Finally, we ask how relationships might change in the near future, and consider some of the ethical challenges of the next few decades. We have three points of focus: (1) the potential of love and sex robots to create new intimacies and change human–human intimacy; (2) so-called 'love drugs', existing and hypothetical, which promise to improve our relationships but also raise questions of authenticity or justice; and (3) social changes and new relational possibilities, such as (a) relationship anarchy, (b) plural marriage, and (c) abolition of the family.

We finish the book with a brief conclusion and by providing some further questions for readers to consider.

1

Attraction, Intimacy, Labels

1. Introduction

The later years of school are a confusing time of self-exploration. Even before our first significant relationships, it starts to matter deeply how we describe and label who we are and what we do, especially in connection to intimacy. Sex slowly slides into focus as classmates start talking about who is, or is not, doing 'it'. But quite what sex looks like, or involves, is not always clear. Our desires and preferences may similarly be confusing. There is the matter of naming and organizing: how best to organize the tangled mess of our crushes, interests, and aversions? Then there are questions of control and value: are we responsible for our attractions, and are some of them more appropriate than others?

These questions can persist through life. New experiences can prompt us to re-examine our attractions, desires, and sense of identity. Falling in love, starting relationships, making commitments are no guarantee that we will not have to ask these questions again. This chapter explores some of these topics from the perspective of contemporary philosophy. We ask what sex is, what orientations are, and whether we have responsibility for our attractions. Running through these discussions is the important question of to what extent, if any, answers to these questions actually matter. In school, these issues can feel monumentally significant, but it remains possible that our anxieties fail to track the best ways to make sense of human intimacy.

2. Intimacy

a. Are we doing it?

If you're sexually active, when did you last have sex?

For some of you, answering this question is easy. It was recent, and memorable. Others of you have to try harder to remember when, exactly, your last encounter was. For most people, however, this question is one of *time*. We rarely stop to ask what sex is, itself. But when we compare notes or examples, this second sense of the 'when did you last have sex' question can become salient.

To see this, consider how straight and queer people might approach the question differently. In her influential and widely reprinted essay 'Are we having sex now or what?', Greta Christina notes that it became harder for her to keep updating her list of sexual partners once she started sleeping with women:

> between women, no one method has a centuries-old tradition of being the one that counts. even when we do fuck each other there's no dick, so you don't get that feeling of this is what's important we are now having sex, objectively speaking, and all that other stuff is just foreplay or afterplay. so when I started having sex with women, the binary system had to go, in favor of a more inclusive definition. (Christina, 2006)

The traditional method of working out whether sex had taken place was to see if a penis had been inside a vagina. (And even that is vague. How far in, for how long – is orgasm necessary?) Once penises are no longer involved, other criteria have to suffice. But if other criteria are valid, Christina notes, then cases of intimacy between her and men which may not involve penetration might also count as sex, on grounds of consistency, and so her initial confidence about whom she has had sex with is thrown into doubt.

Christina's essay amplifies the confusion around defining sex in other ways. There seems to be a difference between 'being sexual' as she puts it, and having sex; sex does not always appear to involve genital contact; some sex is not enjoyed or particularly wanted; and so on. We can continue this game by grappling with examples. Who is having sex with whom here?

- Dom and Jeff kiss and stroke each other, but neither of them orgasms

- David stimulates Amy with a vibrator, she orgasms
- Mary, who is asexual, has sex with Rosa who is allosexual (i.e. experiences sexual attraction)
- Max gives an unknown man a blowjob through a gloryhole
- Kaz holds and kisses Jane while she's fisted at a sex party by Sophie
- Dr Raul gives a prostate exam to Axel, who has an unexpected orgasm
- Rachel masturbates on a FaceTime call to Chris while thinking about Carl, while Carl is masturbating on a FaceTime call to Sandra while thinking about Rachel
- In England Rob uses his Wi-Fi-connected sex toy to bring Eve to orgasm in Australia via her Wi-Fi-connected sex toy (Arrell, 2022)

It will be difficult to sort these examples systematically. Does Rachel have sex, for example, and, if so, does she have sex with Chris, Carl, or both? Can it be true that Rob and Eve have sex together despite being on opposite sides of the earth? (If not, then what happened?)

Some forms of sexual intimacy involve orgasm, some do not; some people are sexually attracted to each other, others not; some sex takes place between people who know each other, or can see each other, other sex does not; some sex is between couples, other sex is not; some sex involves attention to, or intentional directedness towards, the person in front of you, other sex does not; sex may not even require people to be in the same room, or even the same country.

These difficulties suggest we will struggle to find necessary and sufficient conditions for sex. This is the view of Kristina Gupta who notes there are issues with each of four possible routes to a definition: a *biological* definition; an *extensional* definition based on a 'list' of what we call sex; isolating our social *normative* definition of sex; and building on our *personal* sense of what sex is (Gupta, 2022). Empirical studies show great variance in what people call sex, both within and between societies and specific communities. Queer people, for example, often have an expansive understanding of sex and sexual agency, and downplay the centrality of penetration (Gupta, 2022, p. 12).

That said, some people are more confident about what sex is *not*. Greta Christina, for example, is adamant that the only aspect of the 'What is sex?' question where they find solid ground is 'if there's no consent, it ain't sex' (Christina, 2006). On this view, shared also by the UK charity Rape Crisis, rape cannot be sex. Full consideration of this complex topic would require a detour into thinking about consent, unwanted sex, sexual 'grey areas', and sexual assault (Cahill, 2016b; Gavey, 2018). It is worth noting, however, that some people might want to retain the idea that rape is sex in order to explain why rape is so morally wrong, perhaps by taking the line that sex is particularly special, or involves heightened vulnerability, such that forced sex is horrific.

This example highlights a broader practical point: any definition of sex has social consequences. Certain behaviours receive the attention of lawmakers, doctors, educators, and parents because they are viewed as sex, whereas others do not. Queer adolescents, for example, whose preferred intimacy may not always be socially understood as sex, may struggle to receive the protection, care, or education that would help them flourish.

Pessimism about settling on a clear definition of sex, coupled with awareness of the social stakes here, motivate different strategies: (1) to abandon the search for a definition; or (2) to adopt a definition which works for us. Gupta favours the latter approach. She suggests 'societies should adopt definitions of sex that are flexible and do not rank penetrative intercourse as better or more "sex-like" than other forms of sexual activity' (Gupta, 2022, pp. 16–17). But Gupta's remark can be understood in two ways. One would be to adopt a pluralist approach, where our social understanding of 'sex' is akin to that of loose and overlapping concepts such as 'game'.

But another way of developing what Gupta is suggesting would be to borrow strategies from the philosophy of gender, particularly the work of Sally Haslanger and other feminist scholars, and shift away from a broadly *descriptive* approach to definitions of sex to develop a so-called *ameliorative* approach instead (Haslanger, 2012; Jenkins, 2016).

Ameliorative approaches to concepts are aimed at addressing existing social problems or injustices. Given a particular problem or goal, they ask, 'How can we best understand our target concept to achieve this goal, or solve this problem?' Ameliorative approaches to gender, for example, might want to understand the concept of gender in a way that would eliminate oppression, even if this is not how we (all) currently understand gender.

An ameliorative approach to sex, then, would be motivated by concerns about the social impact of a heterosexual, penetrative, dyadic, understanding of sex and suggest we need to develop a concept of sex which would correct sexual marginalization. This differs from the first interpretation of Gupta's remark because the definition might not be pluralist. We might have other demands of our definition, such that it is workable within legal frameworks or helps us capture the breadth of sexual abuse and assault.

Settling these matters is not straightforward. Ameliorative strategies are controversial, and even if we favour them, it can be hard to resist our tendency to view concepts in essentialist ways (Ritchie, 2021). But it is aways an option to pair the abstract question 'What is sex?' with the practical question 'Why does this matter?'

The more we think about sex, the harder it seems to define, and the less central penises, procreation, sexual attraction seem to be. We might be tempted, therefore, to shift focus away from sex and towards a concept such as *intimacy*.

b. In the zone

We use terms like 'intimacy' and 'intimate' to describe many different kinds of relationship, not just sexual relationships. Friendships, family life, even collegial life, can be intimate in different ways, as can various kinds of care work and teaching. But what is intimacy?

This is a difficult question to answer. Broadly speaking, we can distinguish between views which centre on relationships and those which look elsewhere. In doing so, we are following Jasmine Gunkel, who recently developed a nuanced account of intimacy (Gunkel, 2024).

For Gunkel, on the relationship view of intimacy, 'an act is intimate in virtue of its being performed in certain types of relationships, or from motivations which arise in those relationships' (Gunkel, 2024, p. 426). She focuses on the idea that liking, caring, or loving are characteristic motivations within relationships (a view held by Julia Inness (Inness, 1996)) or that relationships entwine lives in meaningful ways. On a relationship view, X is intimate because X stems from this sense of liking, care, or love, or because X is a consequence of this entwinement.

The relationship account of intimacy seems right initially. Jane's kiss with Jim is intimate since she loves Jim, or their cohabitation becomes more intimate as their habits become visible in the unguarded time they share. This view helps us explain why some forms of sexual behaviour are intimate, and others not, and may also help us capture why some non-sexual or non-romantic forms of human relating are also intimate, such as relationships between parents and children.

Gunkel rejects the relationship account of intimacy in favour of her 'intimate zones' account. The obvious problem is that we seem to be able to be intimate with people we have little to no relationship with, like strangers who help us at moments of great distress, or with whom we share a secret. Appealing to positive attitudes of liking or care also rules out forms of intimacy motivated by money, such as work in care homes or various kinds of sex work, and does not seem to capture horrific cases of weaponized intimacy (in torture) or forced intimacy (forced pregnancy). As well as failing to track our sense of *which* things are intimate, Gunkel thinks relationship accounts of intimacy fail to explain *why* things are intimate.

On Gunkel's 'intimate zones' account of intimacy,

> Certain zones of persons are intimate. Intimate acts are acts that expose intimate zones. Intimate relationships are relationships in which, through intimate acts, there is sufficient exposure of intimate zones. (Gunkel, 2024, p. 427)

An intimate zone is an aspect of ourselves we are disposed to hide, which helps explain how we view ourselves, and which 'renders [us] specially vulnerable' (Gunkel, 2024, p. 430).

Digging a bit deeper, Gunkel suggests an intimate zone is a feature of us which satisfies two specific conditions: the *hiddenness* condition, and the *importance* condition. A feature of us is intimate if we are disposed to hide it because it matters to us. (This is how we interpret Gunkel, but we can also imagine cases where one set of reasons explains why something is important (e.g. our religion informs our identity), and an unrelated set of reasons explains why we are disposed to hide it (e.g. our religion is banned by the state). We assume Gunkel has in mind cases where there is a connection between importance and hiddenness.)

Hiddenness plays an important role here. A feature must be one we are disposed to hide from people and one we would feel 'psychological discomfort' about if it was exposed, e.g. by experiencing shame (Gunkel, 2024, p. 438). The disposition to hide must be personal: not present because we fear legal or social consequences. For example, we might want to avoid exposure of our bodies, even if this was legal; or disclosure of our youthful transgressions, even if we would remain respected. Appeals to dispositions here show this condition will often be idiosyncratic since we will be disposed to hide different things, but there may be things most people are disposed to hide, such as parts of the body.

Being disposed to hide some feature of us is not sufficient to constitute an intimate zone, because we often hide things which are not connected to our identity (e.g. passwords). This is why the importantness condition matters; the feature we are disposed to hide has to matter too. Gunkel has a specific sense of mattering in mind: 'A feature X of a person is Important if and only if that person believes, fears, or worries that X reveals a facet of their identity' (Gunkel, 2024, p. 443). This aligns Gunkel's view with philosophers such as Krista Thomason who suggest our experiences of shame are tied closely to the control we seek to exert over the parts of our identities which other people can see (Thomason, 2018).

The intimate zone account promises to tie together seemingly disparate acts that we are prone to call intimate, from sharing a secret with a stranger to having sex with a long-term partner. The generality of her account, and the subjective aspects of the two conditions, mean the account can accommodate different approaches to intimacy, and the account does not privilege sexuality as a source of intimacy.

That said, here are some aspects of Gunkel's view which help tease out some further dimensions of intimate life. First, notice how her account rests on the concept of *vulnerability*, since that lies at the heart of the hiddenness condition. But what it is to be vulnerable is itself disputed. Philosophical discussion of vulnerability is under-developed and the relationships between being vulnerable, being intimate, and being dependent need unpacking (Whitney, 2011; Dodds, 2013; McKenzie, Rogers, and Dodds, 2013; Garrau and Laborde, 2015; Tsai, 2016).

Vulnerability can mean something like a propensity to be physically hurt but also a propensity to be *pained* by an experience of nakedness, or shame, or loneliness. Some vulnerability seems to emerge only when we have interpersonal relationships (Tsai, 2016, p. 175).

Philosophers also disagree about whether intimacy and vulnerability are two sides of the same coin. Some think to be intimate *just is* to be vulnerable. Anca Gheaus suggests, for instance, that 'vulnerability to emotional harm in relation to an individual, i.e. their power to inflict such harm with impunity, is part and parcel of what it means to be intimate' (Gheaus, 2024, p. 31). Others, including James Humphries, think that 'the mere fact that relationships may cause pain does not render us (relevantly) vulnerable, because – given the kinds of creatures that humans are – we are at risk of pain or suffering in indefinitely many activities' (Humphries, 2018, p. 410). Clearly, we cannot reach for the notion of vulnerability without clarifying what this involves. Can Gunkel's view cover all of these forms of vulnerability?

We can raise other questions. Gunkel's view seems to preclude the possibility of being intimate with people who cannot experience the right kinds of shame or psychological harm. This might be the right result; perhaps one reason why shameless people are challenging is because they struggle to share intimacy. But it seems less plausible when we consider young children – their identity is under-developed but breastfeeding and play seem intimate. The example of children also highlights how contingent the body is on the intimate zones approach. But perhaps intimacy is essentially an embodied notion, not something so cerebral (Maclaren, 2014).

We might also want to resist accounts of intimacy that focus on our ability to feel negative, rather than positive, emotions. Intimacy could be defined in terms of our propensity to experience excitement, joy, or wonder. Anchoring an account into negative emotions may reflect the broader philosophical prejudice to think of 'negative feelings' as requiring oversight in ways that positive ones do not. But note both that the concept of 'negative' emotions is complex (Kristjánsson, 2003), and that we might have reason to reject this positivity prejudice (Thomason, 2024).

More theoretically, we might wonder if there is actually any value in talking of intimate zones, rather than intimate *facts*. Any feature of who we are can be intimate on Gunkel's view, providing it meets the relevant conditions, so is the notion of a zone redundant? Gunkel probably reaches for this idea for its practical value, since we need to make generalizations both in our relationships and when crafting legislation aimed at protecting people from forced intimacy of various kinds, but it also risks unwittingly suggesting that certain things are commonly understood as intimate, in ways which can make it harder for people with uncommon intimacies to understand their experiences.

What does it mean, on Gunkel's view, to *deepen* or *grow* intimacy with someone? Is this a quantitative matter of revealing *more* intimate zones, i.e. more features of ourselves that we are disposed to hide due to our vulnerability; or is it a matter of spending *more time* with one zone revealed; or a matter of revealing more intimate facts *within* one zone; or some combination of these ideas? Relatedly, can't intimacy *create* importance? Gunkel's account works outwards toward an account of intimacy from the features of us that we already find important, since they are connected to our identity. But we also think that being intimate with someone *makes* aspects of us important. One dimension of engaging with someone in an intimate way is that we are open to them (re)shaping how we view ourselves in ways which can be surprising and valuable. In characterizing intimacy as a kind of revelation, we can worry Gunkel's view does not fully capture the dynamic, relational, aspects of intimacy over time (cf. Daniella Dover's critique of the 'revelation picture' of interpersonal inquiry (Dover, 2022)).

We arrived at a discussion of intimate zones because we were trying to make sense of the nature of sex. *That* question seemed elusive, but also potentially exclusionary in the way common answers to it privilige a hetereosexual, cisgendered, point of view. Some scholars therefore favour notions of intimacy, or the erotic, to capture what is common within different lives, including those of people often excluded, such as asexual people. But intimacy is itself not a straighforward concept. This is useful to notice, as it points to the methodological idea that we are relating concepts to each other, and refining our understanding of each concept in terms of the others, rather than in terms of some foundation concept (a process often called 'reflective equilibrium' (Tersman, 2018)).

Awareness of this complexity might be suitable in a seminar, but will it help with practical and legal questions around sex and intimacy? For example, if we want to retain the idea that sexual wrongs are categorically worse than some other kinds of wrong, we need a workable definition of the sexual that can be used in court to distinguish forced sexualization from other kinds of forced intimacy. How, exactly, to marry philosophical accounts of important concepts with workable legal ideas is a topic for another day, however.

3. Labels

As we write this, our children are three months and three years old, respectively. In two decades, they might be finishing university and developing as people, arriving at a better sense of who they are, what they value, and what they desire. As part of that process, they might reach for labels. Perhaps they will consider themselves *queer*, or *bisexual*, or *asexual*. Perhaps they won't want a romantic relationship at all, and consider themselves *aromantic*. Perhaps they want several (romantic/sexual) relationships and consider themselves *polyamorous* or *relationship anarchists*. Few of these labels were available to us when we were children. Talk of polyamory or asexuality, for example, is comparatively recent.

Pondering which labels will still be used when our children have grown up is an interesting exercise, but not just idle speculation. Labels matter. They shape our ability to understand ourselves, relate ourselves to other people, and they also shape our social norms and laws. It is a common complaint, typically from the political right, that there are 'too many' labels for different gender or sexual identities, and some politicians seek to restrict the use of certain labels in schools – most notably in so-called 'don't say gay' laws in some American states (Tabberer, 2024). These worries and laws are anchored in essentialist views that there are only a certain number of real, or legitimate, categories – e.g. 'masculine' and 'feminine' – as gender descriptors.

But even amongst people who are wary of essentialism, the proliferation of labels can seem overwhelming. It is not always easy, for instance, to parse the differences between *agender, genderqueer, genderfluid, genderfuck, gendervoid,* and so on. Practically speaking, too, we may fear that many labels hinder, rather than advance, political aims, such as fostering solidarity, changing laws, or achieving recognition.

One way of trying to manage this diversity would be to distinguish between notions of identity, on the one hand, and notions of orientation, on the other. Matthew Andler, for example, draws upon gender theory, and the rough distinction between sex as a biological given and gender as the social meaning of sex, to suggest we can separate sexual *orientation,* sexual *identity,* and sexual *self-identity* (Andler, 2021). Sexual self-identity, for Andler, is what we think about our own sexual orientation, whereas sexual identity is, roughly, 'a matter of the beliefs of other social agents about [our] sexual orientation' (Andler, 2021, p. 263).

Andler's view has complexities we sidestep here, but it's worth noting that this taxonomy sets up the possibility of tension between our sexual orientation (whatever that is), how we feel/think about it, and how we are viewed and treated by others. In making these distinctions, Andler hopes to understand how we can resist the oppression of sexual minorities. He wants to reflect the fact that some features of our sexual selves are less 'up to us' than others, but that both the more fixed, and less fixed, aspects (orientation vs identity) have a role to play in oppression (Andler, 2022).

a. Sexual orientation

Reserving prominence for sexual orientation, specifically, is a common move. A loose definition of sexual orientation might be our stable pattern of attraction to other people. On closer inspection, however, we quickly see that we can ask a range of questions about sexual orientation – 'What is a sexual orientation?', 'Are orientations specified in terms of sex, gender, or both?', 'How many orientations are there?', and so on. More specifically, we can ask whether asexuality or polyamory are sexual orientations? The ease with which we can raise these questions might induce scepticism about the value of any orientation talk. Might we need to radically revise, or even reject, the notion of sexual orientation?

There are a range of different philosophical accounts of sexual orientation. Most of them are the product of descriptive, rather than ameliorative, approaches to the concept. This means philosophers are trying to tidy up how we ordinarily talk about orientation. That said, several of the current major philosophical accounts have been developed with one eye to the ameliorative project, which, you will recall, is the attempt to develop a target version of the concept of sexual orientation that will enable us to address the oppression of sexual minorities. (For more on this, see Díaz-León (2022), and for an example discussion focusing on pansexuality, see Pismenny (2023).)

One main philosophical dispute in current thinking about orientations is whether they concern how we are disposed to *behave* (Dembroff, 2016), or how we are disposed to *desire* (Díaz-León, 2022). As Robin Dembroff makes clear, focusing on behaviour alone, as opposed to dispositions to behave, is not particularly helpful as people can be prevented from behaving as they might like to, or behave in ways they do not endorse (due to coercion, say) (Dembroff, 2016, pp. 12–13).

A simple dispositional view, then, would say our sexual orientation is specified by the sexual activities we are disposed to engage in. It is a further question, however, how we taxonomize those dispositions. The typical approach is to focus on the *sex* of the person we are disposed to act sexually with, in relation to our own sex: is it the same or different? Another option would be to focus on the *gender* of the person we are disposed to act sexually with, in relation to our own gender.

Dembroff themself prefers a more complex and interesting view, which they call 'bidirectional dispositionalism'. In summary, it holds that:

> A person S's sexual orientation is grounded in S's dispositions to engage in sexual behaviors under the ordinary condition[s] for these dispositions, and which sexual orientation S has is grounded in what sex[es] and gender[s] of persons S is disposed to sexually engage under these conditions. (Dembroff, 2016, p. 18)

Talk of 'ordinary conditions' for dispositions is intended to block an appeal to ideal conditions. We should not, they think, try to understand what someone's sexual orientation is by imagining situations where there are no barriers to them acting as they would like. Dembroff thinks such idealizing is insufficiently sensitive to cultural difference over time, and the fact that our desires are shaped by the actual contexts we are in (Dembroff, 2016, pp. 14–15).

Dembroff's account gets its name from the second part of the formulation above – namely, the fact that our orientation can be anchored in our attraction to people on grounds of *either* their sex, *or* their gender, *or* some combination of sex and gender. This move is itself grounded in the ameliorative desire to reduce or eliminate 'the presumption that cisheterosexuality is the normatively standard sexual orientation and all queer sexual orientations are normatively deviant' (Dembroff, 2016, p. 5). This view contrasts with dispositional theories like that of Kathleen Stock, which view sexual orientation in terms of our disposition to be attracted towards people of a certain sex but not gender (Stock, 2019).

Dembroff's account also makes no mention of the *relationship* between our sex/gender and the sex/gender of other people, and focuses only on the sex/gender of the people we are disposed to be sexual with. This has the consequence that orientation-talk would not capture notions of sameness or difference. This revisionary consequence of their account would change how we talk about sexuality. As they put it, 'the current concepts of "homosexual" and "heterosexual" do not pick out sexual orientations under [bidirectional dispositionalism]' (Dembroff, 2016, p. 25).

Dembroff's view is exceptionally rich, and rewards careful study. Here, it is intended to represent one version of behavioural dispositional approaches to sexual orientation (see also Stein, 2001). An alternative view, which also approaches sexual orientation in terms of dispositions but which shifts focus away from behaviour, and towards *desire*, is offered by Esa Díaz-León. Her 'desire view' is as follows:

> A person S's sexual orientation is determined by the sex[es] and/ or the gender[s] of persons for whom S is disposed to have sexual desires, under the relevant manifesting conditions. (Díaz-León, 2022, p. 302)

She defines sexual desire as follows:

> A sexual desire (for men and/or women, or people of certain sex and/or gender) involves the combination of a propositional attitude (of the form 'S bears the relation of desiring toward proposition p') plus a disposition to be sexually aroused by, or sexually attracted to, men and/or women. (Díaz-León, 2022, p. 303)

This view aims to reflect the fact that our sexual selves are shaped by desire, not just by action, and that being unable to act, or to be disposed to act, does not rob us of our sexuality. For example, Díaz-León suggests there can be cases where a woman is bisexual even if she is not disposed to act on her desire for women, in a range of close possible circumstances, since she is married to a man.

We might also think we understand our dispositions to act sexually by examining our desires. T. R. Whitlow and N. G. Laskowski put a similar point in these terms: 'plausibly, when we are disposed to behave sexually, that's because some further feature(s) of us grounds the behavioral disposition, such as our dispositions to *want* to behave sexually, our disposition to be *curious* about what some kind of sexual behavior would feel like, our dispositions to *hope* that behaving sexually will achieve some aim, and so on' (Whitlow and Laskowski, 2023, p. 587).

Like Dembroff, Díaz-León favours an ameliorative approach to sexual orientation. She argues that Dembroff's approach hinders this goal in two respects. First, it cannot capture the structural similarities between 'people who identify as male/men and are attracted to other males/men, and those who identify as female/women and are attracted to other females/women'; as Díaz-León puts it, 'these two communities occupy similar social positions regarding many factors such as cultural representations, access to marriage benefits, housing, healthcare', and having the conceptual tools to recognize these similarities is useful (Díaz-León, 2022, p. 305).

Second, she argues that 'just having certain desires is enough to suffer discrimination and prejudice in the form of invisibility and isolation, in a way that is similar enough to those who are discriminated because of their sexual behavior' (Díaz-León, 2022, p. 307), so a notion of sexual orientation which focuses only on behaviour misses this dimension of harm.

Still, Díaz-León's own approach has also been criticized. T. R. Whitlow and N. G. Laskowski raise the specific concern that accounts anchored in desire, although perhaps better than those focusing on behaviour, fail to capture cases where we experience *arousal* without desire:

> imagine a woman who experiences the phenomenal feeling of sexual arousal around women but who lives in an overwhelmingly oppressive patriarchal society that forbids sexual relationships between women. Imagine, too, that this person has managed, sadly, to rid themselves of all their sexual desires for women out of a sense of self-preservation. Desire dispositionalism predicts that this woman is not sexually oriented to women. We think that's implausible. (Whitlow and Laskowski, 2023, p. 589)

Their own view of sexual orientation, 'categorical phenomenalism', is interesting in two senses. First, it is not a dispositional view. They think we should abandon all appeal to dispositions because we seem unable to specify the relevant factors which justify talking in terms of them. Second, instead of focusing on sexual behaviour or desire, their view is grounded in sexual arousal:

> What it is for x to be sexually oriented to y is for x to phenomenally experience sexual arousal in response to y in virtue of the features that constitute y's manhood, womanhood, etc. (Whitlow and Laskowski, 2023, p. 591)

By 'phenomenally experience', they mean to have a conscious *felt* experience of their arousal (something lacked by the so-called philosophical 'zombies' who feature a lot in the rest of Whitlow and Laskowski's argument, but which interest us less here).

This view is intended to produce the right result when we consider the case of the repressed but aroused people. Whitlow and Laskowski also argue that it simplifies the epistemology of sexual orientation too, since to know what our orientation is is just to know what arouses us rather than to know what our dispositions are.

It's worth asking whether appealing to arousal is simpler, however, than other views of orientation. Whitlow and Laskowski are a bit vague on what the phenomenal experience of arousal amounts to. In one example, they refer to someone who 'does not feel his heart race at the sight of another man', which suggests the experience of arousal involves the combination of mental attitudes and bodily responses to other people (Whitlow and Laskowski, 2023, p. 588). As is becoming increasingly better understood, however, experiences of arousal are often 'non-concordant', which means there might be no straightforward connection between our mental attitudes towards someone, on the one hand, and our genital response to them, on the other (Nagoski, 2015, p. 194).

What is even more interesting, given Whitlow and Laskowski's example, is that non-concordance of arousal seems more common in women than men. Emily Nagoski describes research suggesting that the genital response of women overlaps with their subjective arousal only one in ten times (Nagoski, 2015, p. 195). Not only this but, as Lisa Diamond puts it, 'regardless of whether they describe themselves as lesbian, heterosexual, or bisexual, women typically become genitally aroused by sexual stimuli featuring either women or men, whereas men typically show genital arousal only in response to stimuli featuring their preferred gender' (Diamond, 2022, p. 92). These findings suggest we should be wary in anchoring the notion of sexual orientation in arousal *if* this is understood as an experience where someone responds positively to another person *and* their body responds with the physiological signs of arousal (erections, wetness, etc.), since these can come apart and do so more in some groups than others.

Whitlow and Laskowski are right that there can be cases of arousal without desire, but if this emerging research is to be believed, these cases may be less common than cases of arousal non-concordance. At the very least, this muddies the epistemological waters, as people can easily be confused about whether they are aroused or not (especially in a culture where physical signs of arousal are given prominence), but arguably it is sufficient to cast doubt on the project of linking orientation to arousal.

b. A doomed project?

We have explored some recent philosophical attempts to give an account of sexual orientation. But perhaps this is a doomed project? To explore this, let's consider Sari van Anders' influential sexual configurations theory (van Anders, 2015). Her rich, and extensive, article consists of a critique of existing approaches to sexual orientation and then an attempt to offer an alternative framework. We will outline the critique, then outline the positive view, and then ask whether van Anders is right to think we can still make use of orientation talk.

Van Anders suggests that standard approaches to sexual orientation, e.g. those which seem to specify patterns of attraction on the grounds of sex, fail to capture the richness of human sexuality. First, they risk assuming that sexual orientation overlaps with sexual identity (a mistake the philosophers mentioned above avoid). Second, these accounts struggle to capture experiences of sexual fluidity as our attractions and desires shift over time (cf. Diamond, 2008). Third, these theories presuppose that sexuality is dyadic and fundamentally 'defined in part by one's attractions and engagements with others' (van Anders, 2015, p. 1179). Why assume this? If there are important differences between solo sex and partnered sex, why let the latter define the whole? Fourth, standard approaches to sexual orientation centre on ideas of 'organised sameness and difference', but it seems 'unlikely that people generally organize their sexuality around notions of what they do or don't have, such as "I am attracted to those people who have vulvas *because* I have a vulva and they are like me"' (van Anders, 2015, p. 1180). Diamond suggests that, actually, 'mixed patterns of sexual attraction and/or behavior are far more common than exclusively same-gender attractions and/or behavior' (Diamond, 2022, p. 89).

Fifth, these theories typically emphasize sex at the expense of gender, which, in turn, can lead to a fixation on 'discrete binaries' (van Anders, 2015, p. 1180) (both Díaz-León and Dembroff are careful to avoid this).

'Sexual configurations theory' is van Anders' ambitious attempt to address these worries. She wants to capture all sexual phenomena within one approach to sexual orientation; reflect our lived experiences of sexuality; and clarify our understanding. Talk of 'configurations' is intended to capture the ways in which sexuality is multifaceted and dynamic, and to avoid unwittingly privileging hetero-cis-sexuality. Instead, all sexual configurations are understood relative to each other.

There are two broad domains to sexual configurations theory: *partnered* sexuality and *solitary* sexuality. In itself, this is a big departure from most approaches to orientation, which understand it solely in terms of how we relate to others (and so struggle to accommodate, or exclude, solitary sexuality).

Each domain – partnered sexuality and solo sexuality – is understood along four parameters: (1) gender/sex; (2) partner number; (3) 'sexual parameter$_n$'; and (4) eroticism/nurturance. The basic idea is as follows. A full accounting of our sexual orientation encompasses both our solitary and partnered sexuality. In each domain, we exhibit great diversity in how we respond to others. Some people focus on sex, others on gender, others on some combination; some desire no partner, one partner, or multiple partners; some find their sexuality is accompanied by drives to nurture or form other intimacies, whereas for others it is more sexual. 'Sexual parameter$_n$' denotes other, as-yet-not-fully-understood aspects of human sexuality which may feature into a full accounting of our orientation. Possible examples include: 'sexual age orientation', 'consent and physical violence/force', and 'kink identification' (van Anders, 2015, pp. 1197–8). To this, we add *presumptive permanence*, the extent to which it matters to us that a specific sexual focus lasts over time.

Further complexity lurks *within* each parameter. For example, we might care more than others about the sex/gender of our sexual partners, so this gives us the notion of 'gender/sex strength' (van Anders, 2015, p. 1191), whereas we differ in how willing we are to have more than one sexual partner, which gives us 'sexual partner number openness' of varying kinds (van Anders, 2015, p. 1194).

Van Anders is keen to avoid the idea that certain parameters are more naturally grouped or normal than others, or that they can be 'misaligned'. She stresses that even apparently hegemonic sexuality of straightness is 'more queer' than supposed, since 'individuals might be more interested in maleness than masculinity or femininity than femaleness (thus challenging the notion that gender and sex are necessarily congruent or the same thing)' (van Anders, 2015, p. 1204). Instead, she favours language of features 'coinciding' or 'branching' in ways which may be experienced as more or less complex by the people involved, for example, a 'lesbian-identified woman' who 'may feel "unaligned" when she experiences sexual attractions to men' (van Anders, 2015, p. 1200).

The sexual configurations approach enables van Anders to fold polyamory and asexuality within a theory of orientation. She thinks both are understood in terms of the parameter of *partner number*. Taking the example of asexuality, she writes: 'asexuality relates to a set of orientations and statuses that involve nonalloeroticism at their core and are related, not to gender/sex sexuality, but to partner number sexuality. In this way, sexuality as multifaceted is key to understanding asexuality: separating nurturance from eroticism, and dyadic from solitary eroticism' (van Anders, 2015, p. 1202). Traditional approaches to orientation struggle with asexuality, which is presented as a simple lack of attraction to anyone. But van Anders' sexual configurations theory captures the fact that, whilst asexual people may not typically desire partnered sex on the basis of attraction, we can nonetheless capture differences in attitude towards solo sexuality, fantasy, and masturbation, which often feature in their lives (Bogaert, 2015, p. 58; Yule, Brotto, and Gorzalka, 2017); nurturance and gender/sex preference; and maybe dimensions such as interest in kink (Jolene Sloan, 2015; Winter-Gray and Hayfield, 2021).

Clearly, van Anders has outlined a rich and comprehensive approach to sexual orientation (with equally complex diagrams). She teases out, connects, and organizes the many facets of human sexuality and illustrates the internal complexity of their favoured sexual parameters. But has she really described a theory of *sexual orientation*? Why not reject the concept altogether?

Van Anders' own criticisms of traditional approaches to orientation support the case for abolition, but, surprisingly, she wants to retain the concept. Her negative reason for doing so is she is unsure that notions of sexual identity, for example, would serve any better; they risk entrenching ideas of biological essentialism about sex. Her positive reason is also widely shared: she thinks talk of orientation is *useful*. She also offers a reason to motivate her stretching of the concept in claiming that 'orientation is used quite widely to mean just a set of interests without connotations of determinism or permanence' (van Anders, 2015, p. 1182).

We disagree with this last point. People may be more accepting of changing attractions, but still think these are organized within the fixed envelope of orientation, e.g. that a straight man may experience different attractions to women, but they are all to women in a way that is unchosen and stable.

c. Usefulness and politics

Perhaps we are better off appealing to the usefulness of orientation talk. One way in which orientation talk might seem useful is that it seems aligned to *political* projects of recognizing and protecting minority groups. Calls for polyamory to be recognized as an orientation, by people like Ann Tweedy, take this approach (Tweedy, 2011). Writing within an American legal context, Tweedy argues polyamory is a sexual orientation because it is sufficiently 'embedded' as an 'essential identity' for people and it is a source of discrimination and social inequality.

These approaches are also congruent with those seeking an ameliorative approach to sexual orientation, since political change is their goal. But they are not without critique. A good example of this is due to Christian Klesse, who cautions polyamorists against striving to claim their relationship style as an orientation: 'The equation of polyamory with sexual orientation may undermine the disruptive potential of the category polyamory, achieve only selective protection under the law, obstruct the ability of poly movements to pursue broader alliances, and foster a politics of recognition at the expense of a more transformative political agenda' (Klesse, 2014, p. 92). Klesse is drawn, we think, to the more radical possibilities of non-normative sexuality; to the idea that polyamory brings pressure to bear on attempts to categorize and label altogether; that polyamory does not need to align with any specific view about partner sex/gender, or sexual activity type. He worries also about potential divisions between the recognized orientation of polyamory and other forms of nonmonogamy (perhaps relationship anarchy), which might not prioritize love or longer-term relationships. More generally, he is wary of conflating achieving legal recognition with social liberation, and of the pressures towards social assimilation which might increase if polyamorous people secure recognition. Since 'inscribing polyamory into law' will 'only serve a small subsection of people engaged in non-monogamous ways of life', it is best avoided (Klesse, 2014, p. 93).

Klesse has more traditional approaches to sexual orientation in his sights, not something like sexual configurations theory, but his criticisms give us reason to pause before viewing orientation talk as a useful route to taming the oppression of certain groups. At the very least, the political utility of the concept of sexual orientation remains open.

Another important tension to recognize is between a theory of orientation's ability to capture diversity and nuance, on the one hand, and its legal utility, on the other. To claim legal recognition in a workable way, polyamorous people or asexuals need a concrete sense of orientation. Appeal to something as rich, but complex, as sexual configurations theory may prove a hindrance.

With this tension in mind, perhaps we are better just rejecting talk of sexual orientation altogether? Perhaps van Anders and others have shown us that human sexuality consists of many interlinked dimensions and it is best to accept that fact on its own terms, rather than trying to redefine the much more limited notion of sexual orientation to reflect this complexity. We are sympathetic to the idea that only a radical approach to sexuality will help us tackle injustice and discrimination.

4. Types

Chad, who is white, middle aged, and American, is really into Asian women. He thinks they're sexy. His dating app bio and filters are all geared towards dating Asian women, and Asian women only. He likes to watch porn featuring Asian women. His ideal partner is a 'short, smart, submissive, Asian wife'.

If asked about his inclinations, we can imagine different responses Chad might give. He could respond with a narrative which seeks to make sense of his desire. Perhaps, like other white American men of his age, he believes that Asian women are more sexual, or more submissive, or more 'exotic' and interesting than the white women in his community or other women of colour. If so, he might reference these ideas in an attempt to justify or explain his preference. Alternatively, however, he might shrug and say, 'I'm not sure, it's just a preference.'

Is there something amiss, morally, with Chad's preference?

a. 'Yellow fever'

Arguably, Chad has 'yellow fever', which is a racial fetish. Robin Zheng defines racial fetishes as 'a person's exclusive or near-exclusive preference for sexual intimacy with others belonging to a specific racial out-group' (Zheng, 2016, p. 401). Zheng argues that yellow fever is morally troubling, but not everyone would agree. The explicit preference for someone of a certain race is not the same as overt racism, they might suggest – indeed, isn't it good to be the focus of someone else's romantic and sexual interest? After all, some people lack this attention.

To get this discussion going, we lump together sexual and romantic attraction. Zheng is keen to respond to the 'mere preference' account of sexual/romantic attraction which holds that Chad simply has an '"aesthetic" or "personal" preference' for women who look a certain way or a have a particular heritage (Zheng, 2016, p. 401).

Zheng sets out the mere preference argument as follows:

1. There is nothing morally objectionable about sexual preferences for hair color, eye color, and other nonracialized phenotypic traits.
2. Preferences for racialized physical traits are no different from preferences for nonracialized phenotypic traits.
Therefore,
3. 'Mere' preferences for racialized phenotypic traits are not morally objectionable. (Zheng, 2016, p. 402)

She notes there are several ways to attack this argument; most notably, we could deny premise one, or premise two (or both).

Zheng focuses on premise two. In turn, we can approach this in different ways. First, we can explore the racial *stereotypes* underpinning views like that of Chad – stereotypes with rich and complex histories interwoven with racism, colonialism, and other forms of historical injustice, against Asian women especially.

Second, we could focus on the structural impact of yellow fever, and leave open why people experience it. Zheng prefers this second approach. She notes that

it certainly seems possible (even if unlikely) that some individuals' racial fetishes do not depend in any way on stereotypes; we should not rule out of hand the possibility of individual variation here. Racial fetishes might be based on mere accidents of geography and local demography or even more idiosyncratic personal histories – a first girlfriend or sexual encounter, say. But I don't think that any of this stops racial fetishes from being objectionable or that the targets of yellow fever should not feel bothered when fetishists have their preference for these other reasons. (Zheng, 2016, p. 406)

So why is Chad's yellow fever bad, if not because of any stereotypes he might hold? Zheng gives two reasons. One focuses on yellow fever's overall impact on Asian women. The second focuses on the broader expressive meaning of Chad's attitude. These points are perhaps separable, but Zheng thinks the former happens, in part at least, due to the latter.

In both cases, Zheng wants to shift our attention away from people like Chad, and towards the many unnamed women who are the subject of his attitudes and overtures. What is yellow fever like for them? Her answer is that Asian women are prone to undergo experiences of pervasive self-doubt which arises because they are often 'depersonalized' and 'homogenized' (Zheng, 2016, p. 407). Chad's attitudes treat Asian women not as distinct individuals but as tokens of a type who purportedly share properties (sexiness, submissiveness, intelligence) as members of that type. These attitudes position Asian woman as interchangeable.

In addition, Zheng argues that yellow fever serves to 'otherize' Asian women, who are thereby 'separated and held to a different standard' from non-Asian women (Zheng, 2016, p. 408). This is connected to the wider racialized norms and ideals shaping social intimacy, such as the idea that certain people are objects of 'experimentation' or 'curiosity' due to their apparent difference. In writing about the racialized experiences of Black and Asian people on dating apps, for example, Apryl Williams notes that ethnic minority individuals are often viewed as fair game for dating and sex, but would never be considered for more established intimacy or longer relationships – that 'the racially curated sexual marketplace created by racial filters on dating apps is designed for play and private experiential consumption of the racial other rather than for seeking public-facing, long-term dating relationships' (A. Williams, 2024, p. 23).

Consider Zhou, a young Chinese woman on a first date with Trevor. His messages have been friendly and they share interests and went to the same university. Despite this promising start, Zhou is dating in a context shaped by the way Chad, and others like him, express and act on their attitudes. Zhou may doubt that Trevor is interested in her as an individual. Is he there *because she is an Asian woman*? She might also worry that her personality – confident, loud, and passionate – means she risks being replaced in the future by someone 'more Asian', or that Trevor's interest in her will wane once he has experienced 'something different'.

These doubts are harmful, even though Trevor seems well meaning and could become a wonderful partner. Indeed, the possibility of that outcome can layer-up additional emotions for Zhou to deal with, since she may experience shame about her doubt. What is more, the very fact of having to tackle these layers of mental work is often obscured by modern 'post-race' or 'colourblind' discourse, discourse which often lies behind some expressions of the mere preference argument. Zhou's attempts to explain her doubts to Trevor, or her white friends, may go unheeded in ways which heighten her anxieties about the reasonableness of her own doubt. Zheng suggests that predicament can be a form of hermeneutic injustice, since Zhou is systematically disadvantaged in her ability to understand and articulate her own attitudes towards her life situation due to social prejudice (Fricker, 2007; Zheng, 2016, p. 409).

The psychological weight of dating as an Asian woman is thus present irrespective of the person they are with. Arguably, Zhou's experience is a form of what Sandra Bartky called 'psychological oppression', which is to be 'weighed down in your mind ... to have harsh dominion exercised over your self-esteem' (Bartky, 1979, p. 191). Trevor's speech and actions, his beliefs and implicit biases, are less important on this analysis of yellow fever. Instead, Zheng argues, Zhou's inner life is shaped by her social reality, and that reality 'is still ordered according to highly racialized patterns of behavior and outcomes' (Zheng, 2016, p. 409).

The second reason Zheng gives in support of the idea that yellow fever is bad focuses on the expressive meaning of attitudes like Chad's. She suggests that 'the expressive meaning of yellow fever is that there is something different about Asian women, something that must be more than mere phenotype' (Zheng, 2016, p. 411). Crucially, the expressive meaning argument makes no reference to the origin of Chad's attitudes. Perhaps he lacks stereotypes, and arrived at his particular romantic preference due to a quirk of his childhood, but his remarks and actions still resonate with others in ways which subordinate Asian women.

Zheng's argument is nuanced. It has the consequence that even well-meaning people with certain racial preferences and attractions might be harming others. This argument is compatible with the view that explicit stereotypes also negatively impact minorities in intimate life (Bedi, 2019). Zheng's argument dovetails nicely with the work of other scholars who have explored the various ways in which racial prejudice shapes practices of *looking* and *attention* and, in turn, the interior lives of the people seen (Yancy, 2016; Fanon, 2021), as well as with work exploring similar experiences in the lives of disabled people (Garland-Thomson, 2009). Nor does the thrust of Zheng's argument have to apply to women only. Asian men, to take another specific example, have long been viewed through a complex intersectional lens shaped by ideals of whiteness and masculinity in ways which socially marginalize them, especially as potential intimate partners (Shek, 2007; Han, 2016).

That said, Zheng's general view is not without criticism. Raja Halwani argues, for example, that mere preferences based on attraction are morally permissible when *sex* is concerned, even if we are wary about similar dynamics in the cases of *romantic love* (Halwani, 2024). Halwani worries that critics of lookism, even on grounds of race and ethnicity, have often lumped together sex and love without carefully distinguishing them. This view is compatible, however, with the idea that it would be better if we did not have such preferences (since what is permissible and what is good may come apart, as we shall see later in discussing bad sex).

Two obvious questions arise at this point. First, does Zheng's argument apply to other patterns of sexual and romantic interest? Put another way, should we question premise one of the mere preference argument, which held that 'there is nothing morally objectionable about sexual preferences for hair color, eye color, and other nonracialized phenotypic traits'? Second, regardless of which patterns of romantic preference turn out to be problematic, what – if anything – are people like Chad or Trever supposed to do about them, personally?

b. Beauty too?

Zheng is sympathetic to the idea that we should reject the first premise of the mere preference argument. Social beauty norms and standards of attractiveness, not to mention prevalent views about disability, seem to advantage some people over others. Deborah Rhode, for example, argues convincingly that appearance is a core axis of discrimination in the American workplace (Rhode, 2011); Heather Widdows argues that we are subject to a global, moralized, beauty ideal (Widdows, 2020); other theorists have long argued that women's internalization of beauty norms as structured for the 'male gaze' causes a variety of harms to self-image, confidence, and agency (Mulvey, 1975; Berger, 2008). However, later in her argument, Zheng suggests there are important differences between the experiences of female targets of yellow fever, and other people – namely, the former have a distinct *history* and are also *categorically* different (Zheng, 2016, pp. 409–10). She writes, 'blondes and brunettes as such have not suffered histories of exploitation, colonization, slavery, persecution, and exclusion on the basis of phenotype. Nor does hair or eye color track categorical differences across all social, economic, and political dimensions of life, including opportunities for health, education, jobs, relationships, legal protections, and more' (Zheng, 2016, p. 409). Zheng might be right in point of emphasis here, but we can separate out the historical and categorical points and gesture towards other examples where people do seem to suffer across the board as a consequence of a non-racial physical characteristic. People with certain forms of physical disability which shape their appearance, such as individuals with Down syndrome (Wright, 2011) or people with facial disfigurement (Talley, 2014), have historically been ostracized. In addition, as Kate Manne and others have argued forcefully, fat people do currently suffer across 'all social, economic, and political dimensions of life' (Bordo, 2004; Eaton, 2016; Manne, 2024), and this is so irrespective of the complex history of attitudes towards fat people.

Still, one thing to consider is how to distinguish between patterns of attraction which are innocuous, and those which rest on stereotypes or have the kind of psychological and expressive impact charted by Zheng. What about attraction to certain hairstyles, or freckles, or height? Indeed, height features predominantly in heterosexual dating culture, with the ideal outcome being a woman dating a taller man. Socially, 'heightism' seems to place shorter men at a disadvantage across many different domains of life, including dating, yet is rarely viewed as a form of injustice (Yancey and Emerson, 2016; Kimhi, 2020). Perhaps even being drawn to attractive people, as such, is morally problematic (D'Alessandro, 2023).

Consider how far you would extend Zheng's general argument to non-racial patterns of attraction. Her argument – if you find it convincing, as we do – gives us the resources to be critical of patterns of attraction if they seem to contribute to forms of doubt and psychological burden for the people impacted by them, or have negative expressive significance, and that this is so, irrespective of what we think explicitly about our patterns of attraction or the people we are drawn towards. It is possible that the 'mere' preference for taller men could be harmful, or perpetuate injustice, insofar as it leads tall men to doubt whether they are sought after on their own terms, and has negative expressive significance towards shorter people.

c. Responsibility for attraction

A different way of responding to Zheng's argument is simply to say that we can't be obliged to tackle our attractions, because we *cannot* do so. This approach rests on the widely shared, but not uncontroversial, assumption of 'ought implies can', i.e. it is absurd to suggest someone is obligated to do something they cannot do. But is this right? Can we be held responsible for our attractions and potentially change them, and, if we can, how might we? Unlike the characters in Ted Chiang's short story exploring lookism, 'Liking what you see: a documentary' (Chiang, 2024), we cannot undergo brain stimulation so that we no longer see people as attractive or unattractive, but are there other things we can do?

There are lines of response available here, which we label the *indirect*, *semi-direct*, and *direct* strategies. Some people adopt mixed versions of these strategies (Zheng, 2016). All of them presuppose that we, individuals and collectively, are at least *partially responsible* for the social impact of our romantic preferences; responsible, that is, for causing what Tom O'Shea calls 'oretic injustice', or 'a form of injustice which arises from the distribution or character of people's desires' (O'Shea, 2020, p. 588). There is more to say in defence of this overarching assumption, but we leave that off-stage here (c.f. O'Shea, 2020; Barn, 2022).

The indirect view is often motivated by scepticism about the efficacy and desirability of direct attempts to try to shape our desires and attractions. People may think either that the problem of oretic injustice is just a structural problem and so 'requires a structural solution' (Barn, 2022, p. 423), or that it is both a structural and personal problem, but only structural solutions actually work. Below, we shall respond to one important form of concern about direct strategies to troubling patterns of desire and attraction.

Instead of focusing on individuals, the indirect view looks to social structures. In writing about our romantic preferences, for example, Gulzar Barn suggests, 'if any ameliorative work can be justified, it has to do with reforming the background political conditions that lead to the formation of such preferences' (Barn, 2022, p. 423). Potential structural solutions take various forms, from addressing 'residential segregation' (Zheng, 2016, p. 415), or raising 'educational awareness' of the harms of different patterns of attraction (Barn, 2022, p. 434), to 'deeper structural interventions in the social and physical environments within which our desires are formed', such as changes to our legal frameworks around relationships, marriage, and sexuality or attempts to redesign the 'infrastructure of dating', such as our dating apps (O'Shea, 2020, pp. 592–3). These changes do not require us to work directly on our attractions and desires, although they may require us to contribute to broader social projects and political initiatives. Here, our obligations resemble those that structural injustice theorists argue we have towards other forms of complex, collective, harm, such as climate change or the impact of globalized capitalism (Young, 2011).

The *semi-direct* approach suggests we can also work on ourselves, but in indirect ways. For example, we might try to expose ourselves to new situations to try to form new desires. Some in the literature use metaphors of hunger and culinary pleasure here (Mitchell and Wells, 2018). The hope is that exposure to new 'food' will – over time – change our taste.

Ann Cahill rejects metaphors with hunger on the grounds they unwittingly perpetuate a stark distinction between the body and the mind, with the implication that the latter has to master the former. Instead, she thinks our attractions and desires are more akin to our sense of humour and ability to laugh, something which we have some control over but often experience as involuntary, and which is connected closely to the social, stratified, aspects of human existence (Cahill, 2016a). Cahill views our desires/attractions as 'habitual', rather than more explicit beliefs – habits which both shape and are shaped by broad social structures and our more immediate environments (Cahill, 2016a, p. 296). This habit-like, rather than belief-like, approach leads Cahill to think direct forms of reflection are unlikely to work (as they might in isolated cases of prejudice). Instead, we can work to change our environments and try to scaffold new habits. Negatively, this could involve efforts to remove barriers to change, such as 'white ignorance' that makes recognition of racial disadvantage and white supremacy harder for white people (Mills, 2017). Positively, this could involve pro-active attempts to inhabit new environments and spaces of intimate possibility.

Finally, there are *direct strategies*. These come in different forms. Some argue that self-reflection is a vital component of any attempt to address oretic injustices (Emens, 2008; Zheng, 2016, p. 415). A bit like a business examining its systems and workplace, to see if they are accessible to people with disabilities, we explore our romantic assumptions and desires to see if we can 'accommodate' those people whom we may have been previously excluding. This self-reflection strategy is often viewed as an achievable addition to wider structural views.

Other direct strategies focus less on our beliefs and assumptions, and more on how we attend to other people. In turn, these come in different varieties, depending on the problem. On the one hand, we have strategies to come to see people *as attractive*; on the other, we have strategies to come to see attractive people *as people*.

Ann Eaton, for example, argues we need to address our 'collective taste in bodies' which excludes fat people, because she thinks this absence is partly constitutive of the oppression fat people experience (Eaton, 2016). For Eaton, it is not enough to simply change our beliefs, or modify our social structures, we have to change how we actually feel, and what we find attractive. Her view also focuses on the formation of habits, following Aristotle, but is more active than other views in that she thinks we can take steps to train our taste. Part of this involves wider representation of fat people; we need to 'produce and widely promote vivid, imaginatively engaging, and artistically interesting representations that celebrate fat bodies and encourage us to see them as likeable and attractive' (Eaton, 2016, p. 53). But the active part is contained in this notion of 'seeing as'. Eaton's view involves what we call 'proleptic looking', where we are encouraged to engage in a process, and involve our imagination as we do so, as if we liked what we are doing, *in order to bring it about* that we like what we are doing. She makes another culinary comparison. Craig is not a fan of vegetables. He could simply expose himself to them more often and hope for the best (a kind of semi-direct strategy), but Eaton suggests the following is Craig's 'best bet':

> Craig tries to alter his feelings about vegetables by acting as if they were tasty. He starts with vegetables that are most similar to things he does like, such as meat, and he incorporates them into dishes that he already likes. Finally, it is important that he create positive associations with vegetables by initially restricting his consumption of them to times when he is enjoying himself, and performing visualization exercises where he vividly imagines himself eating vegetables with vigor and enthusiasm. (Eaton, 2016, p. 51)

Other direct strategies are aimed at people who already experience attraction, but in troubling ways. People like Chad, for instance, need to work not to see Asian women as attractive, but rather to see them as individuals. Different options are available here. One might be to retain the force of sexual attraction, but imbue it with a more subjectifying dimension. Sheila Lintott and Sherri Irvin take this approach in developing their feminist 'revisionist notion of sexiness that treats people not merely as sex objects, but as sexual subjects' (Irvin and Lintott, 2016, p. 300). They suggest 'there is an ethical imperative to shape one's aesthetic judgments regarding the sexiness of others so as to respect their subjectivity, rather than just assessing their physical attractiveness or their appeal as objects for sexual use' (Irvin and Lintott, 2016, p. 301). This involves recognizing sexiness is an animated 'way of being' rather than a property of bodies 'as lifeless surfaces'.

For them, seeing people as sexy is fine, as long as we realize and appreciate this is a 'way of being' which is visible in moments of 'genuineness' not performance, where 'evidence of genuineness will be found in originality, comfort, confidence, playfulness, and a sense of improvisation' (Irvin and Lintott, 2016, p. 306). To see people as sexy in this way, they argue, is partly a matter of increased representation and exposure, but partly an effort to see others with empathy, and partly an effort to expand our aesthetic boundaries by learning to be comfortable with ambivalence, playfulness, and looser forms of gender identity.

Similar calls to look with empathy are central to the work of disability theorist Rosemarie Garland-Thomson, and her analysis of staring. She argues, perhaps surprisingly, that staring, with all its fraught sense of tension and exposure, has 'generative potential' (Garland-Thomson, 2009). Those moments of staring can result in dis-identified looking, where we distance ourselves from someone, or view them with pity, or under the grip of our imposed narratives; but they can also result in identified looking, and forms of 'sympathetic response' which 'can be transformed into an ethical relation if it is mobilized into political action' (Garland-Thomson, 2009, p. 186).

Finally, another direct strategy might be to embrace practices of 'aesthetic exploration' which direct our attention towards bodies as aesthetic, and not just sexual, presences. Sherri Irvin, for example, argues that 'it is possible to reinvigorate our ability to pay attention to a wide variety of aspects of the body that are normally neglected' – perhaps looking beyond commonly sexualized parts of the body, or learning to look at our own bodies (Irvin, 2017, p. 14).

Notice that in 'positive experiences of the unique aesthetic affordances of all bodies, regardless of whether they are attractive in the standard sense', we are not engaged in activities of proleptic looking – looking *as if* someone was attractive – but rather working to appreciate them in a broader way that captures their 'richness'. This approach also resonates with those who want to tackle the raced nature of attraction, such as Paul Taylor's suggestion we need to address 'negrophobic somatic aesthetics', i.e. the way our aesthetic ideals express fear of Black bodies (Taylor, 2016).

Direct strategies face one huge objection, which is that they seem patronizing and demeaning in a way that will also make them counterproductive. O'Shea, for example, asks us to 'consider what controlling or habituating sexual desire would mean for the new objects of desire' and suggests: 'There is a danger that the message is something like this: ordinarily, I would find you too repulsive, plain, or downright unsexy to bother with – but, out of a generous sense of duty, I have trained myself to overcome my aversion or indifference to you. At the very least, there seems something patronizing about that attitude' (O'Shea, 2020, p. 589). And Barn worries that 'Attempts to re-habituate desires along a racial dimension – even assuming this were possible – may be counterproductive to racial justice goals. This is because consciously seeking out members of marginalized racial groups would further the otherization and objectification that I have suggested is present when general views are held about racial appearance and behavior' (Barn, 2022, p. 433). These objections are amplified if the direct strategy in question allocates an active role also to the people seen, not just the spectators. In writing about Harriet McBride Johnson, a disabled and wheelchair-using lawyer and writer, Garland-Thomson suggests: 'By both showing and telling her experience *as if it were ordinary* ... the staring encounter [McBride Johnson] stages will shift her audience from curiosity to knowledge. She will turn them away from arrested stares and set them on a path toward empathetic identification' (Garland-Thomson 2009, 192, italics added).

To our ear, Garland-Thomson overlooks the risk inherent in these encounters: the way people such as Harriet McBride Johnson may experience misunderstanding, failures of uptake, or ridicule and harm in moments of vulnerability, even if they try hard to show themselves 'as if' ordinary. At the very least, it is plausible to think the onus should aways be on the activity of the person looking, not the person seen.

Is there a response to the patronizing objection? One line of reply is to distinguish between an internal and external perspective and the reasons we are responsive to. We might want to try to broaden our horizons, and so head to a Szechuan restaurant for the first time for that reason, but that reason does not account for why we loved eating mapo tofu. We loved the tofu because of how it tasted. Similarly, perhaps the reason why Trevor ended up on a date with Zhou was because he underwent a prior process of reflection, or exposure, or activities of proleptic looking, but the reasons why he is appreciative to Zhou on their date are reasons internal to that context, i.e. things about *her*. Put another way, we have to avoid the genetic fallacy which conflates the causal path we took to be in a situation with the reasons we respond to in that situation.

Still, that kind of response presupposes the process of self-transformation has finished, or is at least substantially under way. Often that is not the case; we are just starting, or are curious about change. In those cases, the *means* we choose to change are vital. Zhou would rightly feel worse if she knew Trevor was sitting in front of her because he wanted to try something different and experiment, or to try to date 'as if' Chinese women were attractive, and so on. Perhaps Trevor has greater licence to explore his attractions if the targets of his efforts were images, films, forms of fantasy. But even then, we can worry about the moral status of those states of mind, especially if it is possible to wrong people purely by having bad thoughts about them (Eskens, 2023).

We have surveyed a few different strategies for responding to morally worrisome patterns of attraction. When discussing how to respond to bad intimacy, we shall pick up a similar theme. As we mentioned, it is possible to combine elements of the strategies, mixing structural and personal efforts to change. Charting the boundaries of our personal responsibility is a complex matter, and it remains to be seen whether a developed response can be provided to the objections that direct strategies are patronizing and counter-productive.

5. Conclusion

When it comes to intimacy, the familiar can often feel universal. It's easy to overlook other ways people might experience attraction, or desire, or arousal; or to forget that not everyone wants sex, or can have sex in the same ways; or that there are now – and have been historically – more labels and ways of describing our intimate inclinations than one person could ever remember. We began the book with asexuality to help bring these differences to light, and so to help us appreciate the likely fact that predominant theories of intimacy might need revising.

Of course, just because a form of intimate life is not central to the social imagination does not mean it lacks significance or has been historically absent. It is certainly possible to retell these stories and give them prominence, as, for example, Elizabeth Hopkinson has been doing with her asexual fairy tales (Hopkinson, 2019). We all need to ask: how might society be different if these stories were more widely appreciated?

2

Finding Someone

1. Introduction

Nothing elicited more anecdotes than telling people we were planning to write about dating apps.

One favourite was an interaction which soured after someone asked a man they were chatting to on a dating app who their favourite musician was. 'I am my own favourite musician', this man replied. The 'ick' set in immediately after this comment, but attempts to let this man down gently were met with increasing hostility: 'you're either being very insecure or discriminating against me for something', he wrote, 'you [have] no internal space to tolerate difference', 'I hope you … don't find anyone [three crying face emojis]', and so on.

Compared to other interactions, this one was relatively tame. Other people are less fortunate; unwanted dick-pics, slurs, harassment, and stalking are common. Equally noticeable from our conversations was the wider fog of frustration and ambivalence surrounding the topic of dating. The consensus seemed to be that dating is a chore, or a necessary evil, which tests our patience, goodwill, and self-esteem. What is interesting, however, is that although 'the apps suck' is a core theme, we still use them in our millions. Tinder alone, for example, has over 10 million paying subscribers, and 75 million users (Iqbal, 2024).

Dating is vastly understudied in contemporary philosophy. Quite why is unclear. Perhaps it is seen as a frivolous prelude to lofty love, which has preoccupied philosophers; or because it is seen, wrongly, as the preserve of younger people, who are taken less seriously by philosophers. Whatever the reason, in this chapter and the next, we will show this neglect is a mistake – that many aspects of dating raise ethical questions.

Our discussion will rest on a somewhat artificial distinction between the process of finding someone, and the activity or practice of dating. Dating is something we do. What dating is, why we do it, how it can be done well, and what happens when we want to stop are all important issues. But to ask those questions in practice, we have to find someone to date. The process of finding someone is the subject of this chapter; the activity of dating is the subject of the next chapter.

The finding–dating distinction is artificial as the process of choosing someone to date often involves some interaction. We message each other on apps, share photos, maybe even call or video-call each other before meeting. By the time some people meet in person, they might know a lot about each other, and may have even been sexually intimate. For our discussion, we'll count those in-app discussions, chats, as parts of choosing someone.

The ethics of choosing a partner need greater study. We focus here on digital intimacy, since it is now so common, but other efforts to seek an intimate partner can be ethically charged. We can massage our intentions, perhaps emphasizing a friendship in an attempt to morph our relationship into something more romantic. We might deceive a potential hookup about our relationship status. We might employ a matchmaker to help us satisfy a particular racial or religious preference. We might cruise for a sexual partner without communicating our sexual health status. Some of what we discuss in this book applies to these cases too, e.g. our discussion of race and dating preferences in chapter 1, but there is more to be said about the ethics of dating and acceptable behaviour.

We focus here on dating apps, since they are one important and increasingly entrenched way in which people seek to find a romantic or sexual partner. Dating apps form only one part of the wider ecosystem of digital intimacy. Wherever people can communicate online, they are likely flirting and being intimate. Message-boards, forums, fan sites, comment pages, workplace software, and so on, will all be used to chat, and arrange in-person meetings, especially for younger people who might be unable to pass age verification used by dating apps. Muddying the waters are apps such as WeChat in China, a powerful communication app used by millions. Since it allows users to search for nearby profiles, it can also be used for dating. Also relevant are forms of mediated intimacy, such as introduction services which may use a variety of digital tools to assist their work. These have a long history (Quinn, 2024).

Also, unless specified, we make no meaningful distinction between 'apps' understood as mobile applications, and websites. Many platforms are multi-modal in the sense that they can be assessed in different ways. The specific mechanics of some platforms, such as the unique opportunities for affordances of swiping offered by mobile phones (but not desktop computers), are relevant and will feature below when we discuss gamification. Some of our discussion in this chapter and the next applies also to intimate chatbots and apps such as Replika or Meeno, and perhaps even responsive sexbots (Devlin, 2018), but our primary focus is on use of technology which could, potentially, lead to us meeting a real person (although there are apps like Nevermet, which allow you to date via your avatar in the metaverse, which somewhat blur this restriction).

Finally, unless specified, we use 'dating' broadly and make no assumptions about the specific goals of daters. Some daters are looking for committed relationships, or marriage; others are looking for hookups; some are unsure; some have no intention of meeting. Quite what constitutes dating and distinguishes it, if at all, from becoming friends is a question for the next chapter. There are substantial overlaps between people looking for romance, sexual intimacy, and friendship, and some apps offer specific versions of their interface depending on how the user identifies their intentions (Bumble), whereas other apps cater explicitly to friendship (Timeleft).

2. Dating apps

a. The ecosystem

There are many dating apps. Tinder, Hinge, and Bumble might be household names, in the United Kingdom and North America at least, but dating apps feature in most countries. In China, for example, Momo and Tantan are used by tens of millions of users apiece. Badoo is the biggest dating app in Brazil. In Iran, dating apps are banned by the government with the exception of Hamdam, a state-run app aimed at marriage-orientated bachelors (France-Presse, 2021).

Other apps focus on specific communities, from uniform lovers (Uniform Dating), people exploring non-monogamy (Feeld), people with chronic health conditions and disabilities (Datability), through to coeliacs (Gluten-free Singles), *Star Trek* fans (Trek Passions), tall people (Tall Friends), or people with high opinions of themselves (The League).

Different apps scramble to develop and promote their unique selling point, whether that is a specific community of potential users (Ashley Madison and married people), or a specific interface (Grindr's 'grid'), an interactional structure (Bumble giving women the first move), a general strategy (Raya trying to make dating feel like a private members' club), and so on.

One main difference between apps is that some are based on swiping through profiles and others use questionnaires to offer matches (A. Williams, 2024, p. 56). Each offers the user a distinct mode of inter- action with the app.

Bouke de Vries suggests that mobile dating applications are impor- tantly different from websites since they

> track users' geographical locations; feature user profiles that are heavily picture-based as opposed to text-based; and require individuals to evaluate these profiles by either swiping left to express a lack of interest in someone (dislike) or right to express interest (like), whereby users who mutually like each other's profiles (a phenomenon known as 'matching') become able to communicate through the app's chat function. (de Vries, 2024, p. 1)

In a different context, Lik Chan (2021, p. 2) describes five features common to Chinese-designed dating apps:

1. The 'people nearby' feature
2. The 'swiping' feature
3. The 'groups nearby' feature
4. The status update feature
5. The livestreaming feature

Chinese apps can blend together swiping and profiles (often separate strategies in Western apps), as well as aspects of dating, social media, cam work, and even gaming (for example, some of the livestreaming functions have monetized 'gift' dimensions). The Chinese app-ecosystem therefore offers unique possibilities and pitfalls for users.

Some of these features are becoming less exclusive to phones as computer and tablet hardware and software evolve. Indeed, the emergence of devices such as Apple's Vision Pro glasses, coupled with large language AI (Artificial Intelligence) models, is already spawning new dating interfaces, including DateGPT which offers 'a unique service that personalizes matchmaking by understanding and adapting to individual user preferences. The app's AI-powered algorithm analyzes personal tastes, behaviors, and interaction patterns to provide a curated dating journey for its users. This approach ensures that connections made through the app are not only compatible but also deeply resonant with each user's personal preferences' (EIN Presswire, 2024). Apparently, 'users of DateGPT on Apple Vision Pro are pioneers, exploring new dimensions of digital dating and contributing to a broader understanding of how advanced AI and immersive technology can revolutionize the concept of online connections' (EIN Presswire, 2024).

b. Social change

Differences aside, dating apps are a transformative technology, which have shaped, and will further shape, how we meet, communicate, date, and get intimate. In the USA, for example, over half of people under thirty have used a dating app, one in ten of people in long-term committed relationships met their partner on an app, and a third have used a paid feature on an app (Vogels and Mcclain, 2023).

The rise of dating apps is interlinked to broader social changes, from globalization, the rise of the gig economy, through to the lasting impact of the Covid-19 pandemic. A central way in which dating apps have changed intimate life is by *privatizing* it (Bergström, 2021). Society changes as we live longer, work differently, delay marriage and family, have more flexible family units, and shift our social routines away from community and towards more selective forms of association. But Marie Bergström makes a strong case that dating apps 'take this privatization into the realms of love and sex and accentu[ate] it' (Bergström, 2021, p. 10).

Anyone, practically anywhere and at any time, can use their phone to connect with other people. They do so free from the oversight of peers, friends, or family. Instead of dating within familiar networks bound by ties of work, geography, or kinship, we can now look for sex or love in parallel networks of our own, networks sustained by shared values, interests, desires, and kinks.

Bergström argues that the practice of using apps is changing our norms (not just the other way around). We are more likely, for example, to think it is desirable to have separate networks of friends and of lovers (Bergström, 2021, p. 71), and both the pace and progression of intimacy have increased (Bergström, 2021, p. 84). Dating apps have upended familiar romantic trajectories: talk, meet, commit, have sex (Z. Williams, 2024). These changes are accompanied by a growing desire for autonomy and control over intimate life, free from social influence (Bergström, 2021, p. 88).

As the pursuit of intimacy becomes more private, the reflection and regulation involved become more personal, and 'self-governance' becomes 'the primary mode of control of contemporary sexuality'; as Bergström puts it:

> greater sexual leeway has brought new demands, men and women being expected more than ever before to use their freedom wisely and responsibly. This results in self-examination. Many online dating users continuously question whether their conduct is appropriate and consistent with their personal ideals and values. Self-scrutiny, auto-correction, and self-censorship are common among both men and women; examples are fixing a maximum number of dates per week or month, deciding not to have sex on a first date (a decision common among women), doing 'detox' by temporarily suspending usage, or even quitting online dating altogether. These self-regulating practices, which aim at a sexually healthy and responsible usage, full of respect for oneself and others, are the new sexual morality. Faced with a seemingly unlimited access to sex, each individual is summoned to define for herself or himself a proper sexual conduct. (Bergström, 2021, p. 95)

Interestingly, although some scholars, such as Eva Illouz (Illouz, 2013, 2019), worry that individualistic forms of dating are in tension with commitment, Bergström points to evidence which suggests people are *more likely* to move to committed relationship-statuses, even marry, as a result of using apps (Bergström, 2021, p. 92).

Dating apps are an entrenched but evolving feature of the modern intimate landscape. But the motivations of app users are complex and varied. We can use dating apps for more reasons than trying to arrange an in-person date or hookup. One study identified thirteen different motivations for using Tinder: (1) to seek social approval; (2) to seek a relationship; (3) to have a sexual experience or develop sexually; (4) to practise flirting and social skills, and gain confidence; (5) to connect with people while travelling, perhaps to gain local knowledge or meet people; (6) to attempt to get over an ex; (7) to fit in with friends/peers; (8) as a response to direct peer pressure; (9) to make friends or broaden social horizons; (10) to connect with people of the same sexual orientation; (11) to pass the time or have fun; (12) to procrastinate; and (13) out of sheer curiosity (Timmermans and De Caluwé, 2017).

Some of these motivations are active, where we are seeking something (sex, a relationship), whereas others are more responsive, where the app distracts us from something else (an ex, boredom, peer pressure). Many users will probably relate to multiple motivations at once. Interestingly, in the Chinese context, 'mudixing' – or reducing 'the multiplicity of relationships or nonrelationships afforded by dating apps into a single goal' – is frowned upon (Chan, 2021, p. 123). What is also clear is that user motivations can 'change during the use of an app', since the app interface itself can afford possibilities we had not considered or did not notice (Chan, 2021, p. 123; Newerla and van Hooff, 2023).

The list of motivations above is not exhaustive. Dating apps have been used for political campaigning (O'Brien, 2020), to spread information during war (Bielskytė, 2022), and by firms for marketing (Suresh, 2024). Some have suggested using the quiz functions of apps helps in 'discovering yourself' and learning about your intimate preferences (Weiss, 2024). In China, dating apps are often associated with business activity, especially amongst male users (Chan, 2021, p. 60). Chan's analysis of the Chinese context centres on his notion of a 'networked sexual public' – i.e. the idea that apps can function as a digital social space for people to relate, form shared experiences, or organize around common goals. Since these apps have more social networking features, they can function as slightly more open 'third spaces' away from home or work (Chan, 2021, p. 38). For queer users in China, specialist apps (like Rela and Ledso) are sources of *quanzi*, or community, which provide 'emotional support, information, and advocacy' (Chan, 2021, p. 98). Nor is that function unique to China: an acquaintance (a middle-aged queer woman) told us that she'd turn to dating apps first if she needed to borrow a screwdriver. It is worth noting, however, that some apps facilitate community, whereas others are put to use – or bent to use – by members of a community.

Some reasons for using apps anchor us to other people in physical space. We want to meet them, have sex together, or form relationships with them. But other reasons do not require this. As apps develop, and hardware develops, some users may find apps are a source of satisfaction and value separate from physical interaction. Neil McArthur and Markie Twist conjectured that we will see a rise in so-called *digisexuals*, for whom intimate technology is central to their sexual identity (McArthur and Twist, 2017). They coined the term, in part, due to a concern that such people may face discrimination. For such people, changes to apps, whether intentional or due to hacking, could change or end their digital relationships with devastating consequences for some users, as happened when the relationship-bot app Replika changed its product to prevent sexual conversations (Purtill, 2023).

Although dating apps are an entrenched part of global culture, and satisfy different motivations, app companies are under pressure. As we write, for example, Match.com, which develops apps including Tinder, is cutting jobs as paid users decline (McMahon, 2024). Bumble is also struggling with users annoyed with recent changes to the app which make it possible for men to make an opening move, and a mismanaged ad campaign denigrating celibacy (Estrada, 2024). Public discourse around apps feels increasingly ambivalent, even hostile, with users frustrated about the gap between the social prominence of apps, and their own experiences. For example, Pew Research data showed that only 53 per cent of dating app users in the USA thought their experiences where 'somewhat positive' or 'very positive' (Vogels and Mcclain, 2023).

c. Some benefits

With this downturn brewing, and user dissatisfaction seemingly on the rise, it helps to remind ourselves of the benefits of dating apps. First and foremost, apps make it easier to meet people. This is transformative if you are a member of a sexual minority, are disabled, have unusual interests or values, or have a working life which makes it hard to access other forms of dating (de Vries, 2024, p. 30). The same Pew Research data which painted a generally ambivalent picture of dating apps, for instance, found that LGBT app users were more likely than other groups to suggest apps had a positive impact (61 per cent). Location-based apps enable users to make practical choices based on their life circumstances. Dating apps also require minimal initial investment. We can use them anywhere, for as little or as long as we like, and leave with few risks or costs. In-person dating is not always like this. Dating apps also increasingly offer users descriptive categories which enable them to communicate their sexual or gender identity, and romantic intentions and desires. This streamlines the search for comparable partners, increases visibility of smaller intimate identities, and facilitates curiosity and self-exploration. These dynamics might also play a role in the kinds of cultural and normative change widespread app use is bringing about, such as the rise of personal autonomy in dating (mentioned above). We can learn about ourselves, and our desires, just by being on dating apps. Dating apps also enable us to seek advice and input from other people. As the range of motivations for app use illustrated, there are likely to be other benefits to using apps too. Some people might find them fun, or exciting; they might bring social benefits if friends use them.

It is important not to downplay these benefits. Nor should we shy from thinking about the ways dating apps, as a form of technology, could be designed in ways that work for us – which enable us to be safer than we otherwise would, more fulfilled, or more autonomous. That said, clearly people have concerns about dating apps.

3. Ethical issues

We shall outline several ethical issues raised by dating apps, with a particular focus on the idea of gamification.

a. Safety

For many users, and indeed for the apps themselves, personal safety is a core concern on dating apps. Is the person we are talking to who they say they are? Do they have bad intentions? Are we at risk in meeting them? People use apps to facilitate fraud (D. Taylor, 2023), sexual assault (Press, 2024), abduction (Hlophe, 2023), and even murder (Litvinova, 2019; Mooney, 2024). LGBT people are at particular risk.

The use of apps to perpetrate violence is not confined to headline-grabbing crimes. In a recent survey completed by 910 American university students, 54 per cent report that they had experienced forms of 'technology facilitated sexual violence', which 'can include online sexual harassment, gender- and sexuality-based harassment, cyberstalking, image-based sexual abuse, or the use of technology to perpetrate a physical, sexual assault' (Porter et al., 2024, p. 3). The most prevalent form of such violence was being the recipient of uncon-sented-for sexual images or videos. Women and LBGT individuals were more likely than men to be victims of all forms of recorded violence. Three in four women were subject to similar violence in an Australian survey (Criminology, 2022).

Chances are, if you know several women who use dating apps, at least one will have experienced these harms. These harms are inher-ently bad but they also have lasting effects on our mental health, including 'higher depression and anxiety symptoms, higher loneliness, lower self-esteem, and lower perceived control' (Echevarria, Peterson, and Woerner, 2023).

Dating apps make much of user safety. Bumble, for example, is adamant that 'we have a team working around the clock to keep out spam, fake profiles, and anyone who violates our community guide-lines. Bumble is all about safe online dating; sexual harassment, abuse, fraud and violence are not permitted on our platforms' ('Safety on Bumble', no date). Grindr has a useful page of safety tips ('Safety tips', no date). But many safety protocols rely on fallible algorithms which may require compromises in user confidentiality (e.g. by scanning photographs for nudity), or overworked content moderators.

Content moderation is an industry in vital need of ethical study and regulation, resting as it does on outsourced labourers whose working conditions and mental health are often poor. In a study of Match. com's moderation workers in different countries, for instance, investigative journalists revealed clear trends impacting workers:

> Many workers told of mental health issues including symptoms of anxiety, depression and PTSD that they associated with their jobs. One had attempted suicide on multiple occasions. Concerns were raised about understaffing, punishing productivity targets and a shortage of mental health support, as well as the time it took to address users' abuse reports. *A number of workers drew a direct link between their working conditions and the safety of the apps' users.* (McIntyre, 2023, italics added)

b. Discrimination

The connection between dating apps and user preferences is another area of concern. In chapter 1, we explored some ways in which romantic preferences and patterns of attraction can be harmful. There, we focused on race, and to some extent on appearance, but related concerns apply to other social categories, such as social class and disability. Dating apps can contribute to discrimination. First, their algorithms might encode judgements about appearance of compatibility on explicit racial grounds (A. Williams, 2024). Second, apps might offer people the ability, usually for a price, to filter potential matches on lines of race, ethnicity, class, and so on: to 'racially curate' the 'sexual marketplace' (A. Williams, 2024, p. 112). Third, apps can provide users a mechanism which engages their romantic and sexual biases, for example the card-deck swiping structure of apps such as Tinder, which encourages hasty choices based on appearance. Some of these contributions are direct, others are indirect. Evaluating responsibility is thus a complex matter, particularly as dating apps rarely expose their inner working.

c. Ghosting

Behaviour is still another area of ethical concern for app users. Most users of a dating app will have either ghosted or been ghosted – that is, have someone just leave an interaction without prior warning or explanation. You might also have been 'orbited' – that is, ghosted by someone who still lurks on your social media. You might also have experienced breadcrumbing – that is, 'a negative dating behavior that involves repeatedly tossing out just enough titbits of interest to keep another person interested and involved, where the breadcrumber is not truly interested in the person they are dating and is only using the relationship to gain a superficial connection and attention from them' (Khattar, Upadhyay, and Navarro, 2023, p. 2). Or perhaps you have been put on the 'backburner' in the sense that you've been interacting with someone who is already committed, but views you as a potential romantic partner if their existing relationship falls apart (Dibble and Drouin, 2014; Dibble et al., 2015). These forms of behaviour are not unique to dating apps, but dating apps have played a role in facilitating, or at least not discouraging, some of these behaviours. Whether that is a problem or not is an interesting ethical question. People are divided over ghosting, for instance, with some viewing it as a logical strategy when faced with many poor or stalling conversations on an app, and others worrying it can be a harmful and disrespectful form of interactional practice. We return to ghosting in the next chapter.

d. (In)authenticity

Another ethical worry centres on authenticity. Setting aside fraud or catfishing, we can still worry about the character of our interactions on apps. Are we getting to know 'the real them', are their pictures accurate, are they being open with us, have they got a broader dating strategy in mind? These are not new questions. King Henry VIII was famously furious with Hans Holbein's painting of Anne of Cleves when he met her in person, for example. But they raise their head with new force in the digital age.

Of growing concern is the interaction between dating apps and generative AI. LoveGenius, for example, offers to use AI to provide you with a dating biography that is '5x' more likely to get you a better match. RoastDating will use AI to help you generate AI photos for your profile. Like Ken dolls looking for outfits, users can select between 'business', 'casual', 'relax', 'sportswear', and – importantly – 'beach' themes to project the right image. Users are told to 'write your own story, get the perfect pictures for any situations'. Yourmove.ai 'perfects your profile and puts your texting on cruise control. So you can spend less time swiping, and more time dating' through a range of AI-integrated services including 'conversation assist', which generates text for you to use, in a variety of styles, by analysing screenshots of your chats on apps. Even the CEO of Bumble publicly mooted the idea of an AI 'dating concierge' which can date other AIs to improve your matches (Whittaker, 2024).

These are direct ways of shaping the interactions you have with other people. Other services and applications offer indirect ways, too. Apps such as Menno (a start-up by ex-Tinder CEO Renate Nyborg) aim to help people overcome loneliness and interact better by improving their 'social health' by enabling them to practise interactions (Murgia, 2024). A survey by Meeno found that a third of men surveyed, aged 18–34, were using ChatGPT for relationship advice (Meeno Blog, 2024). So even if someone is not using AI to interact with you directly, they may be using strategies they have learnt using AI elsewhere.

These offerings are just the beginning. The integration of AI into dating applications is likely to grow, given current enthusiasm for AI. For the user, the ethical questions are clear. Should we use AI to interact with others? If so when, or under what constraints? Is a bit of AI dating advice, or AI profile writing, any different from asking for the input of a friend when setting up a profile or deciding to swipe right? We suspect people who are unbothered about a bit of profile sharpening will doubt the desirability of having a conversation with someone's AI bot, or of swiping through entirely AI-generated 'photographs' of a potential match.

The ability to trust other people, and have authentic interactions with them, is still prized. We might be dispirited, for example, to realize we were one of the 5,238 women dated and rejected 'virtually' by a ChatGPT bot built by developer Alexander Zhadan (Cleave and Stewart, 2024). Even his 'successful' fiancée might have doubts about the soundness of his method. His whole approach can be critiqued in other ways too. While ChatGPT might make *his* life easier, our colleague Sophie Goddard noted that if each woman his bots chatted with spent one hour doing so before giving up, that is over *half a year* of female emotional labour wasted.

Use of AI isn't the only worry with apps either, as people can adopt various distrustful strategies in an attempt to 'game' the algorithm to their advantage. One radical strategy is men lying about their sexuality (Townsend, 2024), but more common strategies might be lying about height or age, or choosing interests which one thinks are likely to result in matches even if one does not have them.

e. Justice

We can worry about the dating landscape. Just as some people we match with might not be transparent with us, so app companies might be less than transparent about their products. This can be inherently frustrating, as we might want to know how a specific product uses our data or impacts us (Carr, 2016), but there are structural issues here too. We might agree, for example, with Elsa Kugelberg who thinks that dating apps share the 'digital sexual sphere' by playing a substantial role in distributing and patterning romantic goods (who gets to meet and date, etc.) (Kugelberg, 2025). Since collectively they have such power, we should ask when and under what conditions this power is justified. We might think that the power of any institution that shapes our opportunity to access important goods is justified only if it meets certain values – especially that of justice. We can disagree what those values are, but good candidates could be: that the principles under which our intimate fates are shaped have to be made *transparent* and/ or *justified* to us; that the opportunity to access intimacy should be open to everyone, and minorities should not be set back; and that the ongoing ability to structure the digital sexual sphere must be subject to *oversight*. At present, few if any apps meet these conditions, and the general ecosystem of apps is not heavily regulated.

Some of the issues arising from dating apps in general may be due to the involvement of commercial incentives. Bouke de Vries, for example, argues that dating apps are designed to prolong our search for intimacy and love, since the more time we spend using them, the more money they make (de Vries, 2024). This increases the personal costs for the user, compared to non-commercial solutions. Some might go further still, and question whether romantic goods should ever be subject to market pressures and incentives (Frank, Klincewicz, and Jane, 2022, p. 567). All of these views, whether motivated by concerns with justice, unnecessary personal cost, or the nature of the goods being distributed, can prompt us to consider non-market solutions to the problem of how to find people to date, such as state-run dating apps.

f. Gamification

Many of the ethical issues we have raised are not unique to dating apps. Dating prior to the internet could be harmful, racially biased, fraught with poor behaviour, inauthentic, unjust, or shaped by market incentives. So is there anything uniquely problematic about this technology? To answer that, we shall explore how dating apps *gamify* our search for love.

Dating apps are like casino slot machines. They make the search for love game-like and, in so doing, encourage us to engage in simple but compelling behaviour which can distance us from what we really care about.

We shall focus on the inherently bad features of gamification when it arises in the wrong context via its connection with acting autonomously. Other scholars have noted that the analogy with a slot machine has similar financial resonance, however, since many dating apps make available various in-app purchase options (like 'boosts' or 'superlikes' and membership tiers). As de Vries puts it:

> the use of visibility boosts meets all the criteria for being a (non-conventional) form of gambling defined as 'the act of wagering or betting money or something of value on an event with an uncertain outcome with the intent to win more money or things of value than was wagered'. (de Vries, 2024, p. 6)

Indeed, he argues that 'the use of visibility boosts is *structurally similar to the most addictive forms of gambling such as slot machine games and the use of loot boxes* [in computer games]' (de Vries, 2024, p. 6). Even if money was not involved, however, there are grounds to be concerned about the impact of gamifying systems.

To be clear, gamification is not unique to dating apps, but dating apps may gamify in unique ways due to their specific interfaces. This can be more or less intentional. To gamify something is to make it game-like in some respect. Thi C. Nguyen explores the changes to our agency that gamification can bring about (Nguyen, 2020, pp. 189–215). Nguyen's core ethical worry is that 'features that are crucial to the agential fluidity of games [i.e. which make it easy for us to get immersed in them], when exported clumsily to our non-game life, can lead to moral and social disaster' (Nguyen, 2020, pp. 189–90). When we play games, we are encouraged to adopt simple practical motivations and strategies in pursuit of set goals. We reason in instrumental terms – 'How do I achieve this goal?' – and, temporarily, focus on that goal as if nothing else matters. Good games help us get into this state by making things seem simple. Our objectives are clear, and the values within the game are easy to apply, rankable, and often translated into each other (commensurable). This clarity makes games satisfying.

When gamification occurs outside of games, several bad things can happen (cf. Sicart, 2015). For one thing, Nguyen worries we might be drawn to social contexts and environments which make values seem 'artificially clear' (Nguyen, 2020, p. 199). Some political parties, cults, or wellness providers do this. But the bigger problem he terms 'value capture', which happens in the following way:

1. Our values are, at first, rich and subtle.
2. We encounter simplified (often quantified) versions of those values.
3. Those simplified versions take the place of our richer values in our reasoning and motivation.
4. Our lives get worse. (Nguyen, 2020, p. 201)

When we are value-captured, we are seduced by the simpler, clearer, version of the value we already cared about, and we 'lose touch with the richness of our values' (Nguyen, 2020, p. 206). The underlying worry, here, is that, as we are seduced by simpler and clearer versions of our values, we become less able to act *autonomously* – i.e. in accordance with *our* values.

To this, we also add the problem of *emotional capture*, where our rich, messy, and often ambivalent emotional responses to something – such as a person we are dating – are replaced with simplified, or polarized, or more sentimental versions of those feelings (Pugmire, 2007). (Developing this idea would take us too far afield, unfortunately.)

Most of Nguyen's examples of gamifiers are oppressors and bureaucrats, but gamification is a core part of business design, where it is often viewed positively (Gardiner, 2024). Dating apps arguably gamify the user experience. Karim Nader, in drawing on Nguyen's work, argues that Tinder – to take a specific app's interface – gamifies a user's values as they use the app, and so simplifies their motivations in a way that can distance them from their more subtle, complex, and messy initial intimate values (Nader, 2024). Nader gives us reason to use terms like 'compulsion' with care. He suggests positive emotions, like hope, play a much more important role in locking us into simple game-like structures. We keep going because we are hoping for a good outcome.

Nader argues both that Tinder is designed to gamify and that it achieves this goal (cf. Garda and Karhulahti, 2021). Tinder centres on the game-like continuous physical action of swiping, which locks the user into a loop. A mutual match provides the user with a pop-up box, like a point in the game, and the player can either continue or stop and start a conversation with the match. In itself, this interface reduces the complexities of trying to meet and start a conversation with someone to a fairly simple repetitive process.

Nader's main focus, however, is on the goals and motivations he thinks Tinder is getting us to adopt – what Nguyen would call the 'game-like shifts of agency' involved (Nguyen, 2020, p. 189). This is a shift away from the complex process of interacting with someone to see if there is an intimate spark, and towards the activity of 'matching'. Nader looks at Tinder's marketing and monetized offerings to argue the app is premised on the idea that we should try to match with as many people as possible.

The stated reason for this is that the more matches you have, the better your chances of real intimacy are, but Nader argues Tinder's 'monetization strategies suggest that maximizing matches is a goal in itself' (Nader, 2024, p. 9) and that the app encourages users to think that 'Swiping and matching are more enjoyable than the complexities of dating. Swiping is a simple process that only asks the user to make a discrete yes or no decision. Matching provides quick gratification with quantifiable success' (Nader, 2024, p. 9). Users of Tinder are value-captured to the extent their prior motivations and intimate values are replaced by those visible in this company strategy. Here, value capture leads to profit.

Nader makes the case that this gamification has occurred, that users change their goals from dating someone to matching with people (whom they might not date), and that users change the *activities* they pursue away from spending time with people and towards the curation of their online persona or attempts to game the algorithm (some of which we have mentioned above). These changes may also lead to shifts in emotional response, too, with complex emotional reactions being replaced with simpler hits of positive or negative feeling.

Tinder provides a good example of how gamification is complex. Nader's analysis rests on an investigation *both* of the user interface design and of the broader message, marketing, and monetization structure Tinder uses. It's the whole package – the combination of a simple action repertoire (swipe) with a simple goal (match as much as possible) – that is game-like and which threatens our autonomy.

Nader worries Tinder's gamification has negative consequences. First, we strive after goals that are kept out of our reach – the algorithm is private, and often stacked against us. Second, we risk unethically objectifying people since we treat them as mere means to a match, or as fungible, or as disposable, and so on (Nussbaum, 1995). Third, we risk intimate value capture. We risk, that is, coming to value what Tinder encourages us to value, rather than what we start out valuing, and wanting, in our intimate life.

Nader makes a strong case, and it is one that will apply to other dating apps. We think, however, that value capture is unlikely to be total in the sense that we fully replace the complex (human intimacy) for the simple (matching). Indeed, we suggest something more nuanced occurs, a form of *temporary value alienation* perhaps, where we are gripped by the simplified version of a value that nevertheless still matters to us. This is why many users of apps feel a kind of estrangement or ambivalence – a sense that they are sucked into a form of interaction which isn't really what they want, but which they struggle to reject.

We have surveyed several ethical issues arising from the widespread use of dating apps. Some concern the ends to which apps are used (e.g. sexual violence), some concern the behaviour prevalent on and perhaps encouraged by apps (e.g. discrimination and ghosting), some concern the broader app ecosystem (e.g. unregulated and unaccountable), and some concern the personal impact of engaging with dating apps (gamification).

We lingered over gamification, in particular, because it is a subtle form of potential harm, one connected closely to the specific interfaces and strategies used by apps, and one that may account for the well-documented frustration and apathy around dating apps. One way to account for that apathy is in terms of a growing recognition of the gap between the simplified but alluring offering apps provide, on the one hand, and the richer and more meaningful values which structure our pursuit of intimacy, on the other.

The obvious question to ask, then, is: can these problems be addressed?

4. Better online dating

Let's explore different ways to respond to the ethical problems associated with dating apps. We are concerned with dating apps in general, rather than specific apps, but different apps warrant different approaches. The strategies below can be combined, and some of them might be mutually reinforcing.

We shall also sidestep complex questions about blame and responsibility. You might think, for example, that the onus to change falls on those who have benefited from a specific social arrangement (e.g. for-profit companies). Alternatively, you might think we have collective obligations to reshape social institutions which impact everyone. Note, however, that we can still concern ourselves with strategies to change, which lead to a morally better environment, in the absence of direct blame. (For an example of this with some relevance to interactions on dating apps, see Regina Rini's work on how to address microaggressions without hostile blame (Rini, 2020).)

For convenience, we divide potential solutions into three loose categories: what *dating apps* can do, what *governments* can do, and what we can do, as *individuals*.

a. What can apps do?

We assume that dating app companies could design their products differently, and be more proactive in taking a value-led approach. We explore this using five themes: transparency; safety; user agency; value-led design; and an active social role.

Apps could be more transparent. Efforts to explain how they work would help to go some way to addressing the justification gap at the heart of the industry, where the intimate sphere is shaped by companies whose reasons and procedures are not widely understood.

User safety can also become more of a priority. Apps can invest more into content moderation, and ensure moderators have good working conditions; review their safety policies and revise them to ensure they take a robust stance on sexual racism, for example; review their monetization structures and ensure there are procedures in place to assist users who spend too much (as with problem gamblers); and consider implementing 'share my date' features so daters can let their friends know where they are (Petter, 2024).

User agency can be supported by apps in several different ways. First, apps can do more to replicate some of the networked or community features of some Chinese apps, or do more to help users understand positive and negative connections between people they trust and potential dates. Tinder's attempt to involve friends and family provides some oversight (Thomas, 2023), but in a way that is not transparent to other users. The dating app Feeld takes a different approach with their 'constellation' feature, which enables users to link their profiles to up to five other profiles using a range of different relationship-labels (not all romantic). These features enable some users to benefit from a better sense of the offline networks they might be moving into. Done right, small moves to de-privatize intimacy online may foster trust and reduce abuse. More radical options might include making it public when someone has had a complaint upheld against them, or has been banned on other apps, or is a serial reporter of other people. These options would require careful consideration by ethicists, since app report functions are often used maliciously (Prendergast, 2020).

Second, apps can be more proactive in educating their users. This can happen on sign-up, for example, and periodically as users are on the app (perhaps with educational 'cards' on a swipe-based apps 'deck'). Apps might also consider making user data accessible to users themselves to enable them to better understand how they are actually behaving, as opposed to how they think they are behaving (perhaps like music app Spotify's end-of-year snapshot of user's music tastes). Well-intentioned daters who think they are not racially biased might be surprised to see they disproportionately favour people of their own race. When users are better informed about their preferences, they are better able to reflect on how they use, and want to use, a product.

Third, apps can do more to help users signal their intentions and frames of mind, which, in turn, can enable them to better signal what kind of 'discursive' frame they are in (Kukla, 2018). If users can better display their mood – that they are feeling curious, or hesitant – via a status, or emojis, they give others social clues about how they might want to interact or be approached. App interfaces might also consider how to facilitate active transitions between certain kinds of conversation – e.g. between general chat and sexual interactions, or between written conversation and the exchange of images – in ways that ensure consent is respected and which may help reduce unsolicited or unwanted sexualization.

Apps embrace value-led design when they allow explicit human values to shape the process of product development (Frank, Klincewicz, and Jane, 2022, p. 555). Rather than trying to remain neutral on issues of discrimination, sexualization, or ghosting, apps could be more explicit about the kind of interactions they are hoping to foster, and which are commensurate with their brand. In turn, their product could be designed to embody these values. Apps could take a stance on ghosting and design positive 'nudges' to change the default setting away from enabling ghosting, to one where users are asked to reconsider or explain before leaving an interaction. Another example might be taking steps to ensure certain kinds of filtering are not possible, or not possible as a default (height, for example).

There is room for strong and weak versions of value-led design. The weaker version aims to ensure the default setting aligns with the expressed values – i.e. you can ghost but not by default, it has to be something you 'opt into' doing in some sense. The stronger version is to prohibit an option (e.g. by not providing a racial filter (Hunte, 2020)). If this sounds intrusive, it helps to remember that no product design is value-neutral, and that apps already take a stance in the specific interfaces they make available. We can do more to ask: 'What are those values?', 'Are they good values?', and 'How can the product be changed to align it with better values?'

One possibility is that apps embrace forms of 'good gamification'. Their interfaces might make it easier for us to reflect on desires and how we treat others, or whether we ghost. Although there is a profit motive to sustain our attention, this could potentially be accompanied by efforts to encourage periodic personal reflection – indeed, to make that process a virtue of an app itself.

Finally, dating app companies can take a more active social role. Perhaps they could embrace voluntary forms of sector-wide regulation, or the establishment of independent policy review boards, oversight committees, or ombudsmen. Other things they could do would be to include users on their boards, and ensure their products serve the communities that use them. App companies could also build on examples of admirable historical collaboration with public health agencies to assist in addressing sexual and mental health (Garcia-Iglesias et al., 2024). Grindr, for example, has partnered with sexual-health testing charities in several countries to help facilitate HIV (human immunodeficiency virus) testing; many apps promoted vaccination during Covid-19 with stickers to enable people to show they had been vaccinated, and even free in-app benefits (such as boosts) as an incentive (UK Gov, 2021), and some apps have also been active in campaigns against loneliness (Tinder, 2023). Broader collaboration between app companies and other sexual and relationship charities can also help to educate users about good relationships, sexual health, and mental health.

b. What can governments do?

Dating app companies are unlikely to make changes which limit their ability to profit, especially in competitive markets. These companies are unlikely, for example, to adjust lucrative paid-membership options or the provision of in-app boosts, even if they are proven to be structurally akin to gambling. Nor are app companies likely to try to help users leave their products. As Lily Frank and co-authors put it: 'success in most [dating and hookup app] business models relies on a covert failure [to efficiently find people a good match] that must not openly be declared or acknowledged' (Frank, Klincewicz, and Jane, 2022, p. 560). Even people optimistic about the ability for companies to balance profit motives with wider social responsibility might look for more robust government intervention.

Governments have at least three core options when it comes to dating apps: ban them, regulate them, join them by offering a state-run dating app. Let's consider each.

Some countries have banned dating apps. Grindr, for instance, seems to be the most frequently banned dating app, with it being unavailable in thirteen countries (Castro, 2024). Outright bans are possible. This move seems deeply illiberal to many, however, and would deny citizens the real benefits that apps provide, most notably an increase in the ease of meeting people.

Regulation is more palatable. Governments could do more to ensure dating app companies, and other big tech firms, have accountable corporate governance, are more transparent about their products, have to respect privacy and data laws (users may not know that different apps owned by the same umbrella company might share data between themselves), have robust and perhaps independent complaints procedures in place, and have mechanisms to protect whistle-blowers with legitimate concerns (de Vries, 2024, p. 12).

Other forms of regulation may be aimed at preventing monopoly power in the market (e.g. targeting companies, such as the Match group, which own most major dating apps and which have expanded aggressively without much opposition (Mangalindan, 2018)).

Governments may also take steps to regulate the integration of AI into dating technology – perhaps making it a legal requirement to indicate when a photo or profile has been shaped by AI, or when a conversation is mediated by AI.

Regulation can be more or less extensive and robust. In democratic counties, where regulators are in theory representatives of the people and themselves checked by independent courts, regulation of dating apps may help address some of the concerns about justice in the previous section. Citizens may consent, as it were, to having their ability to find partners largely shaped by private companies if they know those companies are regulated by laws written by their political representatives.

Finally, governments can make their own dating apps. As mentioned previously, this is already the case in Iran, and will be the case in Japan (Quiroz-Gutierrez, 2024). As these examples show, this option is compatible both with a wider ban on dating apps (Iran) or with a state-run app playing a role in a wider ecosystem of commercially run digital apps (Japan).

De Vries has argued in favour of state-run dating apps (cf. Kugelberg, 2025). His core positive argument is that the interests of governments and their citizens, when it comes to intimacy, are more aligned than those of companies and citizens (de Vries, 2024, p. 8). Governments, the thought goes, want people to meet and form relationships, whereas companies want people to stay on the app. His core negative argument is that we can defend the idea of state dating apps from objections – most notably, that they need not be too expensive to create and that we can impose regulations to ensure governments do not misuse data.

De Vries thinks there is no need, either, for states to ban other dating apps to have positive benefits. The existence of a free government app alongside commercial alternatives (or of a non-profit app) helps people who want to find a partner – with limited personal cost, greater transparency, and the absence of a commercial incentive – to do so. He suggests that adding a government app to the existing ecosystem is 'less intrusive', as an option, compared to efforts to force dating app companies to modify or publicize their algorithms (de Vries, 2024, p. 12 fn.15).

Adding a state-run app might address some concerns about justice and fairness. But there are many questions about the desirability of this approach. For one, we might agree with de Vries that governments are aligned with citizens who want long-term relationships, but what about people who want hookups, or gay sex, or to pursue BDSM (bondage, discipline/domination, sadism/submission, and masochism), and so on? The Japanese app in development, for example, was motivated by the government's concern with declining fertility, rather than with sexual pleasure and the enjoyment of intimacy. Moreover, what a government is *able* to justify to its taxpaying citizens, in pragmatic terms, is not always what is required by the demands of justice (as LGBT people will confirm). We also have concerns about government mismanagement, use of data, political interference, the protection of minorities, the use of app-generated location data by security services, and the provision of facilities to forge intimacy offline (all substantive issues in themselves).

That said, the case for a state-run app is much stronger than it first appears, and dovetails nicely with arguments in support of other state interventions aimed at providing equal access to the digital sphere (Zuckerman, 2020), such as access to the internet (Reglitz, 2020).

c. What can individuals do?

Finally, we consider what individuals might do to address some of the ethical challenges raised by online dating. We placed this last, in recognition of the fact that many of those issues are structural in nature, and some of them – such as gamification – can inhibit our autonomy despite our best intentions.

With this point in mind, someone might object that structural problems require structural solutions – a point we saw Gulzar Barn making in connection to intimate racism in the previous chapter (Barn, 2022). But it is important to recognize that individuals might have obligations to address matters of structural injustice, even if they cannot be blamed directly for them, or even if their contribution is harmful only in virtue of the contributions of other people (Young, 2011).

In the context of online dating specifically, these obligations might include calling out problematic aspects of online dating – whether that is specific apps, or specific aspects of online dating culture; boycotting particular products, e.g. the consumer backlash against Bumble's use of 'celibate' as a negative term (Beck, 2019; Blake, 2024); campaigning to change the wider dating culture, perhaps by calling for reform or regulation, or through forms of consumer activism such as critiquing poor company practices on social media; or political activism, such as voting for parties who promise to regulate large technological companies or who take a strong stance on moderation, or privacy and data protection, or the safety of minorities.

We can also critique the habits and practices of people around us. After all, we likely know people who use apps in troubling ways – whether in serial ghosting, sexually objectifying women, or using AI – and we can challenge them about those behaviours. This need not be a form of blaming criticism, but rather what Robin Zheng calls 'formative criticism', which we can offer even in situations where we recognize the agency of others has been constrained by their social situation (as seems likely in modern dating culture) (Zheng, 2021, p. 351).

Some might think that supporting structural changes is enough. But might we have personal duties too? We saw this in thinking about romantic preferences, attraction, and racism in the previous chapter. There, people posed various strategies to try to identify and work on problematic patterns of attraction. The strongest of these were aimed at actually changing our patterns of attraction. But such views are not without criticism.

In thinking about dating, Simone Degn has argued in favour of a weak 'deliberative duty' (Degn, 2024). She has several worries about stronger versions of the idea we should work on ourselves. First, because we cannot change our preferences very much. Second, because if we focus too much on morality in dating, we also '[seem] inclined to miss out on a certain kind of joy, a joy that pertains to acting accordingly to one's own interests and inclinations' (Degn, 2024, p. 8). Third, because attitudes can also have a negative impact on the people we end up dating. And finally, because our efforts to shape our attractions to tackle exclusion may not be adequate to tackle other kinds of intimate discrimination, such as an *over* focus on some people. Instead, the deliberative duty is 'about critically reflecting on the restrictions placed on us by social hierarchies and, perhaps with time, leaving them behind' (Degn, 2024, p. 14). As Degn understands it, this is a duty to undergo a certain kind of process, rather than to necessarily bring out certain outcomes.

Her version of the duty has us asking three questions of ourselves:

1. 'What do I consider to be essential functions for being my intimate partner?'
2. 'In a sexist, racist, homophobic, fatphobic, ableist, lookist, classist and so on world, is there a chance my list of essential functions is affected by these structures or that the specific instances of essential functions are making me overlook viable potential dates?'
3. 'In light of these structures, how might I aim to act toward others in the dating sphere while simultaneously acting in alignment with the preferences I currently have?' (Degn, 2024, p. 15)

For example, maybe we consider attractiveness to be an essential feature of a romantic partner. We can then ask if our 'need' for attractiveness is the product of problematic social forces, or whether our specific sense of *this* person as attractive, or not, is the product of those forces (perhaps because their racial features, such as wavy hair, do not feature in widespread ideals of beauty).

Degn's view is interesting, offering as it does a moderate version of a duty of self-examination as a response to discrimination. We mention it here, since a version of this duty might apply to other aspects of our efforts to choose someone to date and navigate dating apps. Being unreflective when looking for a partner, failing to consider the impact of social structures, and failing to consider how we interact and communicate, will exacerbate the ethical issues mentioned above. For instance, we might not give much thought about the wider impact of using AI to 'improve' our profiles, or of ghosting as a way of (not) relating to people, and we might have never heard of, let alone considered, gamification, and the idea that apps are designed to capture and monetize our attention. At the very least, becoming aware of these options as options, and considering their impact on others, and how they relate to our underlying assumptions about good intimacy or a desirable relationship, can go some way to improving our situation.

Degn's deliberative duty is purely reflective; it does not *require* us to change our romantic preferences. Like us, you might find this practical inertia dissatisfying. Even if we cannot change how we are attracted, we can – and perhaps *should* – refuse certain restrictive filter-settings, for example, and so introduce a little more chance of the unexpected into our dating online.

Practical change seems even more important in other aspects of our dating interactions. It's not enough, there is reason to think, to identify the connections between social structures, norms, and our personal circumstances when thinking about ghosting, or the grip of gamification; we might also want to change how we act, whether to benefit ourselves or to treat others better.

So how might we tackle something like gamification? A radical option is to quit all dating apps. But in the modern world this puts many people at a disadvantage. Other options include being more reflective about the specific apps we use, in an attempt to avoid using those which increase our risk of being locked into unhappy patterns of behaviour, value capture, and financial expense. Once on apps, we can try to establish semi-regular 'autonomy audits' – every six months say – to explicitly reflect on why we are using the product, what our initial motivations were, what our motivations now seem to be, whether we have felt any sense of value alienation, and whether we think our values or desires have changed, and potentially simplified, for the worse. This could be a solitary process, or one undertaken with friends or therapists (whom we might ask to audit our profiles and filter settings), as part of a broader effort to use technology in a responsible way that works for us.

Finally, another option is to combine our use of dating apps with attempts to meet people in other ways, such as through events organized around shared interests, or by being more proactive in engaging with our local community. Put simply, we can take steps to adopt diversified approaches to finding intimate partners and – in so doing – reduce the likelihood that any particular mode of interaction comes to dominate.

Some of these efforts are merely reflective, and others connected to practical changes. Those changes can be direct in the sense that we toggle a filter or refuse to use a certain app, or indirect in the sense of trying to reflect on our habits. Together, they can help align our behaviour and values. We have focused on the more subtle ethical issues, such as steps to tackle gamification or our patterns of attraction, but of course these strategies also fit alongside other efforts to be safer in using dating apps.

5. Conclusion

Millions use dating apps every day, typically with hope but not enthusiasm. This ordinary frustration demands ethical consideration alongside more serious harms. As forms of technology, dating apps and websites, and other forms of dating mediated by the internet, have radically shaped how we pursue intimacy. We have shown that there are many challenges associated with dating apps, but also different ways we can meet those challenges, whether as businesses, governments, or individuals. These efforts need not be purely remedial, either. Dating apps can, and should, play a vital role in facilitating flourishing intimacy.

3

Dating

1. Introduction

Dating is hard to define. The *Oxford English Dictionary* (*OED*) has, as one definition, 'to go out, or arrange to go out, on a date with somebody; esp. to go out with a person (regularly) as a romantic partner' (*Oxford English Dictionary*, 2023a). Here, much hinges on the idea of 'going out with', which can clearly mean many things. Confusingly, two people might say they are 'going out' with each other without this involving 'dates' of a typical kind at all, and people may go on occasional dates without thinking they are 'going out' with each other. Notably, this definition does not build into dating the idea that the intimacy is acknowledged to be tentative or uncommitted in some important sense.

The *OED* definition also straddles the two separate ideas we distinguished at the beginning of the previous chapter – namely, the task of selecting a person, and the activity of dating the person selected. Here we want to focus on dating in the second, active sense. Dating is something we understand ourselves as doing. Typically, but perhaps not always, we understand dating to be prior to more committed forms of relationship. But quite what dating may involve, and what is involved in doing it well, are unclear.

Dating has seldom been the direct focus of philosophers.

This is not to suggest that aspects of dating have not been discussed or depicted in philosophy for a long time. Socrates in Plato's dialogues, such as the *Meno* or the *Charmides*, is famously flirtatious. And the twists and turns of philosophical inquiry itself, especially in dialogue form, have often been recognized as having parallels with the twists and turns of erotic desire, with the comparison between desire and philosophy being central to Plato's account of love in the *Symposium*.

The neglect of dating as a topic itself, however, might be because the process of actively and independently seeking an intimate partner for oneself is relatively new, especially for women. The term 'dating' was apparently first used in its modern sense in 1896 in a newspaper (Weigel, 2017, p. 12) and was initially a form of working-class slang, but it has stuck around ever since. Significantly, dating as we now know it was made possible through a complex mix of social, economic, normative, and technological change. The concentration of working people in urban areas, changing social attitudes, new laws around divorce, combined with the growing use of the bicycle and then car, made intimate exploration away from the prying eyes of a chaperone more possible for some (Coontz, 2006).

In this chapter, we shall explore a few aspects of dating in an effort to highlight their potential ethical significance. Our motivations for dating can be complex, and change in the process of interacting with someone. The activities which constitute dating, or which are typical to people dating, are rich and poorly understood and may be conducted with or without respect. Sometimes dating does not go well, and we have to part ways.

Our working conception of dating positions it prior to more committed or formally recognized forms of relationship, as that is how most people conceptualize dating. But we note it also makes sense for people to talk about 'dating' their spouse or having 'date nights' – for example, Christian writer Justin Buzzard offers his male readers '100 practical ideas for how to date your wife' (Buzzard, 2012). Some people might also talk of 'dating themselves' (Scott, 2023), or 'friend dates'.

A question to consider as you read this chapter is: Does dating have distinct value? As a social practice, we may be inclined to view dating with frustration or ambivalence since we see it as a necessary step towards more committed relationships. This is an instrumental picture of dating which sees it as the process of relating to someone prior to a committed relationship. This general view of dating is itself scaffolded by other romantic and intimate norms, such as amatonormativity: the idea that amorous relationships have special value and should be at the heart of life; or mononormativity: the idea that we should only have one romantic relationship at a time. But perhaps there are other ways to think about dating and perhaps you have derived value from dating even if it did not lead to an 'outcome'.

2. Curiosity

So what *is* dating?

One stab at an answer is: it's a process of *getting to know* someone. To date someone is to spend time with them, undergo shared experiences, converse, and share information. Why do that? To ultimately be in a position to decide whether that person is right for us relative to our prior aims, whether that is to find someone to have a long-term relationship with, to marry, or to be our next friend-with-benefits. Understood this way, dating is a search for knowledge, and it is a search relative to a prior sense of what we want. It is a search with the question of compatibility at its heart. Often, this compatibility is *romantic* in nature. We are trying to get to know someone romantically. We are wary of building that into a definition of dating, as it might rule out cases where we have a romantic connection with someone we want to know in other ways, or cases where we are dating with an open mind to see how a potential intimacy might develop – i.e. cases where we are dating to see if we *want* to know someone romantically.

Dating is rarely a dispassionate search. Often, we desire to know, and are driven to date, by more complex and passionate motivations. Central to this, it seems fair to say, is a feeling of curiosity. To want to move from a match on an app to chatting with someone, and from chatting with them to meeting in person, and from meeting in person to the bedroom, we have to be undergirded by curiosity. What is this person like? Are they for me? Will we have a good time together?

But curiosity is a complex emotion. If a dating app understands itself as facilitating curiosity, for example, what might that mean? On a compatibility-oriented, instrumental, understanding of curiosity, the app is providing people with a forum in which to come to know things about other people in order to work out if they are a 'compatible' or 'right' match. But might there be other dimensions to curiosity? If so, might there be other dimensions to dating? Our hunch is that a better understanding of curiosity gives us a clearer understanding of what dating is, or might be.

To explore this possibility, we will introduce Daniella Dover's distinction between two kinds of curiosity and relate it to some work on feminist curiosity. This gives us the resources to characterize two different kinds of dating, and then return to questions of value.

a. Erotic curiosity

Dover's core thought is that the emotion of curiosity is not always an epistemic emotion – that is, oriented towards knowledge (Dover, 2024a). She distinguishes between a standard understanding of curiosity, as a feeling oriented towards knowledge, and what she calls 'erotic curiosity'. On the standard picture, she argues, curiosity is viewed as prompted by a *question*, motivated by a *desire*, and ends in *knowledge* (the 'QDK' model). We might want to know if someone is bisexual like us, for example, or whether they share our values, strive to find this out, and be satisfied with the answer. Note that this might not require us to interact with that person at all – perhaps a mutual friend can tell us.

Erotic curiosity, in contrast, focuses on the object or person in question. If we are erotically curious about someone, we are captivated by them. Full stop. We might not have any prior questions about them or any knowledge that we seek. Interestingly, Dover gives an example of something that looks a bit like dating, even though dating is not her primary focus:

> Compare the mundane case of chatting up an intriguing stranger at a bar. Unless you are doing market research, you do not start talking to someone in order to find out whether they come here often. Rather, you ask whether they come here often as a way to start talking to them. If they are really as intriguing as you hoped, talking to them will lead you to ask further questions. But at the end of the night, you will be grateful not for having obtained knowledge of the answers to a bunch of questions, but rather for having had the chance to interact with someone interesting enough to prompt them. (Dover, 2024a, p. 817)

In many cases, these situations *feel* far from mundane. They can be fraught with excitement and uncertainty.

Dover tries to describe some of the features of erotic curiosity. For one, the form of desire involved is harder to pin down. It can 'take the form of an inchoate longing to intertwine with the object of curiosity' (Dover, 2024a, p. 824), and is 'nervous, prickly, goading' rather than a 'state in which we can rest contentedly' (Dover, 2024a, p. 821). This restlessness is also what Dover thinks distinguishes erotic curiosity from wonder (Dover, 2024b, p. 330, n6). Erotic curiosity is self-sustaining and 'finds ways to replenish itself' by 'prompting ever more probing attention, which in turn discloses new, or newly puzzling, vistas' (Dover, 2024a, p. 826). Dover also thinks that the object of erotic curiosity has to be viewed positively (Dover, 2024a, p. 827), but we are less sure about that; there can be a kind of ambivalent fascination and curiosity towards people we recognize are in some sense bad.

Dover remains neutral about the connection between erotic curiosity and knowledge, but is tempted to embrace what she calls an 'inquiry first' view alongside more familiar 'knowledge first' views, which regard knowledge as a basic notion that explains other notions of belief and justification (rather than the other way around). The basic idea is that we may also need to recognize the ways we inquire for its own sake, without being concerned to arrive at knowledge, perhaps because inquiry as such connects us to those around us, whereas some forms of curiosity can be lonely and solipsistic (Dover, 2024a, p. 829).

In a later work, Dover accounts for the active, dynamic, pulse of loving relationships in terms of erotic curiosity (Dover, 2024b). Her goal is to push back against conceptions of love – like that of Iris Murdoch – which centre on attention understood in passive, visual terms (Murdoch, 2001). Instead, erotic curiosity is 'characteristically prompted by *living objects*. Objects of inquiry are "living" when, in virtue of their synchronic complexity, diachronic malleability, or both, they can sustain indefinitely many interpretations and reinterpretations, at least where human inquirers are concerned' (Dover, 2024b, p. 329). We become bored with people, in Dover's view, when we can no longer sustain this attitude. And part of what is involved in sustaining this attitude is resisting getting gripped by fixed stories about who another person is (cf. Harcourt, 2011). When we start thinking we 'have a read' on someone, or pigeonhole them as being a certain kind of person, our curiosity is effectively over; we risk being no longer interested in them as a living changing subject, with their own perspective (we note, against this, that curiosity can always return when our settled story about someone is challenged – how likely this is, however, is unclear).

In developing this view, Dover's work resonates with other accounts of 'feminist curiosity'. Perry Zurn, for instance, describes feminist curiosity in the following terms:

> Feminist curiosity is a curiosity-with rather than a curiosity-about, and as such it practices a listening-with over a listening-for. In this project of relational inquiry, feminist curiosity necessarily rebuffs claims to transparency, purity, and objectivity; that is to say, it foregrounds opacity, ambiguity, and intimacy. (Zurn, 2021, p. 6)

Zurn's discussion helps us appreciate two ways we might obstruct this 'feminist' form of relating curiously to other people. The 'spectacle-erasure' form of curiosity has us stand to another as a spectator in a way that erases their 'history, multiplicity, and relational depth' (Lugones, 2003, p. 96). An example of this might be someone fascinated with people of a certain ethnicity, or with a certain sexual identity, or with a disability. The 'access-disclosure' form of curiosity has us presupposing an intimacy with someone and demanding 'the other's disclosure' in ways which can force intimacy (Zurn, 2021, p. 6).

Central to feminist curiosity and erotic curiosity is acceptance of potential opacity or ambivalence in another person – either because they are hesitant about being known, or because they are complex, or undergoing periods of change. Put another way, erotic curiosity is playful. Playfulness is again a concept overlooked by many philosophers. Part of Maria Lugones' definition of a good kind of play is that it involves 'finding ambiguity ... a source of wisdom and delight', rather than frustration and disappointment (as it might be for someone seeking a specific goal) (Lugones, 2003, p. 96; Brunning, 2024b, pp. 121–9).

b. Dating styles

Attention to erotic curiosity helps Dover distinguish between two broad attitudes towards other people which are common in intimate life: 'taxonomizing and knowledge-banking' and 'inquisitive attention and appreciation' (Dover, 2024b, p. 338). (Elsewhere, Luke has complicated this binary by suggesting there are three forms of curiosity: those aimed at knowledge, those aimed at understanding, and erotic curiosity (Brunning, 2024a). Defending this tripartite taxonomy would take up too much space, and is controversial, so to keep things simple, we ignore it here.)

We can develop this distinction and apply it to dating to suggest there are two broad distinct dating styles, *compatibility dating* and *erotic dating*. Aspects of these styles can overlap but the differences are useful to chart.

We compatibility-date when we seek someone who meets our sense of what we want. We might be curious about people – on a dating app, say – but only because we want to know whether they are a good match. What do they like? What are their values? They say they are kind, but are they really? And so on. We have a goal in mind, such as finding someone for a committed relationship, and dating is a means to secure this goal. As such, this dating style is often temporary: we want it over and done with. This is not to deny that our concern with compatibility may persist long into a relationship.

We erotically date, in contrast, when we are intrigued by someone, or hope to become intrigued. We might lack a clear goal, but view dating as an activity; indeed, we might want to date even when we have committed relationships. We are curious about people, but without clear questions in mind. Indeed, we might find ourselves surprised to be drawn to someone different from ourselves. This dating style is often ongoing or open-ended, as we have no prior sense of what might bring it to an end.

It is important just to stress that the notion of erotic here is not inherently sexual (cf. Lorde, 2019) The core notion is instead aimed at capturing the sense of captivation or engrossment certain forms of open-ended inquiry can bring about. Nor are we suggesting these two styles of dating are rigidly exclusive. We might start dating in one sense, only to fall into the other, perhaps abandoning a prior mental checklist when we meet someone seriously intriguing, or radically unexpected, or perhaps developing an anxiety about an interaction if it starts feeling so aimless.

c. Good curiosity

The obvious question to ask with this distinction in mind is whether one of these dating styles is better than the other, morally speaking? Dover, in her discussion of erotic curiosity, is ambivalent.

On the one hand, she wants to 'raise ethical concerns about the habit of conceiving of our inquiries into one another in terms of seeking and finding knowledge' (Dover, 2024b, p. 340). One particular worry seems to be that the more we are 'approached with a desire for stable knowledge', the more we are tempted to 'mold ourselves into more stably knowable objects' (Dover, 2024b, p. 345).

But, on the other hand, Dover is also aware that the desire to know people, and judge them against our expectations or desires, can make us feel secure. We want a sense of whether we might get along, whether there are pitfalls ahead, whether someone might hurt us.

Her view is that which attitude we choose 'depends in part, on how stable and consistent we want to insist that they be – in other words, on how much change and complexity we want to allow to ourselves and to one another' (Dover, 2024b, p. 343). In turn, she thinks that our ability to pursue erotic over more knowing forms of curious inter-action 'depends on more material forms of safety'. The rest of her view is worth quoting in full:

The way we live now hardly fosters the backdrop of psychosocial abundance – the sense of having time, care, affection, and vitality to spare – against which it becomes possible to face the 'lack' at the heart of both curiosity and love. If we want our desire to be surprised and remade by one another to prevail more often over our fear of the unknown, our ways of living together will have to change. (Dover, 2024b, pp. 345–6)

There is truth here. Our abilities to engage with intimacy on our own terms are fragile and shaped by many factors outside our control (that is the argument of Brunning (2024b)). It is one thing to want to be erotically curious, and another to be able to withstand the lack of certainty or open-endedness that might be involved. This approach is not immune to critical questioning, however.

For one thing, extreme versions of compatibility dating seem problematic. We might be so fixated on our checklist, for instance, that we fail to really attend to the person in front of us as an individual. This might be objectifying in the sense that one date is interchangeable with another (Nussbaum, 1995). This attitude is problematic even if what is on the checklist, and our sense of compatibility, is good. But we can also worry about the checklist. So-called self-styled 'pickup artists' might be curious whether someone is likely to yield to a sexual advance, and act to try to assuage their curiosity, but in a way that is manipulative (Strauss, 2007). Other people might ask questions that are intrusive, or fixated on someone's intimate zones (e.g. what their body is like, or their sexual tastes). Some variants of this dating style are premised on male entitlement, too – i.e. the idea that men are owed certain forms of attention.

We can also return to Dover's worry that the 'taxonomizing and knowledge-banking' form of curiosity encourages us to mould ourselves to become more knowable. The idea underlying this worry could be that this attitude means we incur a loss of some kind, or end up lying or being inauthentic. Perhaps you have experienced this on a date, for instance, where someone asks questions and seeks to categorize you in one way or another: 'Are you straight or gay?', 'Top or bottom?', 'Sub or dom?' – 'Do you vote Labour or Conservative?' You may find yourself, whether unwittingly or otherwise, trying to express who you are in ways that fit these categories, rather than expressing your complex identity (as a bisexual, versatile, switch, Green Party voter, for example). Indeed, perhaps you are doing this because this is the only way you can really make yourself intelligible to the other person. You're not simply trying to please them by using their language, but their approach to dating and compatibility leaves open no room for alternative forms of identity, self-description, or simple ambivalence. (Expressed another way, an entrenched emphasis on compatibility in dating discourse, combined with dominant identity-terms and descriptors, can mean some people are harmed in being less able to make sense of themselves, and communicate this, on their own terms – i.e. experience hermeneutic injustice.)

In itself, doing this incurs a loss for you. You are unable to be yourself. But if we add premises here about the importance of trust and honesty in intimate discussions (LaFollette and Graham, 1986), or about the moral significance of having integrity (Calhoun, 1995; Walker, 2007), then a dating dynamic like this may be more problematic, since these pressures prevent us from dating with integrity, or risk establishing dynamics where we feel unable to express ourselves to others as we would like. We might also worry, as someone being dated in this way, about a possible difference between the ways a compatibility dater relates to us before and after commitment. We might lack confidence that, once their questions are answered, their curiosity satisfied, and compatibility assured, they will then start relating to us as complex individuals who might be uncertain about ourselves, or be liable to change. Indeed, we might worry about the fragility of our relationship with someone who dates in this way. What if our values evolve, or I develop new tastes, as often happens when we are intimate with others over time (Bagley, 2015)?

We should also wonder whether there can be problematic forms of erotic dating? Earlier, we suggested that erotic curiosity in Dover's sense need not be wholly positive: that we can be erotically curious towards people about whom we are ambivalent, perhaps even mordantly drawn towards.

The erotic dater might also find themselves out of sync with people who need clarity for specific reasons. Someone with a child, or with a disability, or who has experienced a history of abuse, or racism, for example, may be less able to dwell in ambivalence than someone otherwise secure in their life situation, happy in themselves, and privileged enough not to have had many bad dates in the past. At the very least, there may be some ethical limits on the manifestation of erotic curiosity in these situations (Dover's remarks indicate she would agree).

More interestingly, however, are cases where the fascination in another person seems entwined with negative or morally worrying attitudes. The erotic dater may struggle to appreciate the separateness of persons, for example, and not recognize the significant ways in which the object of their curiosity differs from them. Or their erotic curiosity could be anchored in racism or orientalism – where the desire to be close to someone, or interact with them in an open-ended way, is there because we are radically othering them.

More complex cases of problematic erotic curiosity are those where the very fact that someone is erotically curious about others, or dating them on that basis, is itself contributing to a failure of proper recognition. An example of this might be visible in the attitudes of some trans-chasers (people who fetishize trans people, usually trans women). Clara Moreton explores some of these dynamics and the complex forms of recognition that seem involved. Most notable is the idea that, for some chasers, the 'perception of trans women *as* women is understood by the chaser as dependent on his own perspective' (Moreton,unpub. ms, p. 2) – that is to say, without the chaser's desire or interest, the person would not be a woman at all. Moreton's analysis, and their idea of the 'fantasy of creation' visible in some of these examples where chaser's view their own attention as what brings into being a woman, can arguably be extended to other contexts too. Erotic curiosity that is not accompanied by a full recognition of someone, or which is anchored in these fantasies of creation, starts to look very sinister. Being dated by someone who thinks their 'inchoate longing to intertwine' with you is what constitutes your romantic status (because you would be otherwise too ugly, or old, or disabled) is not desirable.

Therefore, although erotic dating seems favourable in comparison to many forms of compatibility dating, there are ways in which erotic curiosity can be compatible with failures of recognition, or objectification, which we have to guard against.

Still, practical questions remain about *how* to date erotically, how to do so with responsibility, and how individuals and even dating apps might nurture this erotic curiosity. Erotic curiosity involves making space for others to be malleable and change, but what *that* means in practice – as we get more acquainted – is unclear. We can wonder whether there are limits to this, or certain core aspects of a person we can legitimately require to remain stable (around which the rest of them can change).

At the very least, however, the distinction in this section between kinds of curiosity and, in turn, between two styles of dating gives us some resources to think about the ways we are being approached by others and also to reflect on our own style of dating. If compatibility and acquiring key information matter to us, we can make more space for uncertainty, ambivalence, and change, and ask ourselves whether we are subtly pressuring other people to respond inauthentically to our conversation or advances. If fascination and open-ended exploration matters to us, as it arguably should, we can check there are not some things the other person needs to know in order to feel secure, trust us, or have confidence we are recognizing them for who they are rather than our projection of who they are.

3. Flirting

Curiosity might lead us to date, and sustain us as we do so, but what – exactly – do daters *do*? This is a complex question and, again, one little considered by philosophers. But we might think it is an important matter, since much dating occurs in a context where people may not know each other well, are building intimacy, and may lack wider networks of supportive friends and family who can hold both parties accountable. Put simply, it is easy to hurt the people we date and get away with it. These harms can vary in strength from trivial frustrations and disappointments through to more insidious forms of gaslighting, and consent violation. Arriving at a better sense of what daters are doing is therefore ethically significant.

We cannot canvass all dimensions of dating, but clearly one typical feature of the dynamic is that daters *flirt* with each other. Of course, we can imagine people on dates who do not flirt. A couple might meet in a serious attempt to exchange information, gauge broader compatibility, and discuss the practicalities of more committed living together prior to the event. But although such people might go out on dates, to discuss these matters, we would not be misspeaking to wonder whether they are really *dating*. Flirting, as a practice, is fairly central to most dating as we understand it.

a. What is flirting?

What is flirting? Almost no philosopher has taken up this question, with two recent exceptions, so we shall start with their views and go from there. Before we do, let's check the dictionary. The *OED* defines the version of the verb that interests us in the following way:

> To behave as though attracted to or trying to attract someone, but in a playful way rather than with serious romantic or sexual intentions. Frequently with a person. (*Oxford English Dictionary*, 2023b)

This is a starting point. But many questions remain. For one, note that this definition leaves it open whether the flirter does in fact care about the other person. Understood in this way, Ade can flirt with Carl without being attracted to him, but we might think flirting implies some interest in the other, and that anything else is appearing to flirt, or feigning flirting. Second, we might ask whether someone can flirt by behaving as if they are not attracted to someone, perhaps in cases where it is common knowledge they are attracted (i.e. adopting a 'negging' strategy (M. J. Taylor, 2023)). Third, and more importantly, surely it is possible to flirt *precisely* because you have serious, or sexual, intentions towards someone?

If anything, definitions like this highlight the challenge in characterizing what flirting is. Flirting seems to involve a complex blend of the implicit, the exploratory, the presumptuous, the deniable, all in a complex dance of to and fro. Quill Kukla puts it nicely in suggesting that 'the language of flirtation, seduction, and engagement, not to mention speech within sex itself, tends to be circuitous, stagy, elliptical, metaphorical, innuendo filled, and connotative' (Kukla, 2018, p. 79). Kukla's remarks here also highlight the fact that flirtation will bear many family resemblances to other explicit attempts to seduce, or be humorous, or be sexual.

Carrie Jenkins defines a 'set of necessary and sufficient conditions' of flirting in the following way:

> First, the flirter should act with the intention to do things which are disposed to raise flirter–flirtee romance and/or sex to salience for the flirtee, in a knowing yet playful manner. Second, he or she should believe that the flirtee can respond in some significant way. (Jenkins, 2010, p. 18)

This is an improvement on the *OED* definition as it weakens the connection between flirting and attraction. This definition is also quite broad, and captures the ways in which one person might flirt with another by saying things like 'Oh, we're definitely not going home together later', a remark which indirectly brings to salience a romantic scenario. The idea of playfulness is central to her account, as it is what seemingly distinguishes that remark above from remarks like 'Shall we proceed to have sex tonight?' Jenkins is clear that flirting is not the same as requesting something, declaring something, or suggesting something (Jenkins, 2010, p. 14).

Still, Jenkins' definition can also be challenged. Consider Ade and Carl again. Can Ade be counted as flirting with Carl in virtue of his attempts to make salient, to Carl, the sexual possibilities between Ade *and Jason*, Carl's other boyfriend? Or can Ade flirt with Carl in virtue of his attempts to make salient to Carl, the ways *Carl* might be romantic with Jason? Put differently, why assume *flirter–flirtee* sex/romance has to be central to flirting? In complex nonmonogamous dynamics, or cases of love-triangles, might it be enough for sex/romance *simpliciter* to become salient?

The second sentence is also interesting. It was included by Jenkins so we can say that we are able to flirt with non-humans such as chatbots, as long as they can respond. This is in slight tension with her other suggestion that we can flirt 'with a purely imaginary person' and that 'in that sense it is possible to flirt without flirting with anyone at all' (Jenkins, 2010, p. 17). Imaginary persons do not have the ability to respond to us. Moreover, is the ability to respond necessary? This can mean different things: does someone have the *general capacity* to respond, and can someone respond *now*? It is certainly possible to flirt with someone who cannot respond now. Ade might toy with Carl as he presents a live TV broadcast, or as his mouth is gagged. These nuances aside, Jenkins' definition does point to a kind of reciprocity that some will want to be central to an account of flirting.

Jenkins' definition and discussion of flirting is a useful development on the dictionary, but we might wonder what, exactly, is involved in knowingly yet playfully raising romantic or sexual possibilities to salience? How is this done? Are there good and bad ways it can be done, or contexts in which it should not be done? To consider these issues, we turn to a recent account of flirting by Lucy McDonald.

McDonald's method is to draw on the resources of the philosophy of language to help us understand what flirters are doing. On its face, this is a hopeful strategy; flirting is a complex and nuanced communicative activity, verbal and otherwise, where the things people are trying to do may not align with the literal content of their words.

Here is McDonald's account. For her, flirting is the 'joint activity' of engaging in a 'conversational game' where 'agents presuppose intimacy that initially does not exist, but which comes into being throughout the course of the interaction' (McDonald, 2022, p. 207). The activity of flirting has several components: the presupposition of intimacy, push moves, and pull moves.

First, the presupposition of intimacy:

> Flirters seem to presuppose the existence of intimacy, and they do this by saying and doing things that would only be acceptable and appropriate if such intimacy already existed. They thereby invite the other person to grant that presupposition (bringing the intimacy into existence) or block it. Intimacy is a relationship of

mutual understanding and mutual vulnerability between at least two people. (McDonald, 2022, p. 210)

Push moves are those which 'presuppose a level of sexual intimacy that is not yet in the common ground, in the hope that this presupposition will be accommodated' (McDonald, 2022, p. 211). These could include bringing romantic or sexual possibilities to salience in the way Jenkins suggested.

Pull moves involve resistance to the intimacy presumed by the push move. Crucially, these are different from flat refusals or situations where someone withdraws from the interaction. Instead, in a pull move:

> one appears to *pull away*, pulling the intimacy that has developed between the interlocutors off the table. Yet one does not actually block the presupposition of intimacy, nor destroy the intimacy in the common ground. Rather, one *plays* at blocking the presupposition, but actually accommodates it, and in the process dares the other person to proceed with their presuppositions despite the apparent rebuke. (McDonald, 2022, p. 211)

Imagine Carl and Ade talking at work, about the trouble Carl got in with his boss.

Carl: He really went for it. I got a proper dressing down!
Ade: Oh that's awful ... [pause]
Ade: Still, I bet you'd *love* a good dressing down ...
Carl: Ha, wouldn't you like to know!

Here, Ade makes a push move in saying, 'I bet you'd *love* a good dressing down', since this rests on the double entendre possible in 'dressing down', which can mean both being told off and to undress. In turn, Carl makes a pull move by responding to the rhetorical question with a question of his own. He does not reply explicitly to Ade, but nor does he end the conversation. Indeed, he brings to salience Carl's evident intimate interest in Ade.

McDonald is keen to stress that flirting 'creates a precarious, fleeting state of intimacy, and that is all' (McDonald, 2022, p. 216). To flirt with someone is not to harass them, nor is it to consent to anything. That someone flirted cannot be used as evidence they agreed to anything.

McDonald's view is interesting. She views flirting as a form of what we would call proleptic intimacy, where we presuppose intimacy in order to try to bring it about that we actually become intimate. This is different from other ways we might seek to build intimacy – perhaps by asking questions to understand someone better (by accessing an 'intimate zone' in Gunkel's sense), or by being physically close to them. Understanding flirting as McDonald does can help us appreciate why people value it. We are shy, and often relucent to disclose ourselves, especially when there is risk of rejection. If revealing aspects of ourselves in response to another person's questions or advances was the only way to build intimacy, then intimacy would require much self-disclosure. But there is another route to intimacy – namely, other people can presuppose it already exists, and all we have to do is accept, or deny, their proposal, or tweak the boundaries of their presupposition. We are saved the brunt of the effort to disclose, since others are able to make assumptions based on what they see. (This is not to say there may be other factors which determine whether this process goes well or badly, and we consider some below.)

We might wonder whether McDonald's definition is too general, however. Indeed, it strikes us that her definition of what flirting is could serve as a nice account of what it is like to teach *philosophy* robustly, and perhaps to do other things, such as build friendships or other caring relationships. There, the philosophy teacher – in the process of exploring an idea, or considering a specific argument – often presupposes a certain intimacy with the class, e.g. the momentary presupposition of a shared perspective, or a shared tolerance of discomfort, in order to bring about a greater sense of understanding which, in turn, makes people more vulnerable to each other. There are certain structural parallels between the joint activity of flirting and the conversational language games in the classroom. But teaching is not flirting. What is missing, perhaps, is a sense of the *kind* of intimacy that is presupposed in flirting. Jenkins' definition was more specific that this is sexual/romantic in nature, although, as we have seen, specifying what *that* amounts to is very challenging.

Since flirting is a joint activity, for McDonald, we cannot flirt with someone who does not flirt back, which can seem like an odd consequence (she is happy to bite this bullet, but you might not be). Her view has the advantage over the dictionary definition that it can accommodate 'negging' moves where we might act as if we are not interested in someone precisely *because* we are interested, but we might wonder whether *both* push and pull moves are necessary for an interaction to count as flirting. It seems possible there may be cases where two people push and push at each other, ramping up the presupposed intimacy, in different ways without either of them trying to pull back. We might also think that there are more options when it comes to conversational moves which presuppose intimacy. Alongside accepting or blocking, we can ignore them, for example, leaving them hanging, perhaps on purpose, to exacerbate intimate tension.

b. The ethics of flirting

McDonald's account helps us think about the ethical dimensions of flirting as a core feature of dating and intimacy more broadly. If flirting is a distinct kind of conversational interaction, then it seems to require people move into a particular 'discursive frame': one 'governed by distinctive local internal norms that shape what words and phrases mean, as well as the felicity and force of various speech acts' (Kukla, 2018, p. 79). But we might worry about the ways we enter and leave these frames.

Writing about sexual contexts where non-literal speech plays an important role, but might have serious consequences, Quill Kukla (writing as Rebecca Kukla) suggests we need 'shared pragmatic markers and tools that flag for us when a nonliteral speech context has kicked in and when someone wants to get back out of it' (Kukla, 2018, p. 80). In this sexual context, this might include scene-setting speech, or the use of a safe-word to signify a shift back to literal speech.

Flirting, however, seems poorly served by these forms of conversational scaffolding. We rarely ask to flirt with people, or seek their consent to flirt with them, and we often try to mask when we are flirting, at least to some extent. The ambiguous, risky, nature of flirting seems to rest precisely in the fact that it is held to be contrary to flirting to be explicit in these ways, or to check. Perhaps this is fine if the 'common ground' is widely shared. But we have reason to doubt it is. Neurodivergence, language barriers, or differences in personality can mean that people do not meet as equals in this conversational game.

Relatedly, we can also worry about power and presupposition. Is there a gendered dimension to what 'counts' as a push or pull move? Are men expected to 'push' and women to 'pull'? If so, as seems likely in societies structured by patriarchal norms, the ability of some people to successfully execute certain flirting 'moves' (by securing requisite uptake from the other person) might be limited compared to others. A woman may 'fail' to flirt with someone who simply does not read her push remarks as presupposing a precarious form of intimacy. Fairness in flirting may require wider social changes.

We can also wonder how to flirt *appropriately* and *authentically* (particularly with people we do not know very well). If McDonald is right, then to flirt with someone is to presuppose we are intimate with them (rather than to do something else in an effort to build intimacy). But we need a sense of *what kinds* of presupposition we can make. To return to Gunkel's notion of an intimate zone, it seems plausible to think there are limits on which intimate zones can feature in flirting. If we were to say things that presupposed we already were someone's long-term sexual and romantic partner, for example, we would potentially sexualize them in ways which are in tension with how they want to present themselves (Morgan, 2023). But we also risk inauthenticity insofar as our presupposition is too 'remote' from how things stand, now, between us and the person we are flirting with. Put another way, good flirting involves sensitive, careful, non-objectifying, presuppositions of intimacy which still provide the other person with sufficient room to define the ways they want the intimate aspects of who they are to be seen and understood.

Finally, are there some people we should not flirt with? In mentioning power and presupposition, above, we suggested people can differ in their ability to secure uptake while flirting, due to the ways social norms and expectations shape our sense of what counts as a presupposition of intimacy, or of who gets to make these presuppositions. We can also worry about the burdens and double binds of responding to presuppositions of intimacy in flirting. A rule of thumb here might be that flirting is morally acceptable only with people who are able to track the differences between rejection of a push move and pulling back at that move, and who do not face significant costs in doing either. A young student, for example, may both lack the competence and experience to navigate their teacher's presupposition of intimacy in a flirty remark, and also worry about the costs to themselves of doing so. As such, teachers should not flirt with their pupils. (There are, of course, other reasons why this is wrong (Kukla and Herbert, 2018; Srinivasan, 2019).) Similar conclusions may apply to other groups too.

We have explored flirting as it is a common part of dating, understood as an activity we do. Viewing dating in this way aligns nicely with our remarks about erotic curiosity, since the activity of flirting is a potentially open-ended exploration of, and play with, the other, which is quite different from other efforts to build intimacy by acquiring knowledge (efforts which we have largely not discussed here, but which may also comprise an important part of dating). A compatibility-dater might ask the same question of everyone they date, but they will struggle if they try to replicate the same flirting each time. Flirts take risks in assuming an intimate stance, rather than arriving at that stance by eliciting the revelation of another person's intimate zones.

To flirt well, then, with sensitivity, appropriateness, and authenticity, will involve empathy and the imagination, since we require a good sense of what kinds of presupposition can be made in a specific context when interacting with a specific person. Contrary to the view of some pickup artists, flirting cannot be a matter of following rules or using 'lines' and stock phrases. Instead, it is a skill – which rests on careful appreciation of another person in their particularity.

Put another way – in full knowledge that this may seem provocative – perhaps flirting is even a *virtue*: that is, a disposition to act in a stable and intelligent way, in a manner which deepens over time, out of commitment to the value of intimacy (Annas, 2011).

4. Ghosting

'Hey', 'Hi', 'Got any pics?', 'DTF?', 'Are you trans?'.

When you get lots of terrible messages on dating apps, from the boring to the toxic and misogynistic, ghosting people can seem like a reasonable strategy. For Lily Frank and her co-authors, to ghost means to 'abruptly sever conversations that don't seem to be leading directly or swiftly enough to the desired outcome' (Frank, Klincewicz, and Jane, 2022, p. 562). We ghost by simply leaving, with no warning or explanation. On a dating app, a simple 'unmatch' is all it takes.

a. Ghosters and ghostees

Ghosting is one way we move on from an interaction. Paradigmatic forms of ghosting concern people who leave reasonably established interactions, sometimes even well-developed committed relationships, rather than simply fail to respond to a poor opening advance. Although people have been able to walk out of dates, not return calls, leave town, or even exit marriages without telling their partners, ghosting online can be seen as a 'new break-up strategy' – a form of engagement made easier, more common, and perhaps motivated, by the widespread use of dating apps (Timmermans, Hermans, and Opree, 2021). Before considering the ethics of ghosting, and other forms of breaking up and moving on, it's worth thinking more about this form of behaviour.

Elizabeth Timmermans and her co-authors studied ghosting to understand why people do it, and how it impacts them. Of relevance here is the private form of dating made possible by apps (which we described in the previous chapter). For the most part, apps allow us to date outside the social networks that sustain our in-person interactions, to easily pursue several potential matches at the same time, and to act in secret: three factors which make ghosting more likely to occur than other forms of more explicit break-up (Freedman et al., 2019; Timmermans, Hermans, and Opree, 2021, p. 784). The use of mobile phone apps, in particular, means our search for intimacy is gamified, which 'may create more emotional distance towards other users', and is structured around the physical manipulation of an object (phone) which is thought to 'reduce personhood perceptions' of those individuals depicted on the phone (Timmermans, Hermans, and Opree, 2021, p. 785).

Timmermans and colleagues surveyed hundreds of mobile dating app users and found a range of reasons why people ghost (Timmermans, Hermans and Opree, 2021, pp. 791–3). These include concerns about the 'personality' of the ghostee, the 'undesirable actions and behaviours' of the ghostee (such as being 'pushy, disrespectful, racist, withholding important information, or sending unsolicited sexual content'), questions about the ghostee's motives for using dating apps, a response to a bad or unpleasant date with the ghostee, and finding the ghostee unattractive. Other app users ghosted because they wanted to 'protect themselves' by avoiding a potentially painful confrontation with the other person, because they did not feel 'emotionally ready' to move to in-person dating, because they wanted to retain control and avoid being potentially twisted back into dating the person they wanted to reject, or simply because they were busy. Some app users explicitly mention how apps are designed, suggesting that ghosting was made to be easy; or that they simply deleted the app and so lost all conversations; or that apps provide too many possible matches, which is overwhelming. A small percentage of people surveyed suggested they ghosted out of concern for the ghostee, since they did not want to hurt them through other forms of break-up or rejection, or lead them on.

Also of interest is the finding that prolonged dating-app use actually decreased, rather than increased, the likelihood someone would ghost, perhaps because they are no longer overwhelmed by choice or have become more selective. The negative impact of ghosting also seemed the same for people who had been sexually intimate with the ghoster and those who had not (Timmermans, Hermans, and Opree, 2021, p. 796).

Sadness, hurt, anger, and disillusionment were the common emotional responses to being ghosted. In Timmerman's sample, 44 per cent said that being ghosted 'has had long-term effects on their mental health', such as lowered self-esteem or increased distrust (Timmermans, Hermans, and Opree, 2021, p. 793). Other people felt shame, or even relief, whereas some people felt nothing much at all. Many tried to rationalize their experiences, or develop coping strategies to move on.

Two additional aspects of this study stand out for us. The first is that some people said they ghosted since they felt 'they did not owe the other person anything' and that 'ghosting is part of mobile dating app use' (Timmermans, Hermans, and Opree, 2021, p. 792). The second is that a lack of *closure* was a common theme in the study, with some ghostees attempting to contact the ghoster in other ways to find out why they were ghosted.

These points suggest that ghosting is an emerging strategic response to the world of online dating in particular, which is partly supported by emerging intimate norms, but which impacts people in ways similar to other break-ups. This complicates the search for a general strategy to approach ghosting. Two options stand out. The first is to suggest that ghosting is a distinct phenomenon, and so any ethical discussion has to proceed on its own terms. The second would be to suggest ghosting is just one method of breaking up with people, and that break-ups – in general – need ethical analysis.

Our view is that we get a better grip on what might be problematic about ghosting when we consider it alongside breaking up. (Below, we raise one complication when it comes to viewing ghosting as a species of breaking up, at least according to one account of what breaking up is.) Dating often comes to an end because one party decides enough is enough and wants to move on. If we can understand what breaking up is, at least partially, we might get a sense of whether it generates obligations, whose obligations those are, and when those obligations come into play. With this in mind, we shall turn to breaking up and then ask whether our discussion applies to ghosting. To be clear, this will not be a full treatment of the complexities and ethical implications of breaking up. Such research is waiting to be done.

b. Break-ups

Frustratingly, break-ups have been subject to very little philosophical study (with some exceptions (Lopez-Cantero, 2018)). This omission is strange when you think about it, since breaking up with someone is one way we can really disrupt their life. Thankfully, Richard Healey has recently explored break-ups, so hopefully more research is on its way.

Healey focuses on 'committed romantic relationships' (so we will have to ask how much of his analysis applies to ghosting on dating apps) (Healey, 2023, p. 174). Healey's central thought is that break-ups involve the 'exercise of a normative power' – simply by declaration, we can change our normative relationship with someone. (Other examples of putative normative powers might be promising or legislating (Raz, 2022).) Healey notes an interesting asymmetry here, since we often *acquire* various obligations and responsibilities without explicit declaration. Spending time with someone, being close to them, loving them, caring about them, can lead to a relationship, which, we might think, creates responsibilities even if they have never been made explicit (perhaps through a marriage vow, or other form of contract).

The normative power of breaking up requires us to communicate it to the other – not just 'break up' with them in our mind – and needs their uptake to be successful. Healey embraces a 'value based' account of normative powers, which means we identify which powers exist by identifying the values that justify them (e.g. promising might be grounded in the value of 'control' we have over the normative world (Bruno, 2022)). In this case, the power of breaking up with others is justified, Healey thinks, in terms of the value of being in relationships which are 'voluntarily maintained', since the ability to leave whenever we like is what constitutes voluntariness for him (Healey, 2023, p. 184).

To say that breaking up is a normative power may seem uninformative – not many people would doubt breaking up changes the normative situation between people. The more interesting part of Healey's argument is his attempt to say what the exercise of the power does – how, that is, breaking up actually changes the landscape of obligation between the people concerned.

Consider Celine and Dagmar. They have been in a relationship for a few years, are committed, and have relatively entangled lives. One day, Celine says, 'Dagmar, we're done.' What happens? One view is that Celine has broken up with Dagmar, and this takes them back to a situation in which she has no substantial obligations to him, a bit like before they met. Healey thinks this option does not seem right since he can imagine cases where we are more tempted to say Celine would have obligations, e.g. if Dagmar suddenly fell ill, or required special help (Healey, 2023, p. 185). Healey thinks these cases show us that, perhaps under the surface, we do think that people who break up with others retain some obligations towards them. Specifically, he thinks that these are anchored in the duty to care for someone that constitutes a committed relationship, and distinguishes it from other impartial relationships.

There is an interesting question in the background here: what is the difference between an act that ends a relationship and starts a new one, and an act which changes a relationship? The back-to-baseline view which Healey rejects looks more plausible if we say that breaking up with someone creates a *new* relationship or role – namely, that of being someone's ex. Viewed in this way, we might think that after a break-up two people go back to baseline as romantic partners – i.e. have no more duties towards each other than do strangers – but create new obligations towards each other *as exes*. If *that* role has its own internal duties, then we can account for why we have to act towards our exes as we do. As an analogy: Xan might relinquish command of the ship to Axel at the handover ceremony. As such, Xan is now Axel's subordinate and Axel is captain. Xan's words at the ceremony – his exercise of a normative power – bring it about that he now occupies a new role. His duties towards Axel thereafter – to obey orders, etc. – are understood in virtue of his new role as subordinate, rather than the content of his prior role as captain. You might think that this is splitting hairs, but if duties arise because of the roles we occupy, then exes *qua* exes might have obligations towards each other irrespective of the nature of their prior relationship.

Even on Healey's interpretation that the duties we have to our exes are present due to the prior care we had for the person we are breaking up with, this leaves us wondering what breaking up does, and does not, achieve. Healey suggests break-ups have three 'normative effects' (Healey, 2023, p. 196):

1. Many relationship-based duties will be cancelled and many will be weakened
2. Relationship-*sustaining* reasons will be cancelled
3. A new duty is created: 'a duty to transition out of the relationship' (Healey, 2023, p. 197).

Healey thinks these changes might be distributed 'asymmetrically' and he implies that people who instigate break-ups may have to do more than those who are subject to them.

On this general picture, many of Celine's relationship-based duties will end, and she does not have to try to sustain her relationship with Dagmar. She might wonder what this duty to transition means. Here Healey is brief, but mentions 'omissions' such as spending less time together and not drawing on one's ex for emotional help, supporting them to do certain things themselves, and working on habits they formed during the relationship (like talking to each other about their day, sharing memes, or going for that Sunday run). This duty to transition might require substantial efforts on Celine's behalf. She might have to be proactive in helping Dagmar step back from the relationship (e.g. if he has nowhere else to stay at short notice, but she does), and work on her own engrained habits of reaching out to him.

Healey suggests that failure to act on the duty to transition, by either side, means that they wrong the other person (Healey, 2023, p. 199). This is quite far removed from the alternative view, which is that break-ups leave people back where they were, with no obligations to each other. On balance, Healey's account here wants to capture both the radical and immediate ability to exercise our autonomy by breaking up relationships, and the obligations that doing so might generate.

Still, many questions remain. For one, can people forgo or waive the duty to transition by making it clear to each other that they don't need or desire the presence of the other person at all? Here we might face a tension between the value of care towards someone, which generates duties to transition, and the value of voluntariness, which might generate the ability to waive these duties. How do we make sense of the apparent asymmetry of obligation in break-ups, and which factors shape that unequal distribution of responsibility? It seems implausible to suggest that merely breaking up generates this asymmetry, as there will be cases where the person broken up with has wronged the other, or benefited disproportionately from the relationship. We can easily imagine horrible examples when someone finally manages to break up with an abusive partner, for instance, only for that partner to play victim of the break-up itself.

c. Duties to transition

Thinking about the duty to transition raises other important questions. *What*, precisely, does such a duty to transition demand of us, to whom does it apply, and what is the underlying value that this duty is designed to protect? Healey seems to focus on the wide impact a break-up can have:

> A breakup can leave individuals distraught and disoriented, uncertain about who they are and what kind of life they should live. For these reasons, a failure on one or both parties to take the steps that will allow them to transition out of the relationship could be seriously detrimental to their well-being and their ability to go on to form future relationships. (Healey, 2023, p. 198)

Break-ups impact our emotions, our sense of identity, and perhaps even our agency. But if this is true, we might think the duty to transition needs to be stronger, and that it also applies to people

outside the relationship, such as friends and family. We can also inter-
rogate the general picture of what moving on involves, which might
shape these questions. To do this, we suggest it is helpful to recognize
that break-ups are often experiences of *grief*. Such a view is becoming
accepted as a response to divorce, for example, but applies to the
ending of many relationships, not necessarily those that have lasted a
long time (someone might grieve the end of a short but transformative
relationship, e.g. their first queer intimacy; or grieve the end of a
relationship laden with a felt sense of potential).

Let us assume that grief unfolds like a process, which is shaped
by the stories we tell ourselves about the loss involved (Goldie, 2011;
Ratcliffe and Byrne, 2022). One view of what grief proceeds towards is
that it is aimed at severing our connection to the person we care about.
But another view, one with substantial traction, is that grief 'aims' to
modify the bond we had with someone, and that bond can remain and
play a role in our life even if the person is not around (Bowlby, 1977;
Goss and Klass, 2005; Ratcliffe, 2015; Klass and Steffen, 2017). This
distinction is important, as the things we might need to do to modify a
bond are different from those we might attempt to do if we are trying
to sever a bond.

We assume that grief in general is best understood from the
'continuing bonds' perspective, where grieving people are trying to
modify the internal bond they formed with someone. An ethical
response to grief of this kind is to both not impede this process, and
support it where we can. But what does that involve? Is it just a matter
of giving people space and changing some habits? Arguably not. What
was clear, even from the discussion of ghosting, is that closure – the
ability to make sense of an experience – is vital after loss. To process
loss more generally, people benefit from the ability to *corroborate* and
commemorate their experiences (Higgins, 2013). This can happen in
lots of ways – from being able to tell stories and have friends listen and
validate our perspectives, through to the ability to remember someone,
talk about their ideas, or display valued items they gave us.

The duty to transition out of a relationship must also, we suggest,
mean we do not get in the way of people's attempts to corroborate or
commemorate what matters to them. This may be a case of getting
out of the way, as Healey suggests, but it can also involve more active,
narrative-oriented, efforts to ensure we do not disrupt someone's
ability to explain the break-up.

One interesting but under-explored area is how social norms about
grief following break-ups of romantic relationships, as opposed to
death, can really disrupt our ability to transition well by modifying the

intimate bonds we formed with the people who left us. Luke Brunning, for example, argues in unpublished work that the social background surrounding romantic break-up is often unreceptive (Brunning, unpub. ms). Our social norms are ambivalent, with some people stressing we should 'get over' romantic loss and others emphasizing the value in 'staying friends'. Third parties often take sides, or are defensive and angry to 'support' a friend, or take to social media. The ways people respond to break-ups are also fraught, or polarized, and often make it hard for someone going through a break-up to express ambivalence. Their friends might either downplay the loss – 'They were no good for you anyway' – or try to shift attention: 'Now you can be free and single.' The difference in tone and feeling between friends rallying to our 'defence' when we are subject to a break-up, and how we feel, can be huge – and lead to a marked 'dissynchrony' of grief (Gross, 2018, pp. 55–6), in which we are out of step with the people around us.

Break-ups also generate questions about blame, which can frustrate our ability to modify the bond we have with the other person. We can feel a sense of care, but also anger, or self-doubt. Break-ups can also feel like personal injustices in ways that bereavements might not.

Exes can also get in the way. You might occupy shared roles with them (like being co-parents or working together) which force proximity. Your ex might lurk in ways that hint at possible reconciliation, or they might be actively disruptive, hostile, or support others in taking sides. They can also severely disrupt your ability to make sense of what happened, or fail to corroborate your interpretation of events.

Things get worse if you are *attached* to an ex, in the technical sense of having an attachment bond to them, since disruptions to attachment can also make it harder for us to act as we would like, in broader ways. As Monique Wonderly puts it: 'Not only does extended separation from one's attachment objects cause one to experience a reduced sense of security – and thereby a kind of agential impairment – but such separation also typically motivates the agent to direct her remaining agential resources toward reacquiring that object. In this way, loss of an attachment object can both impair and focus one's agency' (Wonderly, 2021, p. 167). The combination of social norms around breaking up, the lack of clear 'scripts' to commemorate romantic loss, and the potential impact of exes and their 'side', and disruption to attachment mean that break-ups can be turbulent and lasting. The effects of this are complex. Beyond obvious emotional pain, which may be substantial, we might also struggle to secure meaning after a break-up, be tempted to just accept whatever the ex says as a way of drawing a line under things, or find ourselves motivated to spend time trying to reattach ourselves to the person lost.

Why does all this matter? First, it points to the need for a richer account of any duty to transition – one that acknowledges the range of ways break-ups can be disruptive. Second, this complexity points towards a possible tension in the content of any duty to transition between the need to give people space, and the need to support them in their efforts to make sense of what is going on. Third, things get especially complex when break-ups seem to threaten someone's agency, as the person best placed to support them through changes, or to recognize when their agency is undergoing a shift, might be the person who instigated the break-up. Acknowledging this in practice, while avoiding paternalism or manipulative meddling, will be tricky. Fourth, one reason why people often need support after a break-up, even support from the person breaking up with them, is precisely because of how third parties, such as their friends and family, are acting. This gives us reason to think the duty to transition, or something like it, might also apply to people *beyond* the couple breaking up; friends who leap to say 'He was never good for you' or 'You can do much better' might be meaning well, but they can make it hard for someone to sit with their grief. Indeed, we are tempted to say these duties can often be stronger for third parties, as those are the people the person broken-up with will be turning towards for support. Fifth, the duty to transition dovetails with more general social duties to try to resist overly constraining norms and social scripts about how people should feel or behave in response to romantic loss. Finally, we need to better understand when the duty to transition is not present – i.e. what, if anything, someone has to do to forfeit this duty.

Our discussion here is compatible with Healey's broad framework. His account just needs more elaboration, especially since its practical implications remain unclear. For example, relationships rarely concern only the people directly involved. Dagmar's family, for instance, may have formed their own friendships with Celine. If Celine breaks up with him, does he have the standing to tell his family not to contact her, or invite her to significant events, or involve her in their life? On the one hand, such a demand might align with some of the worries Healey raised, since Dagmar needs space and a degree of emotional reconfiguration in order to move on. On the other hand, such a demand seems in tension with the idea that people can form relationships voluntarily as an expression of their autonomy (which undergirded the normative power of break-ups in the first place).

d. Good ghosts?

As with many aspects of intimate ethics, how we understand the practical implications of a specific break-up will depend on the precise context and reason for the break-up. Still, you might agree with that point but think none of this applies to the cases of ghosting where we began. Ghosting, you might argue, often happens in cases where people do not have committed relationships, or happens under a different framework of normative assumptions, which mean that ghosters do not wrong each other, and talk of any 'duty to transition' does not apply.

This is a complex topic, but one worth unpacking. To make sense of it, we can distinguish between thinking about ghosting in real life, and thinking about breaking up interactions which have not made it offline (such as conversations on dating apps). We might think Healey's account shows straightforwardly that ghosting someone in real life, by just never coming home, or by never replying to their messages after we have been dating for ages, is wrong. The ghoster, in these cases, does not seem to uphold any duty to transition at all, and will likely leave the ghostee sad and bewildered.

But one complication here is whether to consider this a break-up *at all* since, for Healey, the duty to transition arises from break-ups. Since ghostings lack uptake, which was a necessary feature of break-ups for Healey, it is unclear whether ghostings should count as break-ups. (Remember that uptake is different from refusal or disagreement. The ghoster simply does not make a communicative move that requires recognition by the other person. They just up and leave.) The fact that they may not could be the right result; it could help us capture the sense in which just never coming home would typically feel worse than other kinds of break-up (due to the doubt and ambiguity involved, perhaps, or the intense disorientation this may induce (Harbin, 2016)). But this does suggest that in thinking of ghosting as a kind of break-up, we might need to tweak our analysis of what break-ups are. Or, to consider ghosting in terms of duties of transition, we need to show that such duties can be generated from *both* breaking up and ghosting.

We shall not settle these issues here. Although this is less than ideal, we can consider the moral demands of romantic endings without a fully developed account of what break-ups and ghostings are, and whether they are the same or different. Either way, it is useful to think in terms of duties of transition. With that in mind, let's ask whether the digital context where ghosting mainly occurs changes things.

To many, the answer is clearly 'yes'; things are different online, and ghosting, if unpleasant, is not like other kinds of relationship ending.

Our main suggestion is to urge some caution here. Remember that our segue into talking about break-ups was motivated by noticing the role that the absence of closure arguably plays in the distress of many people who have been ghosted. One reason for this is that being ghosted might be similar to other kinds of romantic loss, and so occasion similar grief, at least in cases where there was some developed interaction between the people involved. In both break-ups and ghostings, people want corroboration.

With this in mind, we can canvass the options when it comes to classic modern ghostings – i.e. abruptly cutting off online interactions with no explanation or redress. This is a complex topic as there are two relevant dimensions in play when comparing these cases to other forms of romantic loss: the length or status of the relationship (committed vs casual) and the mode of interaction (in-person vs online). To simplify, we shall ignore a lot of this complexity to focus on similar kinds of intimacy in both contexts – namely, leaving semi-developed romantic interactions. These are cases where people have been chatting online for a while, or dating for a time in real life, not cases where we unmatch with someone we chatted to once, or cases where we leave someone after a chat at a cocktail party. (We accept there may be strange cases where those interactions could generate strong expectations.)

We have several options when it comes to thinking about moving on from an online interaction. First, we might think there is *no duty* to transition in these cases. Second, we might think there is such a duty, but think it is *weaker* than in other cases of committed relationship break-up. Third, we might think there is such a duty, and that it is *the same* as in other cases of relationship break-up. Fourth, we might think there is such a duty and that it is even *stronger* than in in-person cases.

If there are no duties to transition away from online interactions, then ghosting would be morally fine (but perhaps deficient in other ways, like being rude, or aesthetically inferior). Why might people take this view? One reason was visible above: the idea that some people think that 'They did not owe the other person anything' and that 'Ghosting is part of mobile dating app use.' This can itself be understood in two ways. First, as a radical expression of voluntariness and autonomy, i.e. the idea that nothing is ever 'owed' to another, in any relationship. People might express these views to try to capture the sense that modern intimacy is ideally for its own sake, and not held together by external factors (such as social obligations) (Giddens,

1992), but in practice few people seem to believe that *nothing* is owed – instead, some accountability to other people seems part of being a moral agent at all, even if this is compatible with great personal change (Walker, 2007).

Second, and more specifically, people might suggest that they *waive* these general obligations to be accountable when they download and use dating apps or other forms of digital environment – that they enter a new normative arena and, like a boxer waiving the right not to be punched, accept the consequences. This would be an interesting view, but it also seems implausible. Widespread frustration and sadness at being ghosted, coupled with negative social attitudes towards the practice, suggest this approach to the issue is not held by sufficiently many people. Moreover, we might suppose a waiver of this kind is valid only if explicit.

So perhaps there are duties to transition when we move on from an online interaction, but they are weaker than in in-person committed relationships. The implications of this analysis are unclear, however. On the one hand, we might think that, if anything, we should refrain from ghosting. We may not have to discharge other duties of transition, perhaps we do not have to do much at all, but we do have to say when we are leaving and explain why. On the other hand, this 'weak duties of transition' approach could be thought to license ghosting under certain conditions. For example, perhaps we can ghost people as long as we do not 'orbit' them – that is, lurk on their social media or in other ways cause a nuisance (Pancani et al., 2021). Avoiding orbiting will at least not hinder their ability to move on, and reduces the amount of confusion our ghosting may cause. Or perhaps we have duties not to be mean about them to others, or post their pages and messages on social media, and so on.

On the third analysis, ghosting online seems ruled out, since we have the same duties to people online as we would have in person. The fourth analysis is particularly interesting, as it holds that our efforts to end online interactions can be *more* demanding than those in person. We might think this since online interactions, as has been shown, still have a great ability to impact people's self-esteem and sense of meaning, but often occur outside wider support networks. As a result, the potential for ambiguity, confusion, doubt, and denial is arguably increased, and so particular care needs to be taken when transitioning away from such intimacy.

We take no firm view on this matter here. What we have done is suggested there is some value in thinking about ghosting alongside break-ups despite the possible nuances involved; explored one analysis of break-ups as the exercise of a normative power which generates duties; added to that picture the fact that break-ups can occasion grief, which is why people crave closure and corroboration; and proposed that there are a range of different positions we can take when it comes to thinking about the moral status of ending online interactions – and on some, ghosting is acceptable, and on others it is not.

5. Conclusion

Dating is more central to modern life than it used to be. Longer lives, more fluid relationship patterns, and the social acceptability of leaving bad relationships mean that more people will spend more time exploring intimate possibilities. The character of this exploration is itself in need of more philosophical attention. We have only covered a few possible topics, and in passing. Underlying the whole discussion, however, is the sense that there are better and worse ways to interact with people in conditions of uncertainty.

4

Intimate Ethics

1. Introduction

You don't need a hard-hitting anecdote to know how challenging intimacy can be, and how wrong things can go.

Everyone reading this, irrespective of sexuality or romantic inclinations, has grappled with the ethical challenges of relating well to the people they care about. You've likely annoyed friends or family by doing things they didn't like, or without sufficient clarity; you've likely had experiences where someone is interacting with you as a means to their end, or through the lens of their own desires, and not you as an individual; you've likely questioned whether you're focusing too much on one kind of relationship at the expense of others. Sex and romance are just one part of life in which these challenges come to light.

We avoided calling this chapter 'sexual ethics' because we wanted to stress that discussion of consent and good intimacy has wide relevance. Sex is hard to define, as we saw in chapter 1, and matters of ethical conduct apply to many kinds of interaction. Indeed, we want to acknowledge that the implicit close cultural association of consent with sex, specifically, contributes to the wider social blind spots around consent and autonomy in many different kinds of relationships. Behaviour within friendships, or the family, or towards young children, or people with disabilities also needs to be consent-conscious (but often is not, e.g. adults rarely ask whether they can hug children), and people of all orientations and inclinations, even those who do not have sex or want romantic relationships, benefit from thinking about intimate ethics.

2. Consent and its significance

'How many things have you consented to today?'

It's an odd question, but perhaps by now you are used to philosophers asking odd questions. Still, how would you answer it? What leaps to mind? Did you consent to your alarm going off; to the radio playing *that song* again; to the train company taking your money as you bought a ticket; to the café barista making that pattern on your coffee; to the publisher profiting from your writing; to another drink; to someone coming back to your house; to that touch …

Our grasp of when we consent and what we consent to is imprecise. This might be because we lack a clear sense of what consent is, but it might also be because we do not care about consent in all cases.

This is not to say we do not care about consent at all. Consent matters very much in high-stakes situations: on the hospital bed as the doctors tell you they highly recommend an immediate operation; or in the morning, awaking in an unfamiliar bed, as we try to remember what happened the night before.

The literature on consent is vast and growing. We cannot cover it all here. (Some classic texts include Archard, 1997b and Wertheimer, 2003; for more recent work, see also Dougherty, 2021; Liberto, 2022.) Our goal will be to set out some waymarkers before turning to more recent work in philosophy that urges us to think differently about consent, or about the significance of consent for intimate ethics.

a. Waiving rights goodbye

We both teach applied ethics around the university to people studying many different degree courses, from medicine to engineering, theatre to dentistry or business. Consent is a common topic. 'But what *is* consent?' we ask, with sufficient emphasis on the 'is' to imply this is an important topic. After some prodding, a student usually responds 'giving permission' and the conversation develops from there.

A simple definition of consenting is giving permission. (So-called 'permissive consent' is to be distinguished from consent understood in connection with promising (Schaber, 2020).) Permission to do what? To cross one of our 'normative boundaries'. A way of making sense of a normative boundary is in terms of *rights*. We have rights that people do not interfere with our bodies, for example, and those rights generate corresponding *duties* that other people must uphold. We might also have normative boundaries constituted by agreement, or contract. However, since we occasionally want people to touch our bodies, perhaps for sexual pleasure or to undergo a medical procedure, we need a way of waiving our rights, at least temporarily. Consent can be understood as the mechanism which waives those rights to enable others to cross our boundaries on our own terms (Healey, 2019; Liberto, 2022). On this understanding, if we did not have the ability to consent, we would be stuck living lives restricted by the general normative boundaries defined by the rights we have, with no ability to change them. (Understanding consent in terms of a rights waiver helps us see that we might not have rights over all of the actions listed at the start of this section, e.g. the radio playing *that* song again, and so consent might not be relevant in all those cases.)

Sometimes, people talk of consent as a kind of 'moral magic' which transforms the impermissible into the permissible (Hurd, 1996). As Heidi Hurd puts it, 'consent can, by itself, turn a battery into a handshake; a sexual assault into a kiss; a trespass into a dinner party; a theft into a gift' (Hurd, 2018, p. 48). Some try to understand consent as the exercise of a 'normative power' (similar to the idea that breaking up is a normative power, discussed in the previous chapter) (Wertheimer, 1999; Dougherty, 2015; Manson, 2016). Although the general idea of permissive consent seems simple, there are many interesting questions to consider. Can *groups* (such as a polycule) consent to things (Varelius, 2008)? Does it make sense to talk of *hypothetical* consent (Stark, 2000; Enoch, 2017)? Are there activities, such as extreme BDSM, that perhaps no one can consent to (Hanna, 2000)? Does our consenting to something generate obligations for us *as consenters* – perhaps obligations to help facilitate what we have consented to (Müller, 2018, p. 120)? (Is it palatable to talk of an obligation to 'facilitate' intimacy we have consented to (Liberto, 2017)?)

Much of the literature consists in trying to work out when consent is valid, i.e. when we *count* as having consented (Bullock, 2018). This is crucial in discussions with our medical students, for example, as they might face situations when they are unsure whether someone is consenting to the treatment they recommend.

Those students are taught that appraising consent requires them to gauge whether someone has the *capacity*, in a specific situation, to consent. Someone who is unconscious, or severely drunk, or who has brain damage, usually lacks capacity. They are also taught that they need to ensure their patients are engaging *voluntarily*, and not being threatened by their family. Finally, they are taught that they need to ensure their patients are sufficiently *informed*. Does the patient grasp what a procedure actually involves, what the risks are, and what recovery will be like? Similar questions might enter our mind in intimate contexts too. Perhaps we have been drinking a bit with someone, and as things get more heated, we might ask whether they and/or we have the capacity to decide to proceed, and are doing so without undue influence or a lack of understanding (Wertheimer, 2003).

Each of these notions – capacity, voluntariness, informedness – is complex and subject to significant debate. Does a fourteen-year-old boy have the capacity to consent to sexual activity with a fifteen-year-old girl (Brennan and Epp, no date)? Does a women in a patriarchal religious society voluntarily consent to wearing a veil (Narayan, 2002)? Do we give informed consent when agreeing to have website cookies harvest our data (Utz et al., 2019)? Different theorists will give different answers. We can also wonder whether these conditions apply in the same way in all contexts; if they do not, then the resulting picture is even messier (Bullock, 2018, p. 92).

To take just one example, how do we specify what it means to be sufficiently informed in a particular consent-giving case? Is this meant to be a demanding condition, such that consent is hard to obtain, or relatively easy? Are we required to *disclose* certain facts, e.g. facts about our relationship status or sexual health? Or do we wait to be questioned, and take the lack of questions to communicate a desire not to know? And, even if we should disclose certain facts, do they all need to be *understood*? For example, if Will is to consent to having sex with Van, does Van have to *disclose* he has the herpes simplex virus for Will's consent to be valid? Even if Van does disclose this, does Will have to understand what this means, e.g. what a virus is, how this one spreads, that it can cause certain symptoms and be managed in certain ways (Walker, 2012; Millum and Bromwich, 2018)?

So far, we have set out a common approach to consent. On this approach, prominent debates when thinking about consent, especially intimate consent, centre on the *act* of consent-giving, the *scope* of consent giving, and the connection between valid consent and *deception*.

b. Thought or talk?

Philosophers disagree whether consent is a *mental attitude* (Hurd, 1996; Alexander, Hurd, and Westen, 2016), or whether consent has to be *performed* (Wertheimer, 2003; Healey, 2015; Dougherty, 2021). We use 'performed' not 'communicated' as the latter term can sound as if it implies consent has received successful uptake, and some philosophers deny that consent requires uptake in all cases (Dougherty, 2021).

Support for the idea that consent is a mental attitude comes from cases where people are unable to communicate, but still do not permit what is happening to them, as can happen as part of a victim's response during sexual assault where they freeze (Hurd, 1996; Alexander, Hurd, and Westen, 2016). Support for the idea that consent must be performed hinges on intuitions about the consent-receiver's perspective, especially the idea that consent must be accessible to them (Dougherty, 2015). Some philosophers also argue that consent has to be understood as a social practice which functions to change the status of interpersonal relationships (Dougherty, 2021).

Even if we favour the performative view, as we happen to do, questions remain. For instance, what counts as communication, and must communication be verbal? Many people are wary of this position as they think consent becomes too stilted and unsexy, and so suggest that consent can be nonverbal. We are familiar with nods, for example, as ways of giving permission in some contexts (Dougherty, 2015, p. 230). But would a nod be sufficient to consent in a sexual context (Archard, 1997a)? What else counts as non-verbal communication?

In an influential discussion of different approaches to rape in the law, for example, Michelle Anderson compares the 'no' and 'yes' models of consent. The former model holds that we assume consent unless people say 'no'. The latter, often touted as an advance on the 'no' model, holds that people have only consented to intimacy if they say yes (we have seen subsequent variants of this idea in advocacy around so-called 'affirmative' or 'enthusiastic' consent practices (Dougherty, 2018; Freitas, 2018)).

Anderson worries about Stephen Schulhofer's influential expression of this view. Schulhofer writes that 'if she doesn't say "no" and if her silence is combined with passionate kissing, hugging, and sexual touching, it is usually sensible to infer actual willingness [for penetration]' (Schulhofer, 1998, p. 272). One of Anderson's concerns with this approach is that it collapses back into the 'no' model of consent in giving a prominent place to the absence of refusal. Another concern is that research evidence suggests men frequently *misinterpret* sexual willingness from the behaviour of women (Anderson, 2004, p. 1417). Perhaps the key concern, however, is that the view allows us to infer consent to one activity from our willing participation in another activity. Usually, we do not seem to think this way, especially when the inferred consent concerns a 'higher stakes' activity. For example, permitting a doctor to take our temperature does not mean we consent to them taking a blood test. Yet on Schulhofer's account, there may be cases where we infer consent to penetration (which many view as higher stakes than kissing), from enthusiastic participation in kissing. (We can also worry about Schulhofer's approach in terms of the scope of consent – on which, more below.)

Instead of the 'yes' and 'no' models of consent, Anderson herself favours the 'negotiation' model, which it is helpful to set out here:

> The Negotiation Model requires consultation, reciprocal communication, and the exchange of views before a person initiates sexual penetration. It requires communication that is verbal unless partners have established a context between them in which they may accurately assess one another's nonverbal behavior. (Anderson, 2004, p. 1422)

The absence of a 'no' or a simple 'yes' are not sufficient on this view. Instead, penetration is morally acceptable only if the people involved have negotiated it beforehand, and – crucially – reached agreement, as only this maximizes 'the opportunity for sexual partners to share intentions, desires, and boundaries' (Anderson, 2004, p. 1423). In a way, this is a hyper-performative view of what permissible sex requires.

Anderson's view is interesting for several reasons. First, the status of her view needs clarifying. Her main concern is to arrive at a legal definition of rape, but there are two ways we can interpret her strategy. One is as offering the negotiation analysis *in the place of* a consent-focused approach to rape. But the other is offering an analysis of when consent has been given. On the former, negotiation is what matters morally. On the latter, consent is what matters morally, but in sexual contexts, we only secure consent via negotiation.

This kind of tension is visible elsewhere in the consent literature. Manon Garcia, for example, works towards an account of sex 'as conversation'. It is unclear, though, whether this is a description of the ideal process via which we secure consent – perhaps a process that also makes sex morally good as it involves respect, reciprocity, and attention to someone in their particularity – or whether it is intended as a new understanding of the ontology of consent, i.e. what consent is (Garcia, 2023).

Second, Anderson focuses on penetration, but sex is hard to define and we might think the value and moral significance of consent and negotiation apply in many other areas of sex and intimate life, and so any ethical analysis of these ideas must be able to apply more widely.

Third, even Anderson's talk-heavy approach to sexual ethics allows for people in longer committed relationships to infer consent based on body language:

After partners establish a pattern of engaging in sexual penetration that serves as the necessary negotiation, the Yes Model provides sufficient protection for sexual autonomy. Partners may proceed to follow the custom between them when they both indicate affirmative nonverbal agreement. A longer-term relationship, therefore, provides a context in which partners may reliably read one another's nonverbal behavior. Without a custom, however, partners have to negotiate penetration verbally. (Anderson, 2004, p. 1426)

An example of such a 'custom' might be a woman handing a man a condom 'at an appropriate moment' to signal consent to penetrative sex (Tilton and Ichikawa, 2021, p. 148). If negotiation is so important as a bulwark against potentially troublesome inferences, why does this not remain the case in longer relationships? Indeed, might 'customs' increase the likelihood of misunderstandings if people are not talking to each other? Views such as Anderson's seem to neglect the fact that most sexual assaults occur within contexts where people know each other.

The debate about the nature of consent, whether it is mental or performative, led us to consider what counts as communication, which, in turn, led us to touch briefly on views which allow us to make inferences about what people are consenting to on the basis of behaviour and context. This connects with a second debate around intimate consent – namely, specifying the *scope* of consent.

c. Setting scope

We often talk about consent in general terms: 'Did you consent to having sex with them?' – 'Yes I did.' But what, exactly, are people consenting to when consenting to 'sex'? We saw in a previous chapter that sex itself is understood to mean different things by different people. Does consent to 'sex' mean consent to oral sex, to sex without a condom, to sex in front of other people, to sex involving pain, and so on?

One attempt to understand how we specify the scope of consent is due to Tom Dougherty (Dougherty, 2021). As we have seen, Dougherty embraces the communication view of consent. More specifically, he favours the idea that consent is an expression of our will, which happens in a public, interpersonal, manner and which can justify our behaviour. For Dougherty, we can give consent either by permitting people to do things, or by directing them to do things. The hard question, however, is working out *what* people have consented to. Dougherty suggests this is determined by two factors. The first is the reasonable evidence we have available to us. The second is the evidence we have a duty under due diligence to find out.

You might ask us, 'Can I borrow the textbook you wrote?', and we say, 'Yes, sure!' What have we consented to here? (Setting aside any complications that may arise from it being a 'we' that consents.) For Dougherty, the scope of your permission to borrow our book is set in part by social conventions on book borrowing, and in part by the things you ought to find out, e.g. whether that includes you taking the book on your forthcoming six-month work trip, or whether you can mark the book with a permanent pen.

Dougherty's emphasis on due diligence stresses the role of the consent-receiver in clarifying aspects of the exchange. But the practical implications of his view are unclear, since it rests on our wider intuitions. We need moral intuitions to distinguish between moral and immoral social conventions, so we can exclude the latter from our sense of what fixes the scope of consent; we need intuitions about what it is 'reasonable' to think is evidence that an action falls within the scope of someone's consent; intuitions about how thorough we need to be, when being diligent; we also need clear intuitions about the 'stakes' of being wrong. People disagree on all of these counts, especially in intimate ethics.

Moreover, what happens when people have different senses of what is reasonable, or what a moral convention is? Ross may think it is conventionally understood that consenting to have penetrative sex also means that people consent to have oral sex (on the grounds that oral sex is seen as 'less serious' than penetrative sex), whereas Carli disagrees (on the grounds that, for some women, oral sex is felt as more intimate than penetrative sex). Ross and Carli may also disagree about the demands of due diligence. Yes, they agree consent to sex needs clarification when it comes to use of contraception, but they disagree that they have to check whether a partner agrees to have sex with a latex condom specifically. 'That's way too specific', says Carli; 'That's just common sense', replies Ross, 'some people are allergic to latex.'

We can also wonder whether due diligence to find evidence about the scope of consent can be asymmetrical, or change in different relational contexts? Does a background of patriarchal social norms which privilege men over women and contribute to rape culture and the 'cultural scaffolding of rape' (Gavey, 2018) mean that men have to be more diligent than women in acquiring evidence? Or would such a view actually perpetuate harmful stereotypes or impede efforts to make relationships, and intimate labour, more equal? Can we be less diligent in a long-term relationship than in a causal encounter?

Finally, it is worth highlighting the nature of Dougherty's analysis. He is working towards an account of what consent is and how we set its scope. With this framework in hand, we then turn to our moral intuitions to flesh out the detail. But perhaps this gets things the wrong way around, or, at the very least, our general approach to the nature and scope of consent should be open to the influence of moral intuitions about power or patriarchy, say, from the beginning (a matter we shall return to below).

d. Deception and dealbreakers

The matter of the scope of consent dovetails with a final debate about the links between intimate consent, being informed, and deception (some argue that these issues are often conflated (Tilton and Ichikawa, 2021)). The main worry is that consent is not valid if it rests on deception or if we withhold information that might be someone's 'dealbreaker' (Dougherty, 2013). At stake here is a tension between, on the one hand, people having requisite information to make informed choices about themselves and their bodies and, on the other hand, people having the ability to protect or withhold parts of themselves.

Views diverge wildly. At one point, Dougherty took a radical position that withholding *any* information that would be a dealbreaker for the other person relative to the proposed action invalidates their consent (Dougherty, 2013). This is radical as the information might seem trivial or unrelated to sexuality, and because some deception is common in intimate life (Buss, 2005). It might be a dealbreaker for your sexual partner, for instance, to have sex with someone who weighs between 64 and 66 kg. If you withhold that you are 65 kg, their consent is invalid. Dougherty took this result to show us that consent is less significant than we might think, in the sense that we can invalidate consent in ways which seem far less grave than in cases of rape.

Hugh Lazenby and Iason Gabriel, in contrast, argue in defence of the idea that we can have 'permissible secrets'. This means we can have a strong enough interest in some aspect of ourselves – e.g. that we have been a victim of sexual assault – for the other person to lack a claim-right to that information, even if it would otherwise be a dealbreaker for them (Lazenby and Gabriel, 2018). Note that this view aligns nicely with Gunkel's account of intimate zones, as some things might be so intimate we want to withhold them, since their exposure could subject us to psychological harm.

Even if we find the permissible secret view plausible, we might disagree about its consequences. Perhaps we are justified in withholding information, but have to take steps to avoid intimacy with someone for whom that information would be a dealbreaker. We also face challenging questions about *which* features of a person may count as permissible secrets (Tilton and Ichikawa, 2021). Is the fact that we have transitioned gender, for example, something that we can reasonably not disclose even if we know someone would not consent to sex with us if we did disclose it?

e. Alternative approaches to consent

So far, we have set out a common approach to consent, which understands it as a rights waiver – typically giving permission – that enables people to do things they have a duty otherwise not to do. Consent, on this view, has to be given in an informed, voluntary way by someone with the capacity to do so. Philosophers disagree whether consent has to be communicated, quite what non-verbal communication might involve, and about how to specify the scope of what we consent to. Another debate swirls around consent and deception.

While these debates continue, and the literature grows larger, some philosophers are urging us to approach consent differently. We shall explore two of these recent approaches before asking whether philosophers have given consent too much prominence when thinking about intimate ethics.

Quill Kukla argues in favour of a 'non-ideal' approach to consent, on the grounds that we rarely, if ever, are fully autonomous (Kukla, 2021). By autonomy, they have in mind our ability to make decisions for ourselves and direct our lives. Unlike more familiar approaches to consent, Kukla wants to resist the idea that consent is linked to a 'cognitive moment of choice' or involves 'an explicit communicative act', instead arguing that 'consensual activity is a kind of agential, self-determining activity, in which everyone involved understands that everyone else is acting in this agential, self-determining way, and in which everyone involved can and would stop the activity as soon as it ceased to be agential and self-determining' (Kukla, 2021, p. 271). The idea, here, is that consensual activity is a quality of activity, rather than whatever follows from a specific choice. Kukla is clear that they want to resist the default understanding of consent as something which removes the duties other people have to leave us alone. As they put it, 'I find it forced and odd to think of people as walking around with duties not to "do sex" to one another, from which they can be released', as this makes sexual activity sound like a passive happening (more on this worry later) (Kukla, 2021, p. 272).

Kukla notes that our autonomy can fluctuate, both in terms of our general capacities and in terms of how we are situated in a given context at a specific time. They think that consent too, as a kind of action, can also come in degrees. But we can also help 'scaffold' the autonomy of other people, so that our activities are consensual, even if our autonomy is under pressure or compromised. Kukla's examples of this can seem controversial. One is the specific case of a romantic couple where one partner suffers from dementia and lives in a care home. The other is the more pervasive issue of women consenting under patriarchy. Kukla's approach to these cases is also shaped by what they take to be our attitudes towards 'people with memory problems, mildly drunk people, people out of their element, and people at a power disadvantage', all of whom, they think, are not incapable of consent (Kukla, 2021, pp. 281–2).

What does it mean to say that consent is possible under non-ideal conditions, or that we can scaffold each other's fluctuating autonomy? Here Kukla draws on feminist theorists of relational autonomy and theorists who explore ways other people can 'hold' us in our selfhood when we are unable to (Kukla, 2021, p. 284), to suggest we can hold each other in agency:

> Just as I can help someone to be themselves by holding them in their identity, I can also help someone act as themselves, and to express themselves in action, especially when their own capacities and circumstances are insufficient for doing this on their own. Holding someone in their agency or their identity is a nonappropriative way of letting them be, not by leaving them alone but by actively enabling them to be. (Kukla, 2021, p. 284)

But what does this involve? For one thing, it can involve resistance to social practices which threaten agency, from care homes which inhibit intimacy, to social norms which castigate female sexual desire.

More individually, however, it involves careful forms of attention and efforts to give a partner 'competent uptake' – i.e. understand what they are communicating in our shared context – and 'being a good, skilled, and caring interpreter of their expressions of pleasure, pain, desire, embarrassment, comfort, fear, and the like' (Kukla, 2021, p. 285). In turn, this involves a kind of *broad contextualization*: the ability to view someone's desires and expressiveness in one context in relation to their wider 'patterns, values, and sense of self' (Kukla,

2021, p. 285). What this means depends on the person and the context. On the one hand, we might not act on someone's sexual desire if we sense it is unexpected or whimsical in a moment when their autonomy is compromised. But, on the other hand, Kukla reminds us 'there is no general reason to assume that we better protect someone's agency by not having sex with them than by having it', which means:

> It is completely possible that someone may genuinely want a sexual encounter, and that that encounter may be a good expression of who they are, their values, and the kind of thing they enjoy, even if they are somewhat drunk, or have an impaired memory, or have limited reflective reasoning skills, or if they have less power than their partner, or are stuck within a system of misogynist norms that discount their sexual pleasures. (Kukla, 2021, p. 286)

A natural question is to ask how much autonomy is necessary for consensual action? Kukla favours a minimal conception, where our choices are not 'directly manipulated, coerced, or extracted' by others, where they flow 'from our own motivations', and where we have 'enough normative responsiveness and reflective capacities to be open to recognizing reasons not to do what [we] are choosing to do' (Kukla, 2021, p. 289).

That said, there are several tools or features which help us engage consensually in ordinary conditions of compromised agency. These include a sense of trust, the ability to exit from an activity, competent uptake from everyone involved, a supportive social context, 'avoidance of activities that are agency undermining', sufficient epistemic standing, means of redress when consent is violated, and forms of social connection (Kukla, 2021, pp. 287–8).

Kukla's account raises many questions. For example, although this view might accurately describe the ways our agency can be compromised and scaffolded, might wider acceptance of this more nuanced approach to consent actually facilitate forms of manipulation, paternalism, or abuse?

We might also wonder about the implications of this approach for situations where we do not know people well, such as when having casual sex. Kukla's general account of agential scaffolding rests on our ability to attend closely to someone in order to situate their desires in the wider context of their identity, life, and agential abilities. Kukla concedes that the sense of trust or ability to give and receive uptake will be different and perhaps limited in the context of a one-night stand, and that such contexts are not places to engage in 'boundary-pushing activities' (Kukla, 2021, p. 287). But many of the other factors they mention are also hard to secure in one-night stands, such as the presence of a shared support network, or redress, or confidence in someone's epistemic standing. Consent understood as a quality of action seems hard to achieve in situations where we do not know someone well. You might find this unconvincing. We also note that close and long-term relationships can involve biases of their own, such as the so-called 'closeness communication bias' which holds that we are actually worse at listening to people we know well than we are to strangers (Savitsky et al., 2011).

Hesitancy towards more casual intimacy might be reasonable. Kukla could argue it captures the risk and uncertainty inherent when people do not know each other well, but also points to the ways society can work to make casual sex better for people by changing social norms or instigating specific policies in clubs and bars to encourage agential scaffolding, good standing, social support, and competent uptake. But this consequence of their view will not appeal to people who have a more minimal understanding of consent as giving permission.

Finally, and relatedly, can Kukla's account of consent shape political and legal treatments of consent? Their view of our agency and consent is purposefully messy, but the law might need to be precise. Could this lead to a tension between our ethical conception of consensual intimacy, on the one hand, and our legal conception on the other? Is this a tension which might itself hold back attempts to change society in the ways Kukla encourages? If you want to shape policy, you cannot shy away from these questions.

Kukla's approach to consent was influenced by theorists of so-called 'relational autonomy' who contest an overly individual conception of the deciding and acting agent. Another philosopher who approaches consent with a similar motivation, but in a different direction, is Ellie Anderson. Anderson develops a phenomenological account of consent which offers perhaps the most radical departure from standard treatments of what consent is (Anderson, 2022). Her goal is to redefine consent as 'feeling-with' someone. Underlying this is wariness towards 'an overly rationalistic account of erotic experience in which agents meet on an even playing field with transparent access to their desires before communicating them' (Anderson, 2022, p. 6). Instead, she views sex (and we would extend this to intimacy) as involving 'complex dynamics of perception, desire, intention, and willing that cannot simply be reduced to giving permission to another person to transgress one's boundaries' (Anderson, 2022, p. 6).

Anderson turns, instead, to phenomenologists such as Maurice Merleau-Ponty to work outwards from our lived experiences of interacting with people, towards an account of consent. Central to this phenomenological approach is the idea of 'embodied consciousness'. We are not minds housed in bodies. We are actively oriented towards the world, in a direct, emotional, and practical way, as a site of continual interpersonal possibility. This involves immediate perception of others as embodied agents (rather than processes of inferring their mental states from their bodies), but also a sense of ourselves as objects for others too.

For Anderson, consent is understood as 'an agreement of feeling' since only this can account for 'the largely prereflective and direct character of our perceptions of others, especially in erotic situations' (Anderson, 2022, p. 14). This agreement of feeling has a specific triadic structure:

> Phenomenologically speaking, we may define consent as an intercorporeal and dynamic coexistence of desiring bodies, where desire has a triadic structure: one erotically desires the other, erotically desires that the other desire oneself, and desires an unfolding of erotic experience with the other. (Anderson, 2022, p. 15)

Anderson also suggests consent could be described as 'attuned erotic perception' – a form of embodied orientation towards someone as an erotic presence (Anderson, 2022, p. 15). This is an experience of ambiguity, since erotic perception mingles the sense in which we are subject and object for ourselves, and for others, and them for us, all at once. Since consent is understood partly in these affective perceptual terms, failures to secure consent are 'a fault of the initiator not only in a moral sense but often also in a perceptual sense: the initiator may fail to see that the *situation* is nonconsensual due to a lack of attuned perception' (Anderson, 2022, p. 21). (Notice that this emphasis on good attention is shared with Kukla's account, and with others who want to think of consent in a way which emphasizes the mutual openness and sensitivity to another, whether understood as teamwork (Gardner, 2018) or conversation (Garcia, 2023).)

We have shared Anderson's view here as it positions consent as something radically other than a single state of mind or communicative act. Indeed, we seem far removed from the land of rights waivers and permissions altogether. Instead, consent is something more emotional and interpersonal. Even if you find it implausible, it is useful to consider alternative ways of thinking about consent.

Unsurprisingly, we have critical questions. First, desire is baked into Anderson's account. To consent, as she defined it, is to 'erotically [desire] the other'. But people typically think we can consent to things we do not desire. One worry, then, is that either Anderson's account would make it hard to make sense of some forms of bad but consensual intimacy, or it has to rest on an unhelpfully broad sense of desire. Neither option is attractive.

A related worry is that Anderson's account makes it harder to account for situations where we seem to consent with the *hope* that we will experience erotic attunement to someone, rather than *because* we experience that attunement. For Anderson, consent arises when there is already a 'dynamic coexistence of desiring bodies'. But how do we get to that point? Imagine Shaun and Shane are considering a one-night stand. Shaun is unsure how things might unfold, but is curious and wants to try since Shane seems nice and kind. On the conventional view, Shaun might consent to sex in the hope and desire it will unfold well. But on Anderson's view, things are different. Shaun and Shane only count as consenting to what they are doing if they are experiencing the kind of erotic attunement and desire she described. But this can seem too demanding.

Relatedly, it seems likely that we will often be wrong about whether we are 'feeling-with' someone. We might misread their ambivalence – as enthusiasm, for example – or be motivated to read into their feelings due to our own strong sense of sexual desire. More interestingly, a nervous couple might worry they are not feeling-with each other during an intimate fumble, only to later realize they were. These possibilities highlight the epistemic barriers such an account of consent throws in our way; these barriers might be substantial if we also suppose that people are often bad at describing and communicating their feelings.

Finally, we can also ask how this account of sexual consent applies to consent in other contexts. As our colleague Danielle Bromwich put it to us, does consent to a root canal require '"feeling with" the dentist'? This seems implausible. If we embrace that implausibility, then consent in sexual contexts looks different from consent in other contexts. But why should we think that? Is it the presence of the body, or the involvement of 'erotic desire', or some other factor? Bodies and eroticism are not confined to sex, which would suggest this account could apply in other contexts too (dancing, sport, romantic intimacy between people uninterested in sex), but it is hard to see how it would extend into medical contexts, let alone find recognition in the law.

f. Consent's significance

Kukla's and Anderson's two accounts push, in different ways, at the assumptions underpinning traditional discussions of consent in intimate contexts. Both of them are revisionary, in the sense they want to retain the concept of consent but tweak it to better fit our lived experiences. Other philosophers, however, want us to think harder about the overall significance of consent for intimate ethics, and some want us to do away with the concept altogether. We end this section by exploring some of their views. Why would anyone think the idea of consent is problematic?

One key reason to worry about the emphasis on consent is simple: consensual intimacy is often bad (West, 2017; Woodard, 2022). To better understand bad sex, we need to focus on notions other than consent, and this requires us to not ask too much of consent as some philosophers have perhaps tended to do. We turn to bad intimacy in the next section of this chapter.

There are other reasons to de-centre consent from discussions of intimate ethics. Writing before their non-ideal consent paper, Quill Kukla worries that the focus on consent overlooks the actual ways we negotiate intimacy, and that sex is often a response to *invitations* or *gifts* where talk of consent seems misplaced. To see this, imagine someone asks you, 'Hey, do you want to join our football team?' and you reply 'Yes!' and then someone else asks: 'Did you consent to playing football?' There is a sense in which *that* question just feels odd. As we saw above, Kukla is wary of thinking of sex in terms of permission. One reason for this is that it distracts us from the positive aspects of intimate agency; and that 'most philosophical, legal, and public discussions of sexual communication have presumed that the difficult or interesting problem is how to enable women to refuse or avoid sex with men ... Women's need for positive sexual agency is invisible in this story' (Kukla, 2018, pp. 78–9).

Part of the problem here, for Kukla, concerns the routes we take towards sex or intimacy. They suggest that standard models of consent present 'all expressions of desires as requests, for which agreement or refusal is the appropriate possible uptake', a view which arguably 'flattens the communicative terrain' (Kukla, 2018, p. 76). A reason for this flattening is that we often have sex on the basis of invitations – 'Would you like to have sex?' – and Kukla thinks 'consent and refusal are not even the right categories of speech acts when it comes to your uptake. One can't consent to an invitation – one accepts it or turns it down' (Kukla, 2018, p. 82). This seems true of other aspects of intimacy.

Noticing the other ways we interact intimately, and the different routes we can take towards sex, highlights the significance of intimate *negotiation* for Kukla. We offer invitations and gift intimacy, and often discuss these in detail ('Do you want me to give you a massage?' – 'Not today, I'm in the mood for something rougher'). But equally important are the ways we talk *about* and *around* our intimate and sexual contexts to set up, maintain, or modify the framework within which we are intimate. A lot of intimate interaction concerns our 'discursive frame', where we establish the 'distinctive local internal norms that shape what words and phrases mean, as well as the felicity and force of various speech acts' (Kukla, 2018, p. 90). Norms, for example, around pleasure (who gets it, in what order, and in what ways) may disadvantage women at the expense of men.

Negotiation, and tinkering with discursive frames, is more visible in alternative sexual communities, e.g. where people explore BDSM or nonmonogamy, since intimacy might be novel or risky and so require discussion. But those situations just make explicit the fact that all intimacy is framed by assumptions and norms which we can make salient and explore. Negotiation matters, thinks Kukla, because it helps us *expand* our intimate agency and enjoyment. Intimate ethics should focus on this negotiation and the ways we can support each other in having better sex, not just on avoiding wrongful sex.

A different reason to worry about the emphasis on consent is that it can contribute to subtle harms. Melissa Ress and Jonathan Ichikawa are interested in how we are prone to approach predatory forms of sexual interest – e.g. between teachers and students, where there are power imbalances – in terms of consent violation (Rees and Ichikawa, 2024). Specifically, this approach views predation as morally wrong because the victim lacks the capacity to consent. Rees and Ichikawa disagree with this analysis. They argue that these victims often *are able* to consent in these cases, and did consent, and that these encounters are wrong for other reasons (which we can set aside here). Their main argument, however, is that the social dominance of consent-talk sets up a dilemma for these victims: either they continue to see themselves as having been wronged, but accept they lacked the ability to consent; or they retain their sense of having been able to consent and give up the idea they were wronged.

Their idea is that these victims risk being subject to the 'secondary harm' of 'agential demotion', which they define as:

A agentially demotes B when: (i) B is an agent capable of consenting, and (ii) A takes B's agency to be compromised in a way that renders B incapable of consenting. (Rees and Ichikawa, 2024, p. 9)

So not only was the student, say, a victim of sexual predation by a teacher, but to be able to articulate their experience as one of harm they are subject to pressure to deny their own status as someone capable of consenting. We note that similar secondary harms may accompany experiences of unwanted or bad sex where predation is *not* involved, because the dominance of consent-talk can crowd out other ways of articulating dissatisfaction or lack of flourishing.

These are reasons to want to de-centre talk of consent. But Jonathan Ichikawa goes further and argues that consent is not *necessary* for permissible sex (Ichikawa, 2020). (John Gardner explores a similar idea, suggesting that 'when the sexual going is good, consent is also unnecessary' (Gardner, 2018, p. 60).) Ichikawa's view is similar to Kukla's in that it focuses on what the concept of consent *presupposes*. He suggests that consent presupposes we are enabling someone to act as they will, where our will does not come into it, and that this has gendered connotations since it is typically women who are expected to yield to the will of men (i.e. that women 'give' consent to men). As he puts it, 'When you are considering doing something at another's behest, the question of consent is an appropriate one. When you are considering doing something for your own reasons, the question doesn't even arise' (Ichikawa, 2020, pp. 6–7). Not only does the question not arise, he thinks, but it does not need to; sex can be permissible without consent:

> I do think there can be cases of permissible sex where the presuppositions of 'consent' are not satisfied. Indeed, many of the paradigms of good sex are like this. Most sex – especially most good sex – does not arrive from one person acquiescing to another's behest. Sexual negotiations that involve suggestions, invitations, brainstorming, the exploration of shared ideas and fantasies, and so on, needn't involve satisfying these presuppositions. (Ichikawa, 2020, p. 14)

To be clear, sex where the question of consent does not need to arise is not thereby non-consensual sex (apologies for the double negatives). It is simply sex that proceeds from a different basis because questions about yielding to another person do not arise since we are equally active partners in the interaction.

Ichikawa worries that consent-talk risks embedding the idea that the people involved have an 'imbalance of interests and autonomy', and so to avoid this 'we have a good reason to prefer other language for discussion of sexual ethics' (Ichikawa, 2020, p. 29).

These are some of the reasons available for being wary of the dominance of consent-talk in contemporary thinking about intimate ethics. Some suggest the need to supplement notions of consent with other ideas, such as negotiation; others urge us to be careful not to presuppose all sexual wrongdoing needs to be described in terms of consent and the capacity to consent; others still are tempted to get rid of talk of consent altogether. These proposals can seem radical. The idea that we can develop an account of intimate ethics without consent at its heart can be hard to grasp.

Another natural question in response to these proposals is: Can the problem be this bad? We might think that the associations between consent, presumptiveness, and especially the gendered dimension of these presumptions, are highly contingent and can be addressed without us needing to jettison the notion of consent itself. Similarly, can't we avoid the problem of agential demotion while also thinking consent is a crucial concept, by acknowledging the breadth of wrongs, and bad intimacy, that can nonetheless be consented to, and supplement talk of consent with a discussion of its broader value, its limits, and other notions in sexual ethics?

3. Better intimacy

Chances are, if you've had sex, you've had some bad sex.

Bad sex, and bad intimacy more generally, is often consensual. But to say something is permitted is not always to say it is good. There are several different senses of good we can appeal to here, and different ethical theorists will make their own different distinctions. One is the prudential sense, in which something is not a good means to an existing end we have, such as to experience pleasure, or to get pregnant. Another is good in the sense of better and worse for us, or conducive to our flourishing, or good relative to some value we take to be objective. Having unprotected casual sex, for example, could be bad in a prudential sense if we want to avoid risk of pregnancy or sexually transmitted disease, but it also might not be something that contributes to our flourishing or aligns with some conception of the good (such as religious views which locate good sex in marriage). Here we are interested in these ethical senses of good, and the ways that something which seems permissible might be problematic in other ways. As others have noted, this is an under-theorized area – and much work needs to be done (Cahill, 2014; Woodard, 2022, p. 302).

To be clear, not everyone will agree with this line of inquiry. Some people may think, as Igor Primoratz argued, that 'consent is sufficient for a sexual act to be morally legitimate' (Primoratz, 2001, p. 201). We do not share this view and want to explore the increasingly common idea that there is more to be said, morally, about the ethics of intimacy, and many kinds of bad sex and bad intimacy.

This is a vast topic. One problem we face is that some ethically troubling dynamics or practices, which are important to discuss in intimate contexts, such as manipulation (Buss, 2005), or gaslighting (Stark, 2019), or 'dark desires' (Morgan, 2003a), may arguably render consent invalid. This is because the person consenting might not be doing so with sufficient voluntariness, or with sufficient information about the other person (their desires and motivations, say), to specify the scope of the consent. There is room for debate in every case however, and our sense of which troubling approaches to intimacy are consent-undermining, and which are not, will depend on the account of consent we embrace. Philosophers including Elise Woodard, for example, in their approach to bad sex, argue that sex can be consensual whilst resulting from psychological pressure from a partner or from social coercion in ways which make the sex bad (Woodard, 2022). Below, we will try to isolate aspects of intimacy which seem clearly compatible with consent, either in the sense that someone might consensually agree to be intimate with someone in full awareness of how they will be treated, or in the sense that the way they are treated is not sufficient to undermine consent.

a. Object and subject

We have already seen some ways in which consensual intimacy might nevertheless be bad. Our discussion of yellow fever, for instance, highlighted the ways that intimacy can involve one person objectifying another person. Martha Nussbaum influentially charted several variants of objectification. We can treat someone as lacking *autonomy*, or *agency*; as *interchangeable* with other people; as lacking in *boundary integrity*; as being *owned* by another (and so as being sellable); and as someone whose states of mind *do not need to be taken into account* (Nussbaum, 1995, p. 257). For Nussbaum, treating someone as a mere means for our own ends is the worst form of objectification as this involves denying them due respect as a rational being (Nussbaum, 1995, p. 265). Developed in this way, this worry with objectification is anchored in Kantian concerns about respect for persons, which also feature in other analyses of how sex which is consensual on the traditional understanding might also be bad (Morgan, 2003a; Garcia, 2023).

Others have subsequently developed analyses of objectification. Rae Langton, for example, noticed that not only can we *deny* someone's agency, as Nussbaum thinks, but we can also *silence* their agency (Langton, 2009). This can mean objectification is more active. Rather than mistakenly treating a person as if they were a thing, the silencer must recognize someone's agency, at some level, only to disregard it. Zhou (from chapter 1), for example, might consent to an intimate encounter after her date with Trevor, only to be treated as a mere body for him to sate a sexual fetish for Asian women.

Talk of objectification is not clear-cut, however, as some people arguably are over-subjectified. Leslie Green argues that, in a hetero-sexist society, 'First, [the gay man] is most often simply invisible or non-existent. Second, when he does occasionally flit in and out of the frame, it is most often in the figure of one of the dominant stereotypes: aesthetic, sensitive, different, fabulous, foppish, and so forth' (Green, 2000, pp. 46–7). Green thinks that being treated as a subject is a 'motif experience' and he argues, tentatively, that gay pornography might be a way gay men can reclaim their sexuality through objectification on their own terms. Disabled people are also not treated as sexual beings in a similar way, due to 'the long-standing societal prejudice that impairments are incompatible with sexual desire and sexual activity' (Shakespeare, 2022).

Concerns about a lack of objectification are not limited to certain social groups, either. Ellie Anderson and Caleb Ward argue, within a phenomenological framework, that *all* of our embodied human experiences with other people contain aspects of objecthood and subjecthood (Ward and Anderson, 2022). For them, our erotic agency rests in part on the ways in which we are able to be erotic objects for others, and them for us, alongside the ways we are experienced, and experience others, as subjects (cf. Cahill, 2012).

b. Epistemically unsafe

Elise Woodard describes another way consensual sex might be bad, related to aspects of objectification, and this is because it is 'episte-mologically unsafe' (Woodard, 2022, p. 311). Epistemically unsafe sex happens when someone 'worr[ies] about finding out their consent was modally irrelevant: if they had not consented, their partner would have proceeded to have sex with them anyway' (Woodard, 2022, p. 306). This fear can arise in prospect, and may motivate us to consent to sex so that it turns out that we were not raped, or it can arise after an encounter as we reflect on what happened with a creeping sense that the person we were having sex with did not care that we consented.

One way to make sense of epistemically unsafe sex is simply that one (or perhaps more than one) partner does not seem to care enough about the role of consent in the encounter. Woodard argues that this is sufficient to make sex bad because 'this would likely feel violating and arguably objectifying', or that 'this realization can make one feel frightfully close to being assaulted' in ways which 'can undermine one's sense of autonomy or agency in deciding whether to have sex' (Woodard, 2022, p. 312).

We note that epistemically unsafe sex is similar to, and may involve, the dynamics of silencing explored by Langton, and the failures of 'competent uptake' that concerned Kukla. That said, it is also possible to imagine non-objectifying epistemically unsafe sex. The wife of a loving husband in a terribly patriarchal society, for example, might feel uneasy since her husband's attentive concern for her arises in a context where consent of women to sex is trivialized, and so feels precarious and contingent. He could change his mind at any moment and no one would care – indeed, perhaps not heeding her consent would improve his social standing as a man. Although he happens to be nice and caring, their sex is *structurally* epistemically unsafe. (Another way to explore these ideas is to connect it to discussion of unfreedom as domination. We are dominated in this sense if others can arbitrarily interfere with us, even if they do not (Pettit, 1997; Lovett, 2022). Domination can render practices of consent-giving epistemically unsafe.)

c. Reciprocity and mutuality

Related to, but distinct from, concerns with objectification is the concern that some consensual sex can be insufficiently *reciprocal*. This is a core theme of John Gardner's influential paper on consent where he advances the view that good sex is a 'team activity' (Gardner, 2018, p. 54). This does not mean the people involved have to be doing exactly the same things at the same time (our anatomy can make that impossible) but that 'there is no *agent–patient* asymmetry' and 'the activity as a whole is not something that is done by one partner to the other, nor, strictly speaking, by each to the other, but rather by both together' (Gardner, 2018, p. 56). Gardner reaches for an analogy with jazz improvisation to convey what this may involve, i.e. multiple people responding to each other with a common purpose, as a 'we', rather than a disparate collection of individuals.

We think it is conceptually possible, if unlikely in practice, for one person to fail to treat their partner as part of a team, but without objectifying them. Gender norms, or social ideals of sexual agency, could position some as sexual agents, and others as sexual patients. It could be integral to this that the sexual patient is approached as a subject, as an individual with distinct feelings and desires, rather than as a means to gratification (appreciation of facts like this seem central to sexual desire in general (Morgan, 2003b)). The issue is simply that they are not regarded as someone who has the standing to shape the sexual encounter. (As an analogy, an Army sergeant may treat his subordinates as individuals, while not treating them as a part of a team of equals.)

Another concern is that consensual sex might not be *mutual* sex. Sharon Lamb and her co-authors argue that mutuality is distinct from reciprocity, since 'for reciprocity it is sufficient that an individual relies on what is offered or withheld in sex, and responds in like fashion', whereas mutuality is more demanding (Lamb, Gable, and de Ruyter, 2021, p. 274). By mutuality in sex (and we would apply this to intimacy more generally), they have in mind a form of 'caring attention' which 'minimally requires that one look beyond consent to seek to understand the other person's intentions and psychological state, to understand if the sex that is about to occur or is occurring may be harmful in some way to the other' (Lamb, Gable, and de Ruyter, 2021, p. 274). To approach someone with mutuality in mind, for them, is to do so with an eye to 'as much context as he or she can' (Lamb, Gable, and de Ruyter, 2021, p. 276). (Note the similarities with Quill Kukla's description of what non-ideal consent involves. Here, Lamb and co-authors view mutuality as something that ought to *supplement* a minimal notion of sexual consent, whereas Kukla *builds into* their theory of what consent requires something like mutuality.) Lamb and her co-authors argue that consensual sex which is not mutual – such as sex with an anonymous partner via a gloryhole – is 'morally wrong' since one partner cannot attend to the other in the right way (Lamb, Gable, and de Ruyter, 2021, p. 281).

Their view forces us to think carefully about cases where two people differ vastly in their ability to attend to each other, or in the ways they are able to attend – for example, due to various forms of physical or cognitive disability. Such intimacy may not be mutual in their sense, but is it thereby morally wrong? We are less sure.

d. Ordinary vices of bad sex

There might be other ways in which consensual intimacy is bad. Sex can be lazy, ungenerous, uncreative, cowardly, passionless, or coloured by anger, resentment, and envy. In fact, we think that much popular discussion of bad sex – sex which is consensual but ethically troubling – is trying to centre on these ideas. For want of a better term, let's call this collection of issues the 'ordinary vices of bad sex'.

Part of the reason why these aspects of intimate ethics do not feature more prominently is because many theorists are working within a broadly liberal tradition – focusing on what is permissible and the avoidance of harm – or a broadly Kantian tradition, with a focus on dignity and respect. Manon Garcia, to take one example, embraces this dichotomy and argues the liberal tradition has been too dominant (Garcia, 2023, p. 37).

But we can approach intimate ethics from other ethical standpoints, too, including that of virtue ethics or care ethics. (A key advocate of the former approach is Halwani (2003).) Virtue ethics is concerned with character. How would a virtuous person have sex or be intimate? What traits of character would the virtuous sexual person have, and how do they manifest? The relative neglect of virtue ethics is quite strange when we consider the shift towards more relational ideas in intimate ethics; talk of attention, and conversation, and engaging with people in the specificity of a context are all central to the kinds of practical wisdom virtuous people have.

In sex, we are often too selfish, or unfeeling, or hasty to reach orgasm, or unimaginative, or afraid to experiment. On some views, these failures might be prudential – they make sex less fun, more disappointing, but are morally untroubling. But from a virtue ethical perspective, there is room to view these as ethical failures too, insofar as they are manifestations of bad character traits in the intimate sphere.

We lack the space, sadly, to explore each of these possible vices in turn, and we accept that it may be controversial to call some of these vices. Each deserves patient analysis. What is clear, however, is that intimacy might lack objectification and be fine in other ways, while nevertheless raising issues for us. We might sense that someone's emotions are out of sync with their desire (perhaps they only get aroused when angry), or they are too timid, or that they are emotionless. Even if we are wary of vice talk when it comes to sex, it seems clear we do embrace virtue talk, praising generous, open-minded, creative, and attentive lovers.

What is interesting about bad sex is how often the ordinary vices of bad sex *coalesce*. Much popular writing about sexual culture tries to draw our attention to bad intimacy as a rich but pervasive phenomenon (Angel, 2021; Hagen, 2024). Where there is one aspect of bad sex, there are often others. Not only that, but these issues are often expressed in structural terms, with an emphasis on gender and other intimate norms. Bad sex is understood as a product of patriarchy – something that men have sustained over women, and something resisted in queer communities.

Jane Ward articulates a version of this idea in exploring the social impact of straight culture (Ward, 2020). She writes from a queer perspective, and one that emphasizes aspects of choice and agency that are neglected even in queer male writing about 'being born this way'. That said, her perspective is one of 'worrying about' straightness, and trying to reintegrate its contradictions, rather than oppose or reject it outright.

Her focus is 'the tragedy of heterosexuality':

> the contradictions and miseries of *straight culture* – the entrapment, the disappointment, the antagonism, the boredom, the unwanted sex, the toxic masculinity, and the countless daily injustices endured by straight women. (Ward, 2020, p. 4)

Ward's basic claim is that straight culture, and the norms and ideals which sustain it, is stifling. Men feel entitled to women's bodies and time. Men are 'emotional gold diggers' exploiting women's emotional labour. The sexual repertoire of straight people is limited, and genitally focused. Straight people shy from imaginative efforts to consider alternative forms of life, and cling to simple binaries, or 'straight' or 'gay', rather than describing erotic interest and experience with nuance. Boredom is a constant threat; complaint is a mode of expression; ideals of intimate sacrifice are praised, not questioned. These are generalizations, of course, but they ring true. Ward is adamant that heteronormativity is an important conceptual lens, often distinct from – albeit intersecting with – patriarchy, since straight women are also attached to and invested in straight culture.

Underlying the tragedy of heterosexuality, for Ward, is the 'paradox of misogyny' – namely, the idea that straight male desire 'is expressed within a broader culture that encourages them to also hate girls and women' (Ward, 2020, p. 27). Ward contends that the contemporary ideal that men should *like* their female sexual partners is relatively new, historically speaking, had to displace entrenched cultural homosociality (i.e. people liking and socializing with their own sex), and has not fully taken root; that straight people 'are struggling to transition from the trauma and legacy of misogyny to something more authentically "straight" – if by straightness, we mean authentic and noncoercive heterosexual love' (Ward, 2020, p. 36). She thinks this tension is visible in the vast self-help industry around heterosexual romance, which emphasizes gender difference, the 'management' of women's heterosexual frustration, and various strategies or 'rules' to game the system. Ward suggests that latent homophobia (and, we add, biphobia) is the 'outward expression of heterosexual misery, a kind of subconscious jealous rage against the gendered and sexual possibilities that lie beyond the violence and disappointments of straight culture' (Ward, 2020, p. 115).

This dynamic is similar to what Elizabeth Emens calls the 'paradox of prevalence' in relation to nonmonogamy, where 'the potential of nearly everyone to imagine him or herself engaging in nonmonog-amous behavior leads outsiders to steel themselves against polyamory' (Emens, 2004, p. 284). In both cases, uncritical investment in one form of life can be so entrenched that alternatives seem at once tangibly close but impossible to obtain.

Ward's analysis might not resonate with your own experience, but a merit of her view is that it looks systematically at the bundle of disappointments, frustrations, and forms of anger so often expressed by people raised in heterosexual culture, especially with one eye to alternative forms of life explored by other people around them. Our thought is that bad sex and intimacy – i.e. intimacy that is consensual but morally deficient – is often a product of this heteronormative structure, and the related norms about gender, monogamy, and the importance of romantic love which intersect with it. This is why it is rare, we think, for bad sex to be bad along one dimension alone. Laziness, objectification, lack of reciprocity and mutuality, disinterest in the interior life of the other, and so on, are packaged within straight culture, and sanctioned by misogyny (Manne, 2017). (See also our discussion of unequal sexual pleasure in chapter 6.)

e. Better intimacy

So how might we resist bad sex and intimacy? Any solution will involve a mix of different components. Some will involve efforts to approach people in new ways – to attend differently. Others will involve efforts to form new beliefs by critically interrogating old ones. Some aspects of this process will be structural, and require social changes. Others will be communal, and require us to gather in solidarity, shape new environments, and nurture each other.

A key starting point is to make clear that consensuality is the start of conversations about intimate ethics, not the end. In other words, there is a lot of work left to be done to bring the very idea of bad intimacy to public notice, and campaigning around notions such as 'bad sex', rather than folding them into talk of assault or rape, is likely to be productive (Woodard, 2022, pp. 314–17). Philosophers have their part to play here, in resisting the hermeneutic injustices that people who experience bad sex face. They need to be able to talk about the badness of their experience without raising doubts about whether they did, or did not, could or could not, consent.

Much can be done, also, to make intimate preference a matter of agency. Faced with the tragedy of heterosexuality, Ward is resistant to the idea that we ought to dismantle – or even queer – straight culture (contrary to the view of Halberstam (2013)). Instead, she advocates something much more interesting: *deep heterosexuality*. The idea of deep heterosexuality is simple: what if men actually liked women? Ward wants men to 'put their politics where their lust is: in alignment with women' (Ward, 2020, p. 165). She wonders: 'is it not possible that women and men could feel an attraction to each other that was so unstoppable, so expansive, so hungry for the wholeness of the other that it forged strong bonds of *identification and deep mutual regard*, rather than oppositeness and hierarchy?' (Ward, 2020, p. 158). There are two dimensions to this project. First, de-essentialize straightness. Ward wants straight people to learn from lesbian feminists, and view their intimate life and identity as something to take ownership over and cultivate: '[straight people] could learn to relate to their heterosexuality as a cultivated desire of which they are agent, rather than victim or passive recipient' (Ward, 2020, p. 161). This is true even if our sexual orientations are relatively fixed and unchosen, since we can still reflect on and endorse who we are. Ward argues that heteronormativity 'erases the need for straight people to justify or explain their sexuality, to others and to themselves', but straight people could reflect on, and be called to answer, the questions that queer people are often posed: 'What does being straight do to them? What do they like about it? When did they first know they were straight?' (Ward, 2020, p. 164).

We note that this strategy applies with equal force to mononormativity and amatonormativity, and we could imagine 'deep monogamy' or 'deep romanticism', where we are asked, with a straight face, 'What does being monogamous do to you?', 'When did you first know you were monogamous?', or 'When did you realize you valued romantic love over friendship?' Simply being posed these questions encourages us to think about our relationship to these common norms and take ownership of our intimate identities.

The second dimension to deep heterosexuality is arguably the harder one: men need to learn to *like* women. Here, Ward alludes to a 'lesbian feminist mode of desire' which involves 'a merging of objectifying desire, on the one hand, and a feminist, subjectifying respect for those who are desired, on the other' (Ward, 2020, p. 166). Taking a similar stance to Irivin and Lintott's position on sexiness, which we explored in chapter 1, Ward thinks that erotic interest and desire can be combined with a deep identification with the subjectivity of the other; that, 'straight men could be so deeply heterosexual, so drawn to women, as to be "women identified", to see themselves mirrored in the faces, bodies, and lives of women' (Ward, 2020, p. 169).

This suggestion echoes our prior discussion of different strategies we could employ to work on our patterns of attraction, whether that is increased representation of good intimacy, efforts to look 'as if' we care about the other, or forms of aesthetic exploration. At the heart of many of those views, and also at the heart of the concerns about sex failing to be teamwork or lacking in mutuality, is the idea that addressing bad intimacy is a matter of better *attention*. We have to learn to really look at people, see them in context, and try to resist our more self-centred impulses (Murdoch, 2001; Hopwood, 2018).

But more or better attention is arguably not sufficient for the kinds of changes that would make bad intimacy less likely, and less engrained in wider society. For one thing, it is possible to attend to, and acknowledge, aspects of other people without really *affirming* what we see (Brunning, 2024b, p. 170). Men might come to recognize women, or better understand their partner's desires and perspectives, without really liking them, caring much about them, or enthusiastically and emotionally seeing value in those desires and perspectives.

Striving for a richer, emotive, sense of affirmation of the other in straight relationships will involve sustained efforts at empathy and self-reflection, but it will also require structural changes to help us to attend, to educate us about the pitfalls of gendered social scripts, and to offer positive alternatives in their place. With respect to heterosexuality, for example, one requirement on the way to tackling bad intimacy is to explore more positive visions of masculinity (Miller, 2022). This is necessary since the kind of change required involves 'a long-term cultivation of [men's] dispositions', not just isolated beliefs or more basic patterns of behaviour (Miller, 2022, p. 175).

Attention can also be understood in a static, quite objectifying way. Talk of really seeing someone brings to mind notions of the male gaze, or of dynamics where some look and some are looked at (Berger, 2008). But concerns that sex is often one-sided, not a joint activity, or that intimacy can be thought of in conversational terms, gesture towards the dynamic, active, and intwined character of good attention. This is central to Daniella Dover's ideal of 'taking each other seriously'. To take someone seriously in this sense is to seek to access and appreciate their perspective and allow it to bear on the matter at hand, to allow our self-interpretations to be shaped by other people's understanding of us, and to encourage the others to take the same stance towards us in turn (Dover, 2022, pp. 201–4). Good intimacy is partly a matter of taking each other seriously in this sense, rather than one person 'attending' to, and acting on, the other.

Playfulness is another name, perhaps paradoxically, for taking people seriously in Dover's sense. Playfulness – understood in Maria Lugones' loving, not antagonistic, interpretation – involves the ability to shift between perspectives, to be creative, to not fetishize rules, and to be friendly towards small errors and mistakes (Lugones, 2003). Being playful in these senses will also enable us to better recognize the ways we are both objects and subjects for each other, and to appreciate the ambiguities inherent in erotic desire (Ward and Anderson, 2022). There are many ways to practise and cultivate playfulness. It could involve sexual play, toying with gender and sexual roles, getting creative when accommodating personal differences or navigating practical constraints, and so on.

A final clarification. We have explored several aspects of bad intimacy, and especially responses to it, through a critical lens organized around heteronormativity. It is worth being explicit that bad intimacy, and consensual but morally troublesome sex, is experienced by queer people too. A gay man can objectify his partner; a lesbian might be a selfish lover; a bisexual man might have sex in ways lacking reciprocity and mutuality; an asexual person may experience forms of epistemically unsafe intimacy. Moreover, queer people are socialized in heteronormative societies, just as nonmonogamous people are socialized in mononormative societies, and so everyone has some share of introspection, unlearning, exploration, and resistance to undergo.

4. Sexuality in a good life

As we were writing this book, the dating app Bumble was forced to publicly apologise after their advertising campaign suggested 'a vow of celibacy is not the answer' (Sherman, 2024). Female users felt this message was patronizing, in tension with the value of bodily autonomy, and seemed to imply that sexual intimacy is necessary.

Bumble fumbled the zeitgeist with its ad campaign, since the notion of going 'boysober' is also swirling around online and in print media as we write. Younger women have been swearing off dating apps, casual sex, and messy interactions with ex-partners in an effort to live more intentionally and avoid the tragedy of heterosexuality (Lavinia, 2024; Portolan, 2024; Schofield, 2024). For some, this is an effort to avoid sexual intimacy altogether; for others, an attempt to 'de-centre' men. For some, it is a response to experiences of assault; for others, a response to frustration with modern dating culture.

Whatever the motivation, talk of boysobriety or celibacy has pushed ethical questions into print, as people ask: what role, if any, should sexual intimacy play in our lives? Is there anything amiss with a life lacking in sexual or romantic intimacy? Or anything virtuous about a life of celibacy, or sexual temperance? More broadly, we can ask questions about sex and motivation. Is there something wrong, for example, in having sex for money, or having sex solely with the goal of getting pregnant? These are questions of value which have us considering different conceptions of the good, and different approaches to intimate ethics.

a. Sex and philosophy

It's hard to think of a historical figure in the analytic philosophical canon who wrote publicly and enthusiastically about sex. Jeremy Bentham famously defended homosexual sex but only in unpublished writing (Dabhoiwala, 2012, p. 135), and he also explored the idea of temporary marriage (Sokol, 2011; Nolan, 2016).

Historically, philosophers have been quite sex-negative, in the sense that they are wary of sex and view it as something to be managed or pursued in tightly defined contexts, rather than a wonderful aspect of human life and important source of pleasure. Whether we have in mind Immanuel Kant, who equated sex outside marriage with a lemon sucked dry and tossed aside (Madigan, 1998), or, more recently, Roger Scruton, who asks us 'to consider the woman who plays with her clitoris during the act of coition' and suggested that 'Such a person affronts her lover with the obscene display of her body, and, in perceiving her thus, the lover perceives his own irrelevance. She becomes disgusting to him, and his desire may be extinguished. The woman's desire is satisfied at the expense of her lover's, and no real union can be achieved between them' (Scruton, 2006, p. 319). Female readers beware!

More systematically, but equally – if not more – offensively, philosophers inspired by natural law theory attempt to argue that sexual activity is acceptable only in heterosexual marriage open to procreation. They tie themselves in knots explaining why sex between knowingly sterile heterosexual couples who do not want children is fine, but sex between loving fertile queer couples who want children is not. John Finnis, for instance, compares queer sex with bestiality, and argues that

> The deliberate genital coupling of persons of the same sex is repudiated for a very similar reason [as bestiality]. It is not simply that it is sterile and disposes the participants to an abdication of responsibility for the future of humankind. Nor is it simply that it cannot *really* actualize the mutual devotion which some homosexual persons hope to manifest and experience by it, and that it harms the personalities of its participants by its disintegrative manipulation of different parts of their one personal reality. It is also that it treats human sexual capacities in a way which is deeply hostile to the self-understanding of those members of the community who are willing to commit themselves to real marriage. (Finnis, 1993, p. 32)

Homophobia aside, passages like this bring to the surface various premises and assumptions to consider. It strikes us that queer people clearly can take responsibility for the future of humankind, can experience devotion, can have sex without threat to their 'personal reality' and without posing a challenge to married straight people.

While its rarer to see explicit anti-homosexuality arguments nowadays, philosophers do have views about the proper place of sex in our wider lives, views which intersect nicely with more recent discussion of celibacy or the desire to focus on friendship rather than romantic intimacy (Cohen, 2020). Indeed, one way to make sense of the sentiment behind notions such as being 'boysober' is in terms of *chastity*.

b. Chastity

The word 'chastity' may seem old fashioned, but philosophers have recently argued chastity remains a useful concept and may be a virtue (Silverman, 2021). We shall focus on the argument of Nancy Snow (Snow, 2021). Snow suggests that 'the disposition to be chaste is built from repeatedly engaging in deliberate and informed choices to forego engaging in certain kinds of sexual activities, as well as from considering the kinds of choices one would make under counter-factual conditions' (Snow, 2021, p. 97). Expressed in those very terms, the actions of boysoberists could be described as the actions of people seeking to be chaste. But as Snow's view develops, she ends up describing chastity in the following terms:

> Chastity as a virtue of sexual autonomy is the disposition to refrain from sexual activity outside of a monogamous sexual relationship. This disposition is built up from making a series of rationally autonomous choices to abstain from sexual activity or to channel it in appropriately circumscribed ways within the bounds of a committed relationship. (Snow, 2021, p. 109)

At the heart of Snow's account of chastity is the *alignment* between our sexual choices and behaviour and our broader identity. To be chaste is therefore not to simply refrain from sex at all, but to have a sense of which desires and activities are congruent with the person we are or want to be, and avoid those in tension with that conception. More specifically, this alignment is the product of our explicit reflection and reasoning, not by accident and circumstance. As the quotation above indicates, this also involves hypothetical reasoning: how would we act if we were able to have more casual sex, or have several partners, or be paid for sex, and so on. Chastity aims after the goal of sexual autonomy (Snow, 2021, p. 104).

Seeking purity is part of being chaste, too, and this involves avoiding mental attitudes or behaviour which 'degrade or demean others and/or the self, and transgress appropriate moral norms' and fail to 'express respect' for the self 'as a sexually autonomous person' (Snow, 2021, p. 105).

To make sense of chastity as a virtue, Snow positions it as the mean between two accompanying vices: *profligacy* and *prudery* (Snow, 2021, p. 102). Profligate people have too much sex, whereas prudes have a 'distorted view' of sexuality and view 'all sexuality and sexual activity as dirty, nasty, lewd, and otherwise immoral or "not nice"' (Snow, 2021, p. 102).

Snow thinks people can be chaste in committed monogamous relationships, or when they are single, but thinks chastity is not available to people with several partners:

> There is something intuitively wrong about saying that one can be chaste if one has many sexual partners. What is behind this

intuition, for me, is the belief that those who choose polygamy run a very serious risk of being deeply mistaken about the kinds of sexual relationships and encounters that can be genuine goods within a truly worthwhile life. (Snow, 2021, p. 103)

The reason Snow thinks this is that the 'nature of human attachments and emotions' means that strong attachment is possible to only one person, and that multi-partner intimacy is liable to prompt jealousy or insecurity (Snow, 2018, p. 103).

Snow's virtue of chastity is different from related notions of sexual temperance, which are concerned with having the right amount and quality of pleasure and avoiding deficiencies and excesses (Halwani, 2021), because of her focus on the alignment between a conception of self and behaviour, and because chastity rules out casual sex (Snow, 2021, p. 108).

c. Intimate ethics

Readers of Snow's argument might be frustrated by the shift from the initial picture of a deliberative virtue of sexual integrity, in which we reflect on our sexual desires and behaviour and seek to pursue a life based on a view of sexuality that aligns with who we are, to a picture of traditional monogamous fidelity.

Central to Snow's argument are her empirical premises about emotions or attachment – that good feeling and proper attachment are inherently exclusive. To us, and no doubt to many nonmonogamous people, these premises look shaky. The concept of *polyfidelity*, for example, is intended to capture the way some nonmonogamous people seek to remain faithful to a limited number of partners. It is far from clear that members of a polyfidelitous triad, for instance, could not be chaste (Strauss, 2012).

Similarly, we might think a sex worker can be chaste too, if we suppose that sex work can be pursued intentionally, with due consideration of our sexual identity and wider integrity, in a way that avoids objectification or degradation of the other, as it might in cases where someone is a sexual surrogate (a person who is paid to have sex with people with disabilities) or a sex therapist, but in other forms of sex work too.

More generally, we have to be careful not to suppose that because sex is casual, or nonexclusive, that it is not considered, caring, mutual, or even loving.

A more fundamental question, however, is whether we need the concept of chastity at all. Can't *integrity* do the job just as well?

Perhaps if it were coupled with some additional theory around avoiding objectification and other forms of bad intimacy? We can understand integrity loosely as the alignment of our actions and attitudes with our values and sense of identity. Polyamorists and boysober celibates can have intimate integrity in this sense. How we individuate virtues is a complex question (Russell, 2009), but the example of chastity brings pressure to bear on the idea that there are specific sexual or intimate virtues. The specific details of Snow's account might have you worrying that attempts to describe more particular intimate virtues are little more than attempts to forward a substantive moral view about what good intimacy is on a more neutral-seeming footing.

We titled this chapter 'Intimate ethics' but our discussion of consent and now of chastity raises a final question to ponder: is there such a thing as intimate ethics? We might think there is simply ethics, and ethical notions, which sometimes apply in intimate contexts. In places, we appealed to such an idea when thinking about consent, since we were drawn to the view that a theory of consent has to apply in a range of situations, not just sexual ones. Some people might be tempted to explore this question by focusing on the matter of whether sex is special, or not, over which there has been some debate (Primoratz, 2001; Benatar, 2002; Woollard, 2019). If sex is special, perhaps we need a special ethics to treat it.

We worry about these debates not because we have a firm view as to whether sex is special, or not, but simply because we lack a clear sense of what sex is, and think a broader focus on intimacy is more productive. The more we focus on intimacy, however, the harder it appears to claim we need a distinct intimate ethics. Instead, our sense of what is right and wrong, good and bad, in general can be applied to contexts where intimacy is relevant. Those contexts are everywhere, however, as intimacy is a common aspect of life and one which crosses many 'domains', such as the public and the private, home and work.

There are many ethical questions around the place of intimacy in a good life. We have barely scratched the surface. What does it mean to be sexually temperate, for example – might there be too little sex in a life, or too much, and how do we know when we are straying from the ideal?

We can also explore the complex relationship between pleasure and procreation. It is commonly held that procreation is one obviously acceptable 'end' towards which sexual activity can be directed. This was visible in the argument of Finnis and other philosophers inspired by religious thought. But few forms of sex are less spontaneous, and potentially alienating, than explicit attempts to get pregnant, so if we are worried about sex which uses someone as a means, or which inadequately centres on attention to someone in their marvellous particularity, should we be worrying about couples tracking their ovulation cycle and rushing to have sex at a precise moment irrespective of whether they really want to or not?

Many people are not having the sex they would like, or struggle to access sexual partners, for different reasons. We can ask whether this is an issue of justice. Might the state have a duty to facilitate sex in some cases – for example, to assist disabled people to access the sex they would like – or perhaps even fund access to sex workers (Sanders, 2007)? These discussions quickly become highly emotive, but it is far from clear they are easily avoided.

Finally, we can ask more abstract questions. Here is one: would there be sex in utopia, and would it be good? Imagine we were no longer subject to imbalances of power, were no longer comparative and competitive, did not need to reproduce, and had unlimited free time – would sex retain its appeal for the many that currently enjoy it (Suits, 2014)?

5. Conclusion

Philosophers of intimacy seem to agree on many points, and often share a sense of which kinds of intimacy seem good, and which seem bad. Where they disagree, however, is how to make theoretical sense of them. For some, consent is a minimal notion – something that is easy to secure but tells us little about whether intimacy is good or not. For others, consent is a maximal notion – something hard to secure and which tells us that the resulting intimacy is good. We incline towards the idea that consent is a rather minimal notion, since that helps free up our attention for the many other things we want to be in place when being intimate with other people. You may disagree. If you do, you need to meet the challenge that over-focusing on consent, or making it too rich a notion, actually inhibits our ability to describe other kinds of intimate harm, and may itself cause harm.

Intimate ethics is an emerging topic, and one that will be shaped by our increasing scientific understanding of sexuality, and also by emerging technologies. The questions of what intimacy is permissible, what intimacy is good, and what is the proper place of intimacy in life will remain as the kinds of intimacy we are able to experience, or the conditions under which we experience intimacy, evolve and we move ever closer to forms of intimate utopia/dystopia (delete as appropriate). It remains to be seen whether we will have to apply traditional ideas – for example of voluntariness, or being sufficiently informed – to new contexts, or whether we will have to develop new concepts entirely. Either way, the ethical study of intimacy is more urgent than ever.

5

Romantic Love

1. Introduction

Jeff and Victor have been working together for quite a while. Initially, Jeff was wary of Victor. He seemed a bit arrogant, and his humour was atrocious. But, over time, as they collaborated on the same projects, Jeff found himself laughing more and realized he was too quick to judge. What he saw as Victor's arrogance was actually just confidence viewed with an insecure eye, and Victor's humour – although terrible – had a certain enviable honesty to it. Jeff soon came to respect Victor, and was quick to seek him out at work events and social evenings.

Some months later at a work party, Jane, a mutual colleague, drunkenly asked Jeff: 'Do you like him?' 'Sure', Jeff replied, 'he's a good colleague, and I admire his confidence.' 'No, do you *liiike* him?', Jane pressed home. Jeff had never thought about this before. With a lurch, he realized that his attitude towards Victor was certainly more than collegial. But how much more? *Liking* someone, suitably italicized, brought home memories of the schoolyard, of fleeting crushes, attractions, and messy confusion. His attitude was different, more stable, more settled on Victor, who, he now saw, often sat at the centre of his thoughts and feelings. 'Maybe you love him!' Jane joked; 'Maybe I do', Jeff laughed, 'maybe I do.'

Perhaps more than any other type of love, romantic love captivates and confuses us, gripping our imagination, and inviting us to seek to understand it. As Troy Jollimore observes, 'one of the few uncontroversial things that can be said about romantic love is that a great many people are interested in it' (Jollimore, 2018, p. 61). But, as Jeff's predicament suggests, the significance of love can also mean it is hard to grapple with personally, since it is bound up with hopes and anxieties we might struggle to confront. Romantic love is the subject of countless poems, songs, novels, films, and television programmes – indeed, romantic love makes a great story. Perhaps because it is so hugely important to many people, but also complex and widely disagreed upon, romantic love has also received a fair amount of philosophical attention. In this chapter, we consider three of the most significant questions relating to romantic love. In the first section, we ask what the term 'romantic love' even means, exploring different ways that the term gets used, often leading to confusion over what we are talking about when we talk about romantic love. In the second section, we ask what *kind* of phenomenon is romantic love? We examine three possibilities – that it is a biological response, that it is an emotion, and that it is a syndrome. Finally, in the third section, we look at what justifies romantic love – is it arational, or a rational response to a person or a relationship?

2. What are we talking about?

Romantic love is sometimes said to have been invented by the troubadours during the medieval period. This is not true: as we discuss later in this chapter, romantic love, as a distinct kind of love, is a near-cultural universal. Ancient Greek philosophers discussed romantic love, and poems expressing romantic love have been found going back millennia and across cultures. Having said that, pinning down romantic love is strangely difficult: people use and understand the term in different ways, and so we are not always talking about the same thing when we talk about romantic love.

a. Romantic love's features

One way that we could try to pin down romantic love is by describing its features. There is disagreement about what these are, but here we outline what we take to be some about which there is broad agreement.

Romantic love is, first and foremost, a kind, or form of expression, of love, and love involves, at a minimum, *caring* for the well-being of the beloved. It doesn't merely involve caring: as we'll later discuss, it is more self-interested than some other kinds of love, such as parental love. But if Jeff did not care at all for the well-being of Victor, then whatever he felt for him would not be love.

One of the reasons romantic love is more self-interested is that it also involves (at least to a certain extent) *liking* the beloved (Shpall, 2018). It is, to an extent, *chosen* on the basis of such liking. This is one of the ways in which it is different to familial love – we do not (usually) choose our family, but rather find ourselves with them. We can say fairly certainly that we would love our children even if we did not like them. Friendship and romantic love, on the other hand, are chosen kinds of love. If we stop liking our friend or our romantic partner, we can end the relationship with them and the love will likely (eventually) dissipate. Therefore, one of the reasons many people value romantic love is that they feel that they have been chosen, and continue to be chosen, to be the object of their lover's love. As Simon Keller puts it: 'among the most valuable of rewards that I can gain from romantic love is the personal affirmation that comes from the knowledge that someone whom I love romantically has chosen me as a worthy recipient of her own romantic love' (Keller, 2000, p. 163).

However, romantic love is not completely in our control. Indeed, the experience of romantic love is sometimes as a force beyond our control – we *fall* in love, and often behave irrationally because of love (McKeever and Saunders, 2022). People sometimes give up a huge amount in the name of romantic love. In this way, romantic love bears similarities to parental love. In both parental and romantic love, we often love our beloveds far more than is warranted by their properties, and we are often willing to give up a great deal to be near them. Though friendship can make us behave irrationally, it tends to be more level-headed; generally speaking, we tend not to idealize our friends that much more than they deserve, and we are less likely to act irrationally for them.

Romantic love is often described as a sexual kind of love; indeed, it is sometimes referred to as 'erotic love' (Solomon, 1995; Scruton, 2006). While it is true though, that romantic love very frequently is accompanied by sexual attraction, desire, and activity, asexual romantic love is possible too. Asexual people do not experience sexual attraction, but only 16–25 per cent of them are aromantic – meaning they do not want to have romantic love or relationships. Thus, the majority of asexual people pursue romantic love (Brunning and McKeever, 2021, pp. 502–3). Indeed, asexual people are not the only people to experience romantic love in the absence of sexual attraction or activity. Young teenagers, for example, are sometimes intensely in love prior to experiencing sexual attraction or desire, and people with certain disabilities or health conditions might love romantically despite not desiring or being able to have sex. People celibate for religious reasons may also experience romantic love. Thus, we might say that romantic love is *typically* sexual, but not *necessarily* sexual.

Romantic love is also often assumed to be *exclusive* – that is, that we can love only one person romantically at a time. For example, Robert

Solomon writes 'Love *is* the concentration and the intensive focus of mutual definition on a single individual' (Solomon, 1988, p. 197). However, while romantic love is *often* exclusive, we do not have to look very far to find examples of non-exclusive love. Falling in love with someone while already in love with someone else is not an uncommon experience. This could involve an affair, or the people in question could be polyamorous and have thereby agreed that their love is permitted to be non-exclusive. Between 0.6 and 5 per cent of Americans are in a polyamorous relationship (Rubel and Burleigh, 2020). Therefore, again, we might say that romantic love is *typically* exclusive, but not *necessarily* so.

Finally, romantic love, as with all kinds of love, typically involves a desire that the love continue into the future. To say 'I love you right now, in this moment, but I have no desire to love you tomorrow' is not, generally speaking, a genuine kind of love. This is not to say that we cannot imagine cases where we might wish we did not love someone, if they are mistreating us, say, or our love for them is ruining our life. But those cases are ones where we wish for the absence of love towards that person, full stop, rather than wishing for the presence of love that is not future-directed. As we'll discuss in the next chapter, it may not be possible to *promise* to love someone in the future, but love implies a kind of commitment to a person that is more than just momentary.

Taking all this together, we can say that romantic love typically involves:

1. Caring for the beloved
2. Liking the beloved
3. Lack of complete control
4. Often, but not always, sexual desire
5. Often, but not always, exclusive focus on the beloved
6. The desire for the love to continue into the future

Clearly, these are features which are shared with other kinds of love and, indeed, other attitudes towards people. So our search for a feature distinctive of romantic love must go on.

b. Falling in love and committed love

As we have seen, romantic love is difficult to pin down. An additional complicating factor is that the term 'romantic love' is used to describe passionate and sexual love, *and* to describe more stable companionate love. Raja Halwani has described these two types of love as RL1 (passionate and sexual) and RL2 – 'being more about commitment, attachments, and companionship' (Halwani, 2018, p. 16). Dorothy Tennov coined the term 'limerence' to describe the intense, almost obsessive, state that we often feel at the beginning of a relationship (Tennov, 1979). Limerence is characterized by 'focused attention, overvaluation and dependence' (Lopez-Cantero, 2022a, p. 118). Confusingly, it is limerence that some people have in mind when discussing 'romantic love'. For example, Helen Fisher and colleagues (discussed below) distinguish between lust, romantic love, and attachment, with their understanding of 'romantic love' being closer to limerence, and their understanding of 'attachment' being closer to long-term companionate love (Fisher, Aron, and Brown, 2006). And Michal Herer proposes that romantic love is a short-term phenomenon, while friendship is stable: 'unlike friendship, which seems to be a stable relation, a *longue durée* phenomenon … Love erupts in a sudden burst and quickly fizzles out' (Herer, 2021, p. 23).

However, others argue that limerence is not 'love' at all. Carrie Jenkins, for example, takes this view, pointing out that 'you can experience limerence for someone you don't know well (or at all), or even for someone you dislike' (Jenkins, 2022, p. 52). We also see this view in the De Bernières novel, *Captain Corelli's Mandolin*:

> Love is a temporary madness, it erupts like volcanoes, and then it subsides. And when it subsides, you have to make a decision. You have to work out whether your roots are to become so entwined together that it is inconceivable that you should ever part. Because that is what love is. Love is not breathlessness, it is not excitement, it is not the promulgation of promises of eternal passion, it is not the desire to mate every second of the day…. That is just being 'in love'; which any fool can do. Love itself is what is left over when being in love has burned away, and this is both an art and a fortunate accident. (De Bernières, 1995, p. 285; quoted in Lopez-Cantero, 2022a, pp. 107–8)

The key idea here seems to be that real love is what is left once limerence has faded, if you make the decision to stay, and so limerence is not, in fact, love at all.

Pilar Lopez-Cantero observes that this kind of view, which she calls the 'negative view' of falling in love, is fairly common in the philosophical literature: the idea 'that falling in love is a phase which has to be overcome in order to arrive at valuable love' (Lopez-Cantero,

2022a, p. 110). She identifies three concerns that philosophers have had regarding falling in love:

1. when we are falling in love, we do not see the object of love for who they really are;
2. falling in love is irrationally partial; and
3. falling in love diverts us excessively from the world. (Lopez-Cantero, 2022a, p. 110)

This is because, when we are falling in love, we often lack detailed knowledge of the beloved, and so we project onto them an ideal of a beloved, and thus the love is 'not grounded on true concern for the other' (Lopez-Cantero, 2022a, p. 109). Secondly, we see the beloved more favourably than is deserved: 'seeing only the good in the person one is falling in love with' (Lopez-Cantero, 2022a, p. 109). And finally, when we fall in love, we shift our attention to the beloved in a way that can take us away from our obligations to other people and other things that matter.

These seem like major concerns, and ones which would justify the stereotype that philosophers are often quite hostile to romantic love, but Lopez-Cantero argues that these worries are actually less significant than they might first seem. On the first, while it might sometimes be the case that the lover lacks knowledge of their beloved, it is not always so. As Lopez-Cantero notes, 'in most cases of love there is at least some accuracy about the other person's characteristics' and, indeed, in some cases, the lover has detailed knowledge of the beloved *before* falling in love with them. She gives examples of romantic love starting with a friendship, or starting with a partnership as in the case of some people in arranged marriages, who marry first, and fall in love later (Lopez-Cantero, 2022a, p. 111). Jeff's love stemmed from his closeness to Victor as a colleague. (We note, however, that these situations are not immune to other kinds of fantasy or wishful thinking.) Secondly, Lopez-Cantero argues that we can accept that falling in love does make us partial to the beloved, while denying that this is irrational in the sense of making us oblivious. Instead, drawing on Jollimore's 'vision' view of love, she argues that seeing the good in the beloved is just part of what love is (Lopez-Cantero, 2022a, p. 112). And finally, again drawing on Jollimore, she reminds us that 'focusing on something is not the same as *not seeing anything else*' and that falling in love can inspire us and give us hope in dark times (Lopez-Cantero, 2022a, pp. 113–14).

To clarify matters, Lopez-Cantero draws an important distinction between:

- Limerence: a state of high emotional intensity, increased partiality and increased focused attention directed towards an individual.
- Infatuation: an unreasonable state of high emotional intensity, increased partiality and increased focused attention directed towards an individual. (Lopez-Cantero, 2022a, p. 120)

Infatuation could thus be considered 'bad limerence', and needs to be overcome due to its unreasonableness, such as when infatuation leads a person to be oblivious to her partner's awful treatment of her. Limerence, on the other hand, does not necessarily need to be overcome – rather, it can transform into love, as indeed happens in many relationships (Lopez-Cantero, 2022a, pp. 119–20). Lopez-Cantero also notes that falling in love is not necessarily limerence or infatuation either (Jeff would likely agree). Tennov's research, which involved hundreds of first-person testimonies of love, found that not all love begins with limerence – some people are 'non-limerent', falling in love without the obsessiveness that characterizes limerence (Lopez-Cantero, 2022a, p. 118). Furthermore, romantic love does not always start with infatuation: for example, two friends could find themselves to be romantically in love with one another in a calm and stable sort of way, never experiencing infatuation for each other, yet being very much in love.

Therefore, it is important to distinguish between these different states: infatuation, limerence, falling in love, and being in love, particularly as the term 'romantic love' can be used to describe all of them. However, we ought not to characterize falling in love negatively and being in love positively: the reality is more nuanced. Having these stages is not distinctive to romantic love either. Parents often describe themselves as 'falling in love' with their babies, and friends sometimes also have a period which could be compared to limerence with each other. We now turn to consider what *is* distinctive about romantic love.

c. Kinds of love?

As has become clear from the discussion so far, romantic love is difficult to pin down. It is also hard to clearly delineate it from other kinds of love. It is, perhaps, easier to distinguish it from familial love, because it is chosen in a way that familial love is not. And romantic love very often does include sexual desire, whereas familial love almost always does not. But, on the other hand, romantic partners often describe each other as family, and, indeed, one of the reasons they might marry each other is to formally become a family. But romantic love is different to unchosen familial love because romantic relationships can be ended in a much clearer way than unchosen family relationships, at least given current social norms. If I say to my partner that I want to break up with them (or divorce them if we are married), then they are no longer my partner; they become 'my ex'. As we saw in our discussion of break-ups in chapter 3, this transition rests on the exercise of a normative power to change how we relate to others. On the other hand, if I say to my mother that I don't want to be in a relationship with her any longer, she does not become my 'ex mother'. She is still, in some sense of the word, my mother; it is just that our relationship has changed. To be clear, this is a complex topic, one which hinges on the nature of terms such as 'mother', which have both a biological meaning and a social-role meaning. You might argue that, while we cannot change biological ties, we can 'break up' with parents in this social-role sense. But even such a suggestion seems contentious in social contexts in which these attempts are unlikely to secure uptake, either from the parent concerned or from other people around them (since uptake is necessary for the exercise of a normative power).

In this way, romantic love is more similar to friendship, in that it can be ended in a much clearer way than family love. Furthermore, if we return to the six features of romantic love that we gave above (repeated below for ease of reference), we can see that (1), (2), (3), and (6) are also all features of friendship, and friendship may also involve sexual desire (4), and could include an exclusive focus on the beloved in the case of best friends (5).

1. Caring for the beloved
2. Liking the beloved
3. Lack of complete control
4. Often, but not always, including sexual desire
5. Often, but not always, involving exclusive focus on the beloved
6. The desire for the love to continue into the future.

On the other hand, if two best friends cared for and liked each other, felt somewhat out of control of the love they felt for each other, sexually desired each other, loved each other exclusively, and desired to continue to love each other, it would be difficult to make a case that they were not romantically in love. Jollimore asks, 'could we imagine two friends who want to have sex with each other, and who love each other, but only as friends?' (Jollimore, 2018, p. 62). We think we probably *could* imagine such friends, but if we imagine two friends who love each other exclusively, and want to have sex with each other exclusively, it is harder not to see them as romantically in love, at least according to the common social meanings of romantic love.

There is a question here over whether we are really distinguishing between romantic *love* and friendship *love* or between a romantic *relationship* and a friendship *relationship*. But perhaps this is not so important, since the relationship and the love are interlinked. Loving someone romantically entails an openness to desiring, under the right conditions, to be in a romantic relationship with them (more on this in the next chapter).

There is a further question about whether we need to distinguish between these kinds of love in the first place, perhaps analogous to the question of whether we need to distinguish between sexual and non-sexual intimacy, which we encountered earlier. Delineating kinds of love can help us to know where we stand with others, and to be able to package up our feelings, attitudes, and desires under distinct labels. But it might also do a disservice to the diversity of our relationships and the different ways in which we can love, perhaps analogous to the more specific wariness some people have about use of sexual orientation talk. Relationship anarchists provide one example of people who strive to see each relationship as distinct, rather than being an instance of a type, and so do not see a need to distinguish between romantic love and friendship. Perhaps they offer a different practical approach to these matters? We discuss relationship anarchy further in the final chapter when exploring the future of intimacy.

Talk of romantic love is complex, and messy. It is hard to keep track of the shifts in sense between 'liking' someone, and something more; between romantic love understood as sexual interest, and romantic love understood as companionate care – not to mention the distinctions between falling in love (Halwani's 'RL1', limerence, or infatuation) and being in love (Halwani's 'RL2', or companionate love). Even if we can do a good job of distinguishing between these senses, as philosophers attempt to do, we still face unanswered questions about the role of sex, exclusivity, and choice in romantic love and relationships. If sexual desire, exclusivity, and choice are not essential to romantic love, then how do we know when we are romantically in love, and not experiencing familial or friendship love?

In the next two sections, we will investigate romantic love in more depth, analysing what kind of thing it is, and how we can justify loving one person and not another.

3. The phenomenon of romantic love

Jeff might ask himself whether he loves Victor. These situations are fairly common. We might suppose, however, that to answer this question, we first need a better grasp on what love is, in an ontological sense. We might doubt whether these theoretical matters would be practically helpful to Jeff as he examines his behaviour and feelings around Victor. But they will have an influence. If, for example, Jeff conceives of love as an emotion, then he might consider only the strength of his feelings towards Victor. If he conceives of love as a biological response, he might examine his bodily response to Victor (heart racing, stomach butterflies, etc.).

Arriving at a satisfying answer to the general 'What kind of thing is it?' question, with respect to romantic love, is (unsurprisingly) actually quite difficult. Here we consider three possibilities: (a) love as a biological response; (b) love as an emotion; and (c) love as a syndrome. This list is not exhaustive: love has also been described as a desire (Kreft, 2022), a disposition (Naar, 2013), and a reactive attitude (Abramson and Leite, 2011), among other things.

a. Love and biology

One suggestion as to what kind of phenomenon love is is that romantic love is merely a biological response to someone: a 'fundamental human drive', akin to our drive to eat food and drink water, that motivates us to do things which are good for the propagation of the species (Fisher, Aron, and Brown, 2006). Perhaps the most well-known and influential proponent of this view is the biological anthropologist Helen Fisher, who, with colleagues, put people who are at different stages of romantic love relationships in functional magnetic resonance imaging (fMRI) scanners. They showed that romantic love activates dopamine-rich areas in the brain associated with 'reward, motivation and wanting' in both early-stage romantic love and in long-term relationships (Acevedo et al., 2012, p. 157). It is the role of dopamine that leads Fisher to conclude that romantic love is 'a fundamental human drive', because the other basic human drives are also associated with dopamine (Jenkins, 2017, p. 21).

Fisher and her colleagues argue that humans have evolved 'three primary brain systems' in order to direct reproduction: the sex drive, romantic love, and attachment (Fisher, Aron, and Brown, 2006). (As noted above, they are using the term 'romantic love' to describe a phenomenon more like limerence than like long-term companionate love.) These brain systems are not unique to humans, but are found in avian and mammalian species too, though Fisher and her colleagues note that animal behaviours associated with courtship attraction (the animal correlate to the human 'romantic love') have often been lumped together with the sex drive (Fisher, Aron, and Brown, 2006, p. 2174). According to them, it is likely that the sex drive evolved so that individuals would be motivated to copulate with a variety of partners; romantic love evolved so that individuals would focus their attention on one partner, conserving their time and energy; and attachment evolved so that they would stay together long enough to raise offspring (Fisher, Aron, and Brown, 2006, p. 2174).

As evidence that we have evolved to love romantically, Fisher and her colleagues point to anthropological work by William Jankowiak and Edward Fischer (1992), who found evidence of romantic love in 147 of 166 cultures across the world, suggesting that it is a near-universal feature of human cultures. Indeed, of the cultures in which evidence of romantic love was not found, Jankowiak and Fischer note that this could be due to 'ethnographic oversight rather than any set of cultural norms that prevent an individual from experiencing romantic affection' (Jankowiak and Fischer, 1992, p. 153), so it is possible that romantic love could be found in an even higher proportion of cultures if the research was repeated. It is worth noting though that, for this study, their understanding of romantic love is similar to that of Fisher's: 'any intense attraction that involves the idealization of the other, within an erotic context, with the expectation of enduring for some time into the future' (Jankowiak and Fischer, 1992, p. 150). More generally, we see that empirical research into love is shaped by our prior sense of what love's features are – a matter we have shown above to be complex and contentious.

We will return to the biological aspects of love in the section on 'Love drugs' in the final chapter. For now, it suffices to say that biology clearly has a role in love, and it is probably fair to say that this role has been neglected by philosophers. This is perhaps understandable: philosophers are not biologists (apart from some notable exceptions, such as Aristotle). But even without a full understanding of the biological processes involved in love, we can appreciate that there are some biological aspects to it. This can explain why love can feel out of our control and why we cannot just will ourselves to be attracted to someone – chemistry, literally, matters. The biological explanation can also help us to understand why love can feel like addiction, because it does biochemically resemble addiction (Jenkins, 2017, p. 32).

On the other hand, even a full explanation of the biology of love would not give us a complete account of love. The way in which love is experienced differs between time periods and cultures, which suggests that it is not *merely* a biological response. This fact could also explain why there was no evidence of romantic love in nineteen of the cultures surveyed by Jankowiak and Fischer. Carrie Jenkins gives the example of a woman falling in love in Victorian England compared to a Canadian woman falling in love in 2017, when she was writing:

> For the Victorian lady, falling in love is a matter of developing a deep and respectful (but probably rather distant) admiration for a man. Sexual desire is at best irrelevant to this process, at worst a shameful distraction. For the contemporary Canadian, however, falling in love is a matter of developing an intimate attachment that normatively includes sexual desire. (Jenkins, 2017, p. 43)

Jenkins also points out that Enlightenment scholars saw romantic love as rational, whereas the Romantics saw it as out of our control, and that the current way that we see romantic love as the basis for marriage and family creation is a relatively recent way of viewing it (Jenkins, 2017, pp. 44–5). Jenkins argues that love has a *dual* nature: it is both biological and socially constructed. In her words, 'it is *ancient biological machinery* embodying a *modern social role*' (Jenkins, 2017, p. 82).

An appeal to biology also can't tell us how we *should* think about romantic love. To take just one controversy, some argue that it is impossible to commit to loving somebody (Brake, 2011), whereas others argue that to love someone just is to commit to them (van Hooft, 1996). Unpicking whether we should commit to loving someone, and what it means to do so, is not something that we decide merely by examining our biology.

b. Love as an emotion

Love is often thought of as an emotion (Pismenny and Prinz, 2017, p. 169) – something comparable to other emotions such as joy, jealousy, or anger. What emotions are is itself an intricate question we leave to one side here (cf. Ben-Ze'ev, 2000; Goldie, 2000; Deonna and Teroni, 2012; Colombetti, 2014; Tappolet, 2022). Most theorists of emotions agree that they involve an affective, or feeling, component and that emotions motivate us to act. (There is some disagreement about whether emotions have content that is world-directed, or 'about' things.) We gesture towards the affective aspect of love in the fact that phrases such as 'I have feelings for you' are almost synonymous with 'I love you.'

The view that love is an emotion is also found in the philosophical literature on love (Brown, 1987), with Simon May, for example, calling a book on love *Love: A New Understanding of an Ancient Emotion* (May, 2019). Love does certainly often come along with many other emotions – both positive, such as joy and excitement, and negative, such as jealousy, fear, and sadness. This way of approaching love can also complement the idea that it is a biological response if emotions are understood as evolutionary adaptive biological responses (Ekman, 1992).

However, there is reason to think love is not *just* an emotion, at least if emotions are understood in a way which foregrounds their feeling component. First, one does not have to *feel* in love to *be* in love. Loving my partner does not mean actually experiencing the feeling of love for them all the time (Pismenny and Prinz, 2017, p. 169). Indeed, there might be long periods of the day when I don't even think of them at all. There might even go days or weeks, where I don't feel anything for them, but still love them. Hichem Naar gives the example of a depressed father who feels nothing for his children whilst in the depths of his depression. However, if he loved them before he was depressed, it seems plausible that we might ask whether he still loves them 'deep down' (Naar, 2024, p. 194). The same could be said for romantic love as well. A woman might feel nothing for her partner, while she is depressed, or distracted, for example by an affair, but may later say to her husband, earnestly, that she had 'loved him all along'.

Further, other emotions are typically short-lived, whereas love can be very long-lasting. As Naar reminds us, 'saying "I loved her for a few minutes" is puzzling in a way that "I was angry with her for a few minutes" is not' (Naar, 2024, p. 193). (Naar's own view is that love is a *disposition* to experience a range of emotions – something similar to the syndrome view we consider below (Naar, 2024, p. 201).)

Love also differs from other emotions in that it is unclear whether it can be appropriate or inappropriate in the way that other emotions are (Pismenny and Prinz, 2017). Fear of peas is inappropriate, for example, unless one has a deathly allergy to peas, but fear of a lion charging at you in the jungle is appropriate. It is less obvious, however, that romantic love can be appropriate or inappropriate. While this is debatable, as our discussion below on love and rational appreciation will show, it is true that it is not always, or even often, possible to give a full justification for why we love one person over another in the way that we could give a full justification for why we felt fear in one situation but not another. As some philosophers argue, emotions have a target – the object of the emotion *and* a 'formal object' – the property of the target which warrants the emotion (Pismenny and Prinz, 2017, p. 170). If I fear the charging lion, the target of my emotion is the lion, but the formal object is its dangerousness. Fear of bananas is inappropriate because bananas do not have the property of being dangerous. There seems to be no formal object of love, however – there is no property or set of properties which causes one person to be lovable over another, because someone being 'lovable' depends on the lover conceiving them as such.

Thus, while love clearly does involve emotions, there seem to be some good reasons to doubt that it *is* an emotion.

c. Love as a syndrome

Perhaps a better way to think about love is, as Ronald de Sousa argues, as a syndrome: 'not a kind of feeling, but an intricate pattern of potential thoughts, behaviors, and emotions that tend to "run together"' (de Sousa, 2015, p. 4). For example, love might involve, for some people at least, thinking that their beloved is a wonderful person, doing kind things for them, and feeling happy when they are together and sad when they are apart. The term 'syndrome' tends to have negative connotations, bringing to mind disease or medical conditions, but we can conceive of syndromes more broadly than this.

Arina Pismenny and Jesse Prinz also take this view, comparing love to depression, which they also regard as a syndrome. They note several similarities between love and syndromes like depression, which are summarized here:

1. Two people with depression can have very different symptoms.
2. Symptoms include emotions, thoughts, and behaviours.
3. Symptoms are context-sensitive.
4. Syndromes don't have formal objects – they don't need to track features of the world.
5. Syndromes are arational.
6. Syndromes can have symptoms which have no bearing on the stimuli present.
7. Syndromes are culturally influenced but are not merely cultural scripts. (Pismenny and Prinz, 2017, p. 182)

It is not difficult to see how these features of syndromes compare to features of love:

1. Two people in love might manifest their love very differently.
2. Love gives rise to emotions, thoughts, and behaviours.
3. Love is context-sensitive – for example, the experience of being in love in middle age would likely differ to the experience of being in love as a teenager.
4. Love doesn't have a formal object (as discussed above).
5. Love has been described as arational (Frankfurt, 2004).
6. A person can love another even if they appear to have no lovable qualities.
7. Love is culturally influenced, but it is not merely a cultural script, as there are biological components to it too (as with depression).

Of this list, the feature which is perhaps most debatable is (5). As will become clear below, the view of love as arational is not shared by all. However, this does not necessarily undermine the analogy with depression, as though depression *need not* track features of the world, it may do, and it could be thought of as rational at least in some instances. We could say something similar about love – that it *need not* be a response to lovable features of the beloved, but it may be.

Talk of 'syndromes' does raise further questions, however, and we simply note them here. How are syndromes individuated? What ties together the various components of a syndrome? How are syndromes to be distinguished from some conceptions of 'personal valuing', like that of Samuel Scheffler, where to value something is to be disposed to experience a range of other emotions about that thing, depending on the context (Scheffler, 2012)? Are the 'types' of love – romantic, familial, etc. – best thought of as types of one syndrome, or separate syndromes of their own? Is the transition from limerence to more companionate love a shift of syndrome, or a shift within one syndrome? If the latter, how do we make sense of the ways syndromes develop over time – is this partly a matter of narrative, i.e. of the stories we tell around them (Goldie, 2012), or a matter grounded in some other way?

Thinking about love as a syndrome, then, can help us to think about love in a way which incorporates the biological and cultural aspects, as well as conceding that emotions are part of it, while also acknowledging that there is more to it than just biology or emotion. Another important advantage of this view is that it can make room for the diversity of ways in which love is experienced. We have not had the space here to consider all the accounts of what kind of phenomenon love is, but we have outlined three prominent views, and gestured to the view we find the most convincing – the view that love is a syndrome. We now turn to how we might justify love.

4. Justifying romantic love

We have considered how we should define romantic love and what sort of phenomenon it is. But there is another important question we often ask in relation to romantic love, and that is: Why do we love the particular person(s) we do, but not others? We are interested in this question in a justificatory sense, rather than an explanatory one. If we asked Jeff why he loves Victor, one way that he could answer is through providing a historical sort of explanation – he loves Victor because they spent a lot of time together at work and that time enabled him to get to know Victor sufficiently well to fall in love with him. This kind of explanation gives us the context in which Jeff fell in love, but it does nothing to *justify* Jeff's love for Victor. If this explanation was all there was to it, then Jeff would have fallen in love with anyone with whom he spent that much time at work. What we want to know is: *Why Victor in particular?* In other words: How do we justify our love?

a. Love as arational

As mentioned above, one view of love is that it is arational. This means that it does not respond to reasons, but is more akin to taste in food. As our preference for raspberries over strawberries might be arational, so is the matter of whom we love. For the arationalist, love cannot be justified. If asked why you love your beloved, on this view, you cannot say more than 'I just do!'

Harry Frankfurt is perhaps the most prominent proponent of this view. He argues that love itself is a source of reasons, rather than love being a reasoned response to an object or person based on their properties. As he puts it, 'love requires no reasons, and it can have anything as its cause' (Frankfurt, 2006, p. 41). We could quibble over this, as some things seem unlikely causes of love, but the important thing for Frankfurt is that we are able to love, since love provides us with reasons for living: 'it is love that accounts for the value to us of life itself' (Frankfurt, 2004, p. 41). Indeed, he called his influential 2004 book *The Reasons of Love*, not 'The Reasons for Love'.

Interestingly, for Frankfurt, a positive appraisal of the beloved is not a necessary condition of love. Jeff might not appraise Victor at all, for example, or even have a negative view of him (Frankfurt, 2004, p. 38), but this does not matter, because, for Frankfurt, love does not depend on appraisal at all: it is arational.

Frankfurt argues that there are 'four main conceptually necessary features of love of any variety'. These are:

1. love 'consists most basically in a disinterested concern for the well-being or flourishing of the person who is loved';
2. love is 'ineluctably personal';
3. 'the lover identifies with his beloved' and
4. 'love is not a matter of choice'. (Frankfurt, 2004, pp. 79–80)

For Frankfurt, the *only* interest of the lover is to serve and promote the well-being of the beloved, and so a lover who loved their beloved only for what they could get in return could not be said to genuinely love. This kind of selfless love sounds a bit like *agape*, an unconditional love for humanity. But Frankfurt's second feature of love – that it is 'ineluctably personal' tells us that the kind of love in which he is interested is the love for particular individuals, not 'instances of a type' (Frankfurt, 2004, p. 80). This links to his third feature of love, that it involves identifying with the beloved. We take their needs and interests as our own. We cannot do this for 'humanity' because everyone has different needs and interests, so we can only identify with particular individuals. Finally, Frankfurt does not think that we can control whether we love or don't love someone – it is out of our hands.

As we've noted above, it seems clear that, for love to be genuine, it must involve caring for the well-being of the beloved. However, perhaps Frankfurt takes the ideal of disinterested concern too far. For one thing, he does not think that romantic love fits the ideal of love:

> Relationships that are primarily romantic or sexual do not provide very authentic or illuminating paradigms of love as I am construing it. Relationships of those kinds typically include a number of vividly distracting elements, which do not belong to the essential nature of love as a mode of disinterested concern, but that are so confusing that they make it nearly impossible for anyone to be clear about just what is going on. (Frankfurt, 2004, p. 43)

Frankfurt provides a few examples of what such 'distracting elements' involved in romantic love might be later in *The Reasons of Love*: 'a hope to be loved in return or to acquire certain other goods that are distinct from the well-being of the beloved – for instance, companionship, emotional and material security, sexual gratification, prestige, or the like' (Frankfurt, 2004, p. 83). These desires are, to an extent, self-interested, and involve reason, and so, for Frankfurt, they make romantic love inauthentic.

Indeed, for Frankfurt, even the desire for love to be reciprocated renders it inauthentic, for 'love does not necessarily include a desire for union of any other kind. It does not entail any interest in reciprocity or symmetry in the relationship between lover and the beloved' (Frankfurt, 2006, p. 41). This seems odd. The desire for one's love to be reciprocated is integral to most kinds of love. As Frankfurt acknowledges, romantic love tends to involve the desire to be loved in return (Protasi, 2016, p. 218; Lopez-Cantero, 2022b). It is difficult to imagine a case of non-pathological romantic love where the lover did not *desire* reciprocation, even if they knew that in practice such reciprocation was not possible. Friendship also includes the desire for reciprocation – we cannot be friends with someone who does not reciprocate our friendship. And even parental love for small children, which is Frankfurt's paradigm of love, and arguably the most selfless form of love (Frankfurt, 2004, p. 43), involves a desire to be loved back by one's children. Parents are more likely than friends or romantic partners to continue to love their children in the absence of reciprocation, but they will still *desire* that their children return their love.

Agnieszka Jaworska and Monique Wonderly suggest that one thing Frankfurt's account is missing is the *intimacy* of love. They observe that 'Typically, one feels a deep sense of connectedness to the object of one's love. One is not only concerned that one's beloved flourishes, but one is also concerned that one engages with the beloved in meaningful ways' (Jaworska and Wonderly, 2024, p. 258). Indeed, aside from certain fairly unusual conditions, to not want to be around one's beloved would seem odd, and we would question the authenticity of the love. Therefore, while Frankfurt's account chimes with the intuition that love is out of our control, it seems wrong to assume that the desire for love to be reciprocated renders it inauthentic. Furthermore, the claim that romantic love is not a genuine kind of love dismisses many people's experiences of romantic love, which is that it is a valuable and significant kind of love involving a great deal of concern for their beloved. (For a more detailed examination of what we can learn about romantic love from Frankfurt's account, see McKeever (2019).)

Another way of conceiving of love as somewhat arational is to look at the way that it involves attachment. Monique Wonderly has drawn on psychological theories of attachment to argue that it is a central element of romantic love. Attachment theory was developed by psychologists John Bowlby and Mary Ainsworth in the 1960s and 1970s as a way to explain how infants form bonds with their primary caregivers, and also to elucidate how these bonds, or lack of bonds, will affect their relationships throughout their lives. If secure attachment bonds are formed, infants will treat their primary caregivers as a 'secure base' and a 'safe haven' (Wonderly, 2016, p. 229), and this security enables them to explore the world feeling secure and confident.

Wonderly argues, drawing on the work of other psychologists, that good romantic relationships also fulfil the function of secure bases and safe havens for us in adulthood: we feel more confident when they are there, and we turn to them for comfort in times of distress (Hazan and Shaver, 1987; Hazan and Diamond, 2000). Because of this, the lover not only cares for her beloved: she *needs* her beloved too. But, Wonderly argues, the romantic lovers' need for each other does not '*spoil* love, but rather adds to its shape and substance' (Wonderly, 2017, p. 241).

Not all attachments are good. A person might feel attached to an abusive partner, feeling more confident when he is there and turning to him for comfort, whilst also being gaslighted and controlled by him. And attachment isn't enough to provide a full justification of love. It is conceivable that someone in a long-term relationship might say something like 'I don't love her any more, but I can't leave her because I'm so attached to her.' However, attachment can help to explain why Frankfurt's account seemed lacking. If romantic love involves attachment, this explains why it can involve self-interested aspects (such as the desire for reciprocation) while remaining an authentic kind of love. And it can help us to distinguish between love and mere liking or admiration. We can admire someone to whom we are not attached, but we can't love someone without attachment.

We might wonder, though, whether we could become attached to anyone who was in the right place at the right time, in a similar way to how ducklings imprint onto other creatures after they've been born. If this was the case, then we would question whether being loved romantically should make us feel good about ourselves due to having been 'chosen'. Further, an appeal to attachment can't provide a full explanation of the difference between friendship and romantic love. Indeed, Wonderly says in a footnote that she suspects that much of what she says about romantic love also applies to friendship (Wonderly, 2017, p. 246). However, if the ways in which we attach to friends and to romantic lovers are different, then attachment theory could be helpful here – but more work would need to be done to establish this.

b. Love as rational

If love is not arational, then it can be appraised as rational or irrational, to the extent that it is reason-responsive. Here, we will consider two rationalist accounts of love: *the properties view* and *the relationship view*. On the properties view, love is a response to valuing a person's properties; on the relationship view, love is a response to valuing a relationship.

It is pretty common for a person, when asked why they love their partner, to make some reference to their partner's properties. Jeff, for example, might refer to Victor's confidence and honest sense of humour. The view that we love people for their properties is also found in philosophy, and can be traced back to Plato. In the *Symposium*, Plato describes love as, in Donald Levy's paraphrase, 'the desire to possess what is beautiful' (Levy, 1979, p. 285), with the love being better the more beautiful the object.

A more recent example of the properties view of love is provided by Simon Keller. He agrees that romantic love is a response to the properties of the beloved, but suggests that the kinds of properties that are especially significant are those that make the beloved a good romantic partner to the lover. In contrast to Plato, Keller proposes that there is no single property, such as beauty, at which all love aims, but rather the properties of a person that make it rational to love them will depend on the lover – and some of them will be relational properties. Keller gives the example of the property of 'knowing how to treat the lover when she is in a bad mood' as an example of a relational property for which the beloved might be loved (Keller, 2000, p. 166). Therefore, the justification for loving a person will depend on how well they are suited to the lover as a romantic partner. Jeff can justify his love for Victor, not (only) because of some generic properties Victor has, but because of his properties that make him the ideal romantic partner for Jeff.

Love cannot *only* be about valuing the properties of the beloved though. If it were, then we would see some odd consequences. First, on the properties view, it is difficult to distinguish love from liking or admiration. When I like or admire someone, I value their properties, but I don't necessarily love them. This is true even for Keller's more nuanced account: I might know that a certain person would make a wonderful romantic partner for me, but this doesn't automatically entail that I will love them.

Second, if love is all about valuing someone's properties, then why do we find it so difficult to explain why we love people, and why is it nearly impossible to persuade a person to love, or not to love, someone? If love was just a response to a positive appraisal of the beloved's properties, then Jeff could give a complete explanation of his love for Victor by listing his valuable properties. And if he did not love

Victor, his friend Jane might be able to persuade him to love him by simply explaining to him how great Victor's properties are.

Third, why does love not change along with changes in the properties of the beloved? Love often remains steadfast despite major changes in the beloved, but if love was simply a response to the properties of the beloved, it would be a large coincidence for it to track the properties in spite of them changing.

Fourth, why do we not always 'trade-up', to use Robert Nozick's expression, when we find someone with *better* qualities (Nozick, 1991)? Jane would likely think ill of Jeff if he dumped Victor for someone with a bit more confidence, or someone whose jokes were less terrible, but the idea that there is something wrong in such a trade is not easy to make sense of on the properties view.

Finally, although we are primarily concerned with romantic love here, we might note that the properties view is inappropriate for familial love – if asked why we love our children, we would not list their properties; responding 'because they are my child' would suffice.

Therefore, although it accords somewhat with our intuitions to say that love, or at least romantic love, is a response to the properties of the beloved, their properties cannot provide a complete justification for the lover's love.

An alternative rationalist approach to love is what might be called 'the relationship view'. The most well-known version of this, and the view we discuss, is put forward by Niko Kolodny. Put succinctly, he proposes that 'the reason one has for loving Jane, in any given case, is that she is one's daughter, sister, mother, friend, or wife' (Kolodny, 2003, p. 136). Therefore, it is *relationships* that make love appropriate, rather than the properties of the beloved, though a person's properties might be the reason for wanting to form a love-generating relationship with that person in the first place (Kolodny, 2003, p. 140). For Kolodny, love consists: 'a) in seeing a relationship in which one is involved as a reason for valuing both one's relationship and the person with whom one has that relationship and b) in valuing that relationship and person accordingly' (Kolodny, 2003, p. 150).

Kolodny makes several compelling objections against both Frankfurt's theory and the properties view, some of which are also offered as reasons to accept his own account. For example, he argues that Frankfurt cannot distinguish between love and mere urges to help another – an urge to help someone could fulfil each of Frankfurt's four criteria. This is because Frankfurt does not take into account that love is normatively appropriate in some cases but not in others. Normativity is central to Kolodny's theory of love: in order to love, we must understand and appreciate why the love is a fitting response to the object, and, in most cases, it will be the relationship shared with the beloved that makes love a fitting response to them (Kolodny, 2003, pp. 145–6). When we stop loving someone, it is usually because our relationship is no longer of the kind that makes love appropriate. Kolodny thus overcomes the problem faced by proponents of the properties view: that they cannot explain why the lover responds to the beloved with love rather than admiration or liking. We can admire someone whom we barely know, but love requires a valued relationship with the beloved. Kolodny also points out that the property theorist cannot explain why we love people 'in different modes'. As he puts it: 'Heather's mother and Heather's teenage friend may both love her, but they love her, or at least they ought to love her, in different ways.... How is the quality theorist to explain this?' (Kolodny, 2003, p. 139). His account can explain this because Heather's mother and her friend have a different sort of relationship with Heather, which they value in different ways.

It seems right that sharing a relationship of some sort with one's beloved is a necessary component of love, at least if we have a thin sense of 'relationship' in mind which could include people who share a history or are otherwise acquainted (even if it is not formalized as 'a relationship'). The idea of 'unrequited love' makes sense only if the lover shares *some* kind of relationship, or history, with the beloved. Furthermore, if you love someone, it seems necessary that you at least *desire* to share some form of relationship with them. It might be that such a relationship is not possible, perhaps because they are abusive, or because you have overriding caring responsibilities or career-related desires which make a relationship near impossible, for example. But if none of these such factors pertained, it would seem very odd for you to say to your beloved that you loved them but did not want to engage with them or spend enough time with them to constitute some form of relationship (note that we are talking about relationships in general here, not only romantic ones).

Kolodny's view also has a way of accounting for the conflicting intuitions we have that love is reasonless and mysterious, but also that we love people for their properties. Love seems inexplicable because the relationship 'just does' make love appropriate, and the beloved's properties are what make such a relationship possible in the case of friendship and romantic love.

Finally, Kolodny can explain the phenomenon of 'loving the relationship' as well as the beloved, an idea described by Thomas Smith: 'each one of two lovers may love, not just the other but the *two of them*, collectively' (Smith, 2011, p. 79). As evidence for this idea, Smith points to activities that couples do together, 'such as snuggling up, or holding hands, or going for walks, or chatting together about the day's events, or looking into each other's eyes, or simply *rubbing along together* (sharing the same space)'. Such activities, Smith argues, are engaged in '*disinterestedly*, for they need have no further end – no "completion" – in sight' (Smith, 2011, p. 77).

On the other hand, Kolodny's account does not tell us why we want to have relationships at all, or why we would want to have relationships with specific characteristics – he does not explain why relationships themselves are valuable. This is significant, because people do sometimes end a romantic relationship because they do not want to have a romantic relationship at all. This is something Kolodny does not consider when he discusses reasons for ending a relationship (Kolodny, 2003, pp. 164–6). He also doesn't fully distinguish between romantic love and friendship. He does make reference to different activities being part of the relationship, writing 'with friendships, the activities may involve spending leisure time together. With romantic relationships, the activities may involve, in addition, living together and expressing, in one way or another, sexual drives' (Kolodny, 2003, p. 149). However, this seems inadequate. Two friends might live together and have sex, but not consider themselves to be in a romantic relationship. This is relevant, given that one of the issues with the properties view, which Kolodny's account was supposed to overcome, is that of love in different modes.

We think that a satisfying justification of love will likely include different elements. This is not mere fence-sitting. Romantic love is complex, possibly a syndrome, and the term is also used to describe both falling in love and more stable, companionate love. Given this, it makes sense that it will have both arational and rational elements to it, and that a full justification for why we love Person A and Person B will need to reference their properties, and the way we value the relationship we share with them. But it is also conceivable that even doing all this will still not feel like a complete justification, and there are arational elements to it too, which might be explained by biology or psychological attachment.

5. Conclusion

In this chapter, we have considered three of the most significant questions relating to romantic love: (1) What are we talking about, when we talk about romantic love? (2) What kind of phenomenon is romantic love? (3) What justifies romantic love? We hope to have drawn attention to some of the different ways in which romantic love can be understood as both a concept and a phenomenon, as well as inviting the reader to consider how, if at all, we can justify love. In the next chapter, we turn to romantic relationships.

6

Romantic Relationships

1. Introduction

Pick a popular romantic comedy at random and it is likely to portray a vision of intimate happiness which centres on an exclusive committed relationship. Perhaps the hapless protagonist lumbers through a series of terrible dates before finding 'the one'; perhaps they manage to collapse a toxic love triangle; perhaps they finally manage to get Mr Right to make a public commitment to them with an engagement ring to match.

It is harder to imagine a romantic comedy centred on a protagonist who is not interested in romantic exclusivity, who does not think commitment is important, and who thinks romantic relationships between men and women are so problematic that they should be avoided due to feminist concerns – at least not someone who challenges all three norms at once in our current social context. But what might make for a cinematic flop might capture the truth. What if monogamy is an optional relationship style, commitment needs re-examining, and heterosexual romantic relationships are unfair, or harmful? These are questions we grapple with in this chapter.

We have looked at romantic *love* in the previous chapter, but romantic *relationships* also warrant analysis. Romantic love and romantic relationships can be pulled apart. We can love romantically outside of a romantic relationship, as in the case of unrequited love, or continuing love for a partner after a break-up. Romantic relationships take diverse forms, one significant distinction being whether or not they are monogamous. This will be the first issue we'll explore in this chapter. We'll then move on to ask whether commitment is valuable, before looking at feminist critiques of romantic relationships.

A caveat: we do not attempt to provide a *definition* of a romantic relationship in this chapter (for more on this, see Brunning, 2024b, pp. 3–5; McKeever, 2025a). This is, in part, because we want to be pluralist about what such a relationship can look like. As with romantic love, we do not assume that a romantic relationship *must* include sexual activity, desire, or attraction, though we acknowledge that it often will include all three, at least for a time. Romantic relationships can also be nonmonogamous and exist between people of any gender. In the section on commitment, we consider briefly how romantic relationships compare to friendship. It is here that we come closest to defining romantic relationships, arguing that they are similar to friendships but have two key differences: they are more exclusive than friendship, and they involve greater commitment to include the other in future life plans (see McKeever (2025a), for a fuller discussion of this).

2. Monogamy and nonmonogamy

a. Definitions

Romantic relationships can differ from each other in terms of how exclusive they are. In monogamous relationships, two partners commit to being sexually and emotionally exclusive to each other. Fiona Woollard and Bryan Weaver explain monogamy as follows: 'for those governed by the norm [of monogamy], sexual activity is restricted to relationships with a certain feature, and the number of relationships with that feature is restricted to one' (Woollard and Weaver, 2008, p. 507). Nonmonogamy is, obviously, 'not monogamy'. However, it can take various forms. A natural comparison to monogamy is polygamy, which is most often practised as polygyny, the practice of one man marrying several wives. A couple could also be nonmonogamous in practice, but pretending they are monogamous, if one or both of the partners is cheating on the other.

Here, we will contrast monogamy to 'polyamory', which comes from the Ancient Greek 'poly' meaning 'many' and the Latin 'amor' meaning 'love'. In practice, the term is used to refer to various and quite diverse relationship forms. One of these is 'polyfidelity', where, for example, three or four people might be in a romantic and sexual relationship with one another, but no one outside of the throuple or quad. Another is 'hierarchical polyamory', where there are primary partners who might share a domestic life together and prioritize each other over others, but also have secondary and perhaps tertiary partners. Polyamorous people might also choose to be non-hierarchical, giving an equal degree of priority to all their partners (see Brunning (2018, 2020) for a thorough discussion of the different forms polyamory might take).

b. Mononormativity

Monogamy can be analysed either as a *practice*, or as a social *norm*. It is perfectly consistent, for instance, to claim that there is nothing wrong with two people choosing a monogamous relationship, but there is something wrong with monogamy being a social norm (though it would be odd to say that monogamy is wrong as a practice but fine as a norm). Most cultures across the world are *mononormative* (Ritchie and Barker, 2006). This means that there is an assumption that all romantic relationships are or should be monogamous – or, at least, that monogamous relationships are privileged over nonmonogamous ones. Although many countries permit polygamy, a Pew Research Center report from 2020 found that just 2% of the global population lives in polygamous households, and in most countries the percentage is less than 0.5%. In no country does a majority of people live in polygamous households (Kramer, 2020).

Monogamous relationships are thus the social default in most places. People often deviate from the ideal in practice through infidelity (a YouGov poll from 2022 found that 54% of American respondents said that they had been cheated on in the past (Bialik, Orth, and Sanders, 2022)). However, by opting for infidelity rather than polyamory, the unfaithful person upholds monogamy as a practice: they maintain the appearance of monogamy in spite of being nonmonogamous in reality.

Polyamory is still marginalized and stigmatized (Séguin, 2019), but it is more widely tolerated and practised than previously. While 80% of American over-65s say that they would only ever consider being in a monogamous relationship, for under-30s the figure is just 49% (Bialik, Orth, and Sanders, 2022). One in five Americans have tried some form of consensual nonmonogamy at some point in their life (Haupert et al., 2017), and between 0.6 and 5% of Americans are in a polyamorous relationship right now (Rubel and Burleigh, 2020). Nonetheless, these figures also suggest that most people still aspire to be in a monogamous relationship. There is also some recent evidence suggesting that some younger people are even fantasizing about monogamy from a perspective of default nonmonogamy (Lehmiller and Feeld, 2024). Many people will spend the majority of their lives in a monogamous relationship.

c. Benefits and harms

Some people claim that it is simply not possible to love more than one person at a time. For example, Robert Nozick writes that 'it is not feasible for a person to simultaneously be part of multiple romantic couples (or a trio), even were the person to desire this' (Nozick, 1991, p. 429), and Matthew Liao claims that 'We should love another person romantically because we want to and not because we have to, especially since loving someone romantically *requires* exclusive focus on the person' (Liao, 2006, p. 16). We won't dwell on these claims – the existence of people who love, or have loved, more than one person romantically at a time, of which there are many, should be enough to show that non-exclusive love is possible.

Others argue that monogamy is irrational, even immoral (Chalmers, 2019, 2022). Sex and love are good and valuable parts of life, so why should we accept them being restricted in our own life, and, further, why should we want to restrict them in the life of someone we love? Indeed, in other parts of life, it seems to go against what it means to love – even to act in a controlling and unloving way – to try to restrict the person we love from having other loving relationships. For example, it is not loving, or indeed morally acceptable, for us to say to our siblings that we will love them only if they do not love any of their siblings but us, or for us to say to our friend that we will be her friend only if she has no other friends but us. And in romantic relationships, while it is widely accepted that it is fine, even obligatory, to say to your partner that you will love them only if they have no other romantic relationships but you, it is debatable whether it is okay to say to them that your love for them depends on them having no other friends. Chalmers invites us to consider this with the following thought experiment:

> Imagine that two partners are in a romantic relationship, and that they are also (or perhaps a fortiori) friends. Yet theirs is not a typical relationship, for the partners have agreed on a most unusual restriction: Neither is allowed to have additional friends. Should either partner become friends with someone besides the other, the other partner will refuse to support it – indeed, will go so far as to withdraw her love, affection, and willingness to continue the relationship. (Chalmers, 2019, p. 225)

Chalmers claims that most people would find this relationship morally troubling, because 'friendships are an important human good, and when we're in a romantic relationship with someone, we should want our partner to have such goods in her life. Or at least, we should want our partner to be free to pursue such goods as she sees fit' (Chalmers, 2019, p. 225). Therefore, if sexual and romantic relationships are also important human goods, as Chalmers argues they are, then if we find the 'no additional friends' case morally troubling, we ought to also find monogamy morally troubling.

One way of responding to Chalmers is to say that consenting adults can agree to whatever relationship conditions they want, so there is not, in fact, anything morally troubling here. Yet, in a subsequent paper, Chalmers also argues that this is not true. If the stakes are high, and the breaking of a restriction would cause significant costs to the person who broke it, then the restriction calls for a strong justification. He uses a further analogy to show this: 'Consider two partners who, instead of imposing monogamous restrictions, impose a "shoelaces restriction" on one another. Specifically, each makes clear that if the other ever wears green shoelaces, the consequence will be, if not the flat-out undoing of the relationship, then at least severe resentment, blame, or loss of affection' (Chalmers, 2022, p. 1012). In such a case, Chalmers argues, the justification for the restriction matters, even though the partners will likely not be put out by it. He suggests that it would be morally troubling for them to impose the restriction for a reason such as each having a moderate dislike of green shoelaces, or because the restriction would amuse their friends (Chalmers, 2022, pp. 1012–13). Such justifications do not warrant the strength of the penalty imposed for breaking the restriction.

Chalmers' point can be compared to legal restrictions. If the government imposes a restriction on people, such that it will punish them harshly for going against the restriction (imprisonment, for example), it needs to have a good justification for doing so, even if the restriction will barely impact their lives (such as not being permitted to grow yellow peonies in one's garden).

What kinds of justifications can we give for monogamy? Chalmers considers five, but argues that none of them succeeds:

1. 'the specialness defence', that monogamy makes relationships more special;
2. 'the sexual health defence', that monogamous partners will be less likely to get sexually transmitted diseases;
3. 'the children defence', that children are best raised in monogamous households;
4. 'the practicality defence', that monogamous relationships are more practical than polyamorous relationships; and
5. 'the jealousy defence', that monogamy protects us against jealousy. (Chalmers, 2019)

Kyle York has responded to Chalmers with a defence of monogamy. One argument York makes is that Chalmers is over-egging the role of sanctions in romantic relationships. While some couples do say things to each other like 'If you cheat on me, I'll leave you', in York's words, 'other couples know they'd be hurt if a partner cheated, don't know how they'd react, and hope they won't have to find out' (York, 2024, p. 107). When their partner does cheat on them, it might be that they are so hurt that they have to end the relationship, and this does indeed impose a cost on the partner who cheated. However, York argues that this is a causal cost – in that the relationship break-up *causes* the cheated-on partner to be upset – rather than a sanction as such. He also points out that the straying nonmonogamist also imposes causal costs, such as jealousy, on their partners (York, 2024, pp. 107–8). Similarly, if my friend betrays my trust, I might stop talking to them for a while. This will make them feel sad, but I am not *imposing a sanction* on them, I'm merely expressing my hurt, which has a causal cost on them.

Further, York thinks that there is more to some of the defences that Chalmers dismisses. Regarding practicality, he argues that it is easier to plan the future together in a monogamous relationship, by asking us to consider the following two examples:

Monogamous Moving Plans: Elio and Oliver are monogamous and live in the same place. They want to be with each other in the long term. Oliver, however, has to relocate to Kathmandu.

Non-Monogamous Moving Plans: Jack is in a non-monogamous relationship with Babette and Murray. Jack wants to be with both Babette and Murray in the long term. Murray, however, has to relocate to Chengdu. (York, 2024, pp. 108–9)

Of course, things will be more straightforward for Elio and Oliver. However, the fact that nonmonogamous relationships are more complex does not necessarily entail that we shouldn't have them. The decision to relocate to another country is often a difficult choice, regardless of one's romantic relationship – we may have parents, siblings, friends, children whom we don't want to leave. There is though, undeniably, the potential for difficult choices in polyamorous relationships. Suppose, for example, that Babette and Jack really want to have a child together, but Babette wants to have Jack's full attention for the first two years of the child's life, so that they spend an equal amount of time caring for the child. In this case, Jack will face a difficult choice. Suppose

Murray does not like children or want to be involved in childcare at all. Jack may have to ask him for a two-year break in their relationship, or he will have to tell Babette that he will need to spend regular time away from her and the baby so that he can be with Murray. Neither situation is ideal. And if Jack already has commitments which take up a large amount of time (such as a demanding job), then maintaining a relationship with Murray, as well as attending to and sharing parenting responsibilities with Babette fairly, might prove impossible.

This situation might be made easier if Babette had an additional partner as well, who could be with and help her while Jack is with Murray. But this would mean that she would have to have another partner who was happy to help care for her and Jack's child, who was available at the same times that Jack and Murray wanted to be together. This is not an impossible situation, but there is clearly potential for the logistics not to work. On the other hand, while there might be increased logistical challenges in polyamorous relationships, particularly those involving children, logistics are a challenge for most parents. Furthermore, in polyamorous relationships, if things go well, there is the possibility of there being more caring and invested adults around to help with childcare and with supporting the parents.

Thus, the answer to whether monogamy or nonmonogamy is more practical seems to be 'It depends'. The wider circumstances of the people in the relationships matter a lot for what sort of relationship will work best for them (Brunning, 2024, pp. 26–7). Relationships are ways of grouping together, and organizing aspects of one's life. Given the huge diversity among people's preferences, needs, desires, and life circumstances, it makes sense that different sorts of relationships will work for different people and at different times. Sex and love are valuable human goods, but that does not mean that everybody desires to have sex and love with more than one person. Some people have anxieties around sex (Pyke, 2020), or health conditions which make sex difficult. Others might struggle with social anxiety, or find themselves to be rarely found attractive by others, and so the thought of dating or trying to find more partners fills them with dread. And there are also those who just genuinely only want to have one sexual and romantic partner, and who flourish best in a monogamous relationship. Chalmers acknowledges this, arguing that such people 'can stick to relationships with only one person at a time; the key is simply that you remain open to your partner's having multiple relationships at a time, should she desire it' (Chalmers, 2019, p. 241). It is unclear what this means in practice though. You can remain open to your partner having multiple relationships at a time in the sense that you are not going to lock her in the house to stop her doing so, but you are under no obligation to stay in a relationship with her if she changes her mind and goes from desiring monogamy to desiring nonmonogamy. We are all allowed to have relationship boundaries (Kirton and McKeever, 2023), just as we are all allowed to change our minds and have periods of being monogamous and periods of being nonmonogamous. Finally, it is worth noting that we value some practices in life seemingly because they are difficult and often impractical. Forms of creative activity, athletic training, or religious devotion might be impractical in a sense, but this does not count against them in our lives (Brunning, 2024, p. 26).

We can accept monogamy and nonmonogamy as practices, while still challenging mononormativity. Indeed, acknowledging that *both* monogamous and nonmonogamous relationships can be valuable, morally acceptable, and important *does* challenge mononormativity. Changing entrenched social norms is not easy, but there are some concrete steps which could be taken to undermine the dominance of the norm of monogamy. For example, there could be more representation of polyamorous relationships in the media, and sex and relationships education in schools could make it clear to young people that monogamous romantic relationships are not the only possibilities. Plural marriage could be permitted under certain conditions, as we will discuss in the chapter on 'The Future of Intimacy'.

Challenging mononormativity could benefit people who want to be monogamous, as well as those who do not. If monogamy was not the default relationship option, then a decision to be monogamous would also be more meaningful, as it would be an actual decision if other options were genuinely available (McKeever, 2017). Making the decision to be monogamous together could also lead to more self-reflection and better communication between partners, and it might make them feel more secure in their relationship if they felt confident that each other's commitment to be monogamous was based on careful thought and genuine desire, rather than just the blind following of social norms. As one of us has explored elsewhere, our choice of relationship style might also have to be made with one eye to our ability to sustain relationships of that style (Brunning, 2024b). Arguably, we should be careful not to jump into forms of relating to others that we are radically ill suited to continue.

3. Commitment

The move from 'casual' to 'committed' is central to nearly all romantic narratives, even those which play with the genre or reject other social norms concerning gender, or sexuality, or exclusivity. To ask, as we shall, whether commitment is good can seem perverse. 'Of course it is good!', we might be tempted to reply. We often praise people for their relationship commitment, and venerate married couples who have been together for decades (Turner, 2022). As Anca Gheaus observes, 'commitment is often considered to be *the* feature that makes marriage admirable', and one of the reasons for this is that it is seen as indicative of the depth of the love the spouses have for one another (Gheaus, 2016, p. 205).

Our intuitions are not so simple, however. Blind commitment to someone, though often romanticized, is not praiseworthy if it leads us to do morally bad things on their behalf, or to protect them when they behave immorally. Further, we might wonder what it even means to commit to another; none of us can know what the future will hold, so can we really know that we will be able to continue to love and support another, come what may? And is it responsible to do so?

Here we consider three questions: (1) Is it possible to commit to loving somebody? (2) Should we commit to staying together? (3) What commitments do romantic partners have to each other?

a. Committing to love

Wedding vows usually include a promise to love 'till death do us part'. And couples who do not marry still often promise to love each other forever. One way of understanding what commitments are is to view them as promises. But *can* we promise to love? Elizabeth Brake argues that we cannot, based on two premises: first, that 'we cannot promise to do what we cannot do'; and second, that 'we cannot command our love' (Brake, 2011, p. 29). The first premise is obviously true: I cannot promise to teleport myself to Argentina tomorrow. The second premise is also true, regardless of whether you think love is arational or rational.

If love is arational, then it is clearly beyond our direct control and command – as I cannot command myself to like the taste of sauerkraut, I cannot command myself to love. But if love is rational, then it is also beyond our control. If it is a response to the properties of the beloved, or to the relationship we share with them, then we are not in complete control of the beloved or, consequently, our relationship. If we fall in love with them because they are an animal-loving, free-spirited, left-wing campaigner, but, ten years on, they have become an animal-hating, uptight, right-wing workaholic, then the qualities which justified our love for them previously simply don't exist any more. Similarly, if the relationship we shared with them, when we fell in love, was strong and built on trust, mutual support, and enjoyment of each other's company, but, later on, we no longer trust, support, or like each other very much, then if love was a response to the value of the relationship, it makes sense for the love to dissipate.

Therefore, we do not have enough control over love to be sure that we could fulfil a promise to love. However, thinking of commitment to love as akin to a promise to love is just one way of conceiving of a commitment to love. Stan van Hooft argues that commitment in love is not a conscious decision, but rather an 'alteration of the will' (van Hooft, 1996, p. 455). For him, commitment means being invested in the object to which one is committed, and 'in its most general form, the commitment of love is a commitment to act for the well-being of another'; he writes that this commitment 'may be the ground of, or reason for, a promise or vow ... but it is not the same as these' (van Hooft, 1996, p. 457). This view has a clear affinity with Harry Frankfurt's volitional account of love, discussed in the previous chapter.

Van Hooft points out that, although we do sometimes consciously make commitments, sometimes we just 'find ourselves' with them. This seems right; indeed, it is often the realization that we are committed to another that leads to the discovery that we are in love with them. One realizes that 'another person will be accepted into one's life as important so that one's exclusive focus upon oneself and one's own interests is relinquished', and, therefore, 'the declaration "I love you", when honestly made, is either the making of this commitment or the announcement that one discovers oneself with it'. This is because romantic love – but also love of any kind – 'involves altering the order of practical priorities in one's life rather than just having an emotion' (van Hooft, 1996, p. 459).

Therefore, if we conceive of commitment as a promise, then it is not possible to commit to loving somebody, but if we conceive of commitment as an integral constituent of love, then it is not possible to love someone *without* committing to them. This commitment need not be lifelong, but it does need to imply some desire to be able to act for the beloved's well-being into the future.

b. Committing to stay

We have established that commitment, understood as being invested in another's life and well-being, is integral to love. But one could respond by saying that when we talk about commitment to love, we often mean something more akin to a promise to stay with our partner and to try to do what one can to keep the love alive. Indeed, this is really what the marriage vows are about. When we marry, we commit to stay together, 'for better, for worse, for richer, for poorer, in sickness and in health', until death. Indeed, these kinds of commitments, particularly when they are kept, are often praised, and 'an ability to make commitments is usually considered the marker of maturity' (Gheaus, 2016, p. 208).

But should we make this kind of commitment? As Gheaus notes, 'commitment has costs; it partially forecloses the future, and so it makes one less attentive and less open to life's possibilities' (Gheaus, 2016, p. 206). She further points out that the instrumental value which commitment provides, in helping secure a long-term relationship, can also be got from *love*, for 'as long as people love each other, commitment seems superfluous' (Gheaus, 2016, p. 215). Indeed, she writes that we are *better off* achieving the ends that commitment helps us to achieve through love instead, because love also has non-instrumental value, *and* does not come with the costs of commitment (Gheaus, 2016, p. 216). We could, therefore, just say, 'I will be with you for as long as I love you.'

Gheaus acknowledges that love might be eroded, and so commitment can step in at that point and keep the partners together. However, we tend to prefer to be loved out of inclination, rather than due to commitment, since when we are loved out of inclination then the 'love is a direct reaction to the reality of the beloved' (Gheaus, 2016, p. 218). This is true also for staying together – for one's partner to say to you, 'I do not love you, but I will stay with you because I made a commitment to do so thirty years ago' would likely be unsatisfying, and there's a good chance the continuing relationship would be unhappy.

Therefore, although it is possible to promise to stay with someone, it is not possible to promise to be happy to stay with them. Given this, we might wonder what the point of committing to stay with someone is. Surely, if Petra loves Paul, then Petra should want Paul to be with her for only as long as Paul loves Petra – or, at least, for as long as Paul is happy to stay with Petra. And if we can promise neither love nor future happiness at being held to a commitment, then why make one at all?

One reason might be that romantic relationships often involve long-term and all-encompassing life projects, such as moving city together, buying a house, or having children. If we are embarking on that kind of project with someone, it makes sense to want to know that – even if they can't really know how they will feel in the future – right now they are committed to the project. Further, these sorts of projects aside, to love someone, romantically or otherwise, is to be vulnerable to them. Commitment can help to assuage feelings of vulnerability. Even if we cannot know for sure that we will be *loved* by our partner in the future, their commitment can give us an additional reason to think that we will be treated with respect and care in the future, even if they break up with us. Feeling confident that we will be treated kindly and fairly by them, come what may, can help us to feel safe in being vulnerable to them.

Another reason is that people are fickle, and do not always know what they want or what is best for them in the long term. Knowing this about ourselves, we might decide to give ourselves an extra reason to stay together in the future, with someone we know makes us happy now, in the knowledge that there may be points in the future when we will waiver. We might be mindful that in the future our domestic life with our partner will feel mundane and tedious, and we will be tempted to leave in pursuit of more excitement. Making a commitment can be a way of tying ourselves to the mast, reminding our future self of what our past self thought to be valuable.

Thus, committing to stay together 'come what may' is either inauthentic or reckless. It is inauthentic if you make the commitment knowing that there really are some things which would pull you apart, such as serious betrayal. And it is reckless to stay with someone, due to a commitment, despite very strong reasons not to (such as that they have behaved in a morally egregious way). On the other hand, committing to work at a relationship when things get tough, unless there is serious betrayal, mistreatment, etc., or at least to not just leave at the first hurdle, can be helpful and valuable.

c. Realistic commitment

It is not possible to promise wholeheartedly to love our partners forever, or to stay together and be happy about that. But commitment is part of romantic relationships, and indeed of any relationship. Without *any* commitment, there is no relationship, just two people living alongside each other and hoping their interests and activities align. With no commitment whatsoever, it would not be possible to plan for the future together, and we would be much more limited in being able to hold each other to account. But what commitments should romantic partners have to each other, and how do these commitments differ from those we have to our friends?

Friendship involves commitment. In much the same way as declaring 'I love you' implies a commitment to care for the well-being of your beloved, declaring 'You are my friend' does too. If a friend lets you down, it usually hurts more than if a stranger or acquaintance does, and you may find yourself thinking something along the lines of 'That's not the way a friend should treat me.' Friends also make explicit commitments to each other, which may be minor – 'I will be at your birthday party' – or more significant – 'I will support you through your grief.' But there are also commitments which are implicit to friendship, and do not need to be made explicitly. Friendship involves, for instance, a commitment to be loyal, to be trustworthy, and to care for the well-being of one's friend. 'Friendships of convenience' also exist, where, for example, two people play in the same sports team and end up in the pub together every Saturday having a chat, but feeling no commitment to do so or to care for each other's well-being. These are not the sort of friendships which are most comparable to romantic relationships though – indeed, it is debatable whether they really count as 'friendship' at all (Nehamas, 2016).

Romantic partners have the same sorts of commitments to one another that friends have, but there are some significant differences. One is that, typically, romantic partners commit to their relationship being more exclusive than friendships. This exclusivity need not be total sexual and emotional exclusivity, as in monogamous relationships. However, even polyamorous people often have explicit boundaries regarding their relationships, in ways that friends do not. A survey of 343 self-identified polyamorists found that 96 per cent had some agreement with their partner(s) about what they could do with others. And for some of the 4 per cent who had no agreement, this was due to the relationship being new and the topic not having come up yet (Wosick-Correa, 2010, p. 50). Friends, on the other hand, very rarely have agreements about what each may do with their other friends, or about how many other friends each may have. Indeed, it seems to go against the nature of friendship to ask a friend to limit the number of friends they have, or to limit the ways in which they interact with their other friends (McKeever, 2025a).

The other salient difference between the commitments shared by friends and the commitments between romantic partners is that being in a (long-term) romantic relationship with someone generally entails the commitment to include each other in significant future life plans (McKeever 2025a). This does not entail committing to live together, or to having children, or to only living in the same city as the other. And people may agree to have a short-term romantic fling over a summer and be explicit that the relationship entails no future commitments beyond the summer. However, given the norms by which we live, it is reasonable, unless explicitly told otherwise, to assume that your partner's conception of the future includes you as a key element, again regardless of whether the relationship is monogamous or nonmonogamous. This is one of the ways in which we typically distinguish friendship from romantic relationships (although there are some exceptions to this, where people place friendship at the centre of their lives (Cohen, 2024)). A friend will tell their friend that they are emigrating to Cambodia, or planning to adopt a child. A romantic partner will make these kinds of plans *with* their partner. If a partner told the other that they were making a significant life plan like this on their own, this could reasonably feel like a betrayal to the other, unless they had explicitly agreed that they would act independently of each other in their life plans.

Therefore, commitment can have value in romantic relationships, but we need to take care to be realistic about it. Being more thoughtful and explicit about our commitments, rather than blindly following social norms regarding what relationships should be like, can only be a good thing. We should also remember that the pressure to commit to partners, come what may, has historically contributed to the oppression of women, a subject to which we now turn.

4. Feminist critiques

In 1970, Shulamith Firestone wrote 'for love, perhaps even more than childbearing, is the pivot of women's oppression today' (Firestone, 2003, p. 126). She was discussing romantic love between men and women here, which she argued had held women back: 'women are not creating culture because they are preoccupied with love' (Firestone, 2003, p. 126). In the late 1970s, the Leeds Revolutionary Feminists started calling on feminists to become political lesbians, which they defined as 'a woman-identified woman who does not fuck men. It does not mean compulsory sexual activity with women' (Collective, 1981, p. 5). They published a pamphlet in 1981 titled 'Love your enemy? Debate between heterosexual feminism and political lesbianism', where they wrote:

The heterosexual couple is the basic unit of the political structure of male supremacy. In it each individual woman comes under the control of an individual man. It is far more efficient than keeping women in ghettoes, camps, or even sheds at the bottom of the garden. In the couple, love and sex are used to obscure the realities of oppression, to prevent women identifying with each other in order to revolt, and from identifying 'their' man as part of the enemy. (Collective, 1981, p. 6)

Arguably, gendered oppression is not as bad as when Firestone and the Leeds Revolutionary Feminists published these pieces: in 1981 in the UK, it had just been six years since women got the right to open a bank account without their husband's permission, and men could still legally rape their wives until 1991. Nonetheless, feminists are still, for good reasons, concerned with romantic relationships between men and women. Here we consider three of these reasons: (1) gendered norms of dating and marriage; (2) the pleasure gap; (3) unequal labour in relationships.

a. Gendered norms

Many social norms around (mainly heterosexual) dating and marriage serve to disempower women and non-binary people. In heterosexual dating and marriage, it is the norm for the man to take the active role – asking the woman on a date and, later, asking the woman to marry him – while the woman merely says 'yes' or 'no'. In both contexts, gender norms which render women submissive are romanticized. There are other norms which are gendered too. In dating, it is the norm for the man to pay for the date. A recent survey of 552 US college students found that men paid for the first date 90% of the time, while women did only 2% of the time, with them splitting the bill just 8% of the time. A majority of both the men and women also expected the man to pay (Wu et al., 2023).

Ellen Lamont interviewed 105 college-educated adults aged between 25 and 40 in the San Francisco Bay Area about dating. She chose this group because they are people with economic resources and progressive social values, who are most likely to reject conventional gender norms. However, she found that their romantic lives were 'firmly shaped by entrenched inequalities' (Lamont, 2020, p. 3). This is particularly the case for heterosexual men and women: despite most of them rejecting the traditional 'male breadwinner; female homemaker' type of relationship, 75% of them wanted 'some semblance of a traditional courtship', and nearly all of them wanted some aspects of one. The gendered expectations included: the man paying for the date; the man wanting to be taller and stronger than the woman; the man wanting to be more sexually experienced than the woman (Lamont, 2020, p. 53). Conversely, 80% of the LGBQ people she interviewed wanted more 'gender-neutral and egalitarian practices', instead of 'traditional dating conventions' (Lamont, 2020, p. 5). As a result of her research, Lamont concludes that 'sexism hasn't gone away; it has simply become subtler and research isn't accurately capturing the nuances' (Lamont, 2020, p. 12).

The heterosexual wedding ceremony is also replete with sexist symbolism: the woman, but not the man, wearing an engagement ring; the woman being 'given away' by her father; the woman wearing a white dress as symbol of her virginity; the speeches being traditionally given by the groom, the best man, and the father of the bride; the wife being carried over the threshold by her husband; the wife taking the husband's surname and adopting the title 'Mrs', while his name and title remain unchanged. While this latter tradition is not as entrenched as it once was, in 2023 46% of men wanted their spouse to take their surnames, and only 1% wanted to take their spouse's surname. Conversely, 49% of women wanted to take their spouse's surname, and only 1% wanted their spouse to take theirs ('The preferred choice of Brits for surnames upon marriage', 2023). Surprisingly, a YouGov survey from 2023 found that 25% of men, and 9% of women, still thought that the tradition of the bride promising to *obey* her husband should be kept. A further 15% of the men and 9% of the women weren't sure (Eydal, 2023). (The recent 'tradwife' social media trend also advocates women submitting to their husbands, as well as adopting traditional feminine gender roles at home – see, for example, Freeman (2020).) Again, these traditions are romanticized, which makes them harder to challenge, for, as Jenkins puts it, 'ancient gender stereotypes somehow look more acceptable when we see them through the rose-tinted lens of a sweet love story' (Jenkins, 2017, p. 125).

b. The pleasure gap

In addition, and relatedly, norms around sex are still heavily gendered. Men are expected, more than women, to initiate sex, and to be sexually dominant. This is reflected in the kind of language we use to describe sexual acts – the woman is 'fucked', 'screwed', 'had', etc., by a man (Baker, 2009, p. 229). Men are also assumed to have a higher sexual appetite (Baumeister, Catanese, and Vohs, 2001) and norms around the kinds of sex which are to be aspired to in heterosexual sex – particularly forms of intercourse involving penile penetration – tend to be those which are likely to make men orgasm more than women, hence the widely reported-on 'orgasm gap' or 'pleasure gap'. Indeed, sex is often assumed to *be* penile–vaginal intercourse, with this being the type of sex people usually think is the one that 'counts' as 'losing your virginity' (McArthur, 2022a).

Women are, in general, much less likely to orgasm when having sex with men than men are when having sex with women. For example, in a survey of 3,990 American adults about their most recent partnered sex (with 90% being sex with someone of the opposite gender to them), 91% of the men orgasmed, compared to 64% of the women (Herbenick et al., 2010). This is true both for one-night stands and for sex with a longer-term partner. However, despite more clitoris-focused sexual activity being more reliable in leading to women orgasming, women reportedly often don't feel entitled to ask for this and worry it would hurt their partner's feelings if they did so – the majority of women have faked an orgasm during intercourse (Mahar, Mintz, and Akers, 2020, p. 28).

It is not just in orgasm that we find a gap, but in sexual enjoyment more broadly. In the survey referred to above by Herbenick et al., where participants were asked about their most recent partnered sexual event, 83% of the men, compared to 66% of the women, experienced pleasure 'extremely' or 'quite a bit', and 4% of the men, compared to 14% of the women, experienced pleasure only a little or not at all (Herbenick et al., 2010, pp. 352–3).

The pleasure gap has often been explained away by claiming that it is due to biological differences – that women have less capacity for sexual pleasure than men do, or that they are less bothered about orgasm (Laan et al., 2021). However, there is evidence showing that women and men have similar capacities for sexual pleasure, and that orgasm is an important predictor of sexual satisfaction for women (Laan et al., 2021, p. 521). It is also possible that women may say they are not concerned with orgasm as a way to reduce cognitive dissonance if they are not experiencing it (Laan et al., 2021, p. 519). Indeed, women are much more likely to orgasm when having sex with other women than with men, and most women orgasm when masturbating (Mahar, Mintz, and Akers, 2020, p. 25). This suggests that it is not that women are unable to orgasm, but rather that the *kinds* of sex that men and women have together causes women not to orgasm. As further evidence for this conclusion, a study of bisexual women found that 64% of them frequently or always orgasmed when having a one-night stand with a woman, but only 7% of them frequently or always orgasmed when their partner was a man (Mahar, Mintz, and Akers, 2020, p. 25).

If women have similar capacity for sexual pleasure to men, but are getting less of it during sex with men, then this is an issue of fairness – sexual pleasure is a good in itself, and it should be distributed fairly. But there is also evidence that sexual pleasure has various mental and physical health benefits, and so women may be losing out on secondary, but important, benefits too (Laan et al., 2021, pp. 517–18).

Furthermore, if women are having (consensual) sex which they do not enjoy, this might be harmful to them. Robin West, in her paper, 'The harms of consensual sex', suggests that engaging in repeated consensual but unwanted sex, even if it is being traded for something of greater immediate value than the sex (such as emotional or economic support), can harm a woman's sense of selfhood in four ways:

1. It harms her ability to assert herself, as what she does and feels do not match.
2. It harms her sense of self-possession, in that she comes to see herself as 'being for others', with her body no longer belonging to herself.
3. When she is having sex because she is dependent on her partner economically, or for affection, it harms her sense of autonomy.
4. It harms her integrity, because she is lying to herself and to the man by telling herself and him that she enjoyed it. (West, 2002, p. 318)

West notes several reasons why women might consent to sex they do not desire, including fear of violence, fear of putting her partner in a bad mood, having 'no reasonable expectation of attaining her own pleasure through sex', or because of peer expectations (West, 2002, pp. 317–18). She also points out that the 'harms – particularly if multiplied over years or indeed over an entire adulthood – may be quite profound' (West, 2002, pp. 318–19).

Amia Srinivasan also discusses the pressure that women in particular might feel to consent to unwanted sex, out of fear of being labelled a 'tease':

It doesn't matter whether Bonsu himself had this expectation, because it is an expectation already internalised by many women. A woman going on with a sex act she no longer wants to perform, knowing she can get up and walk away but knowing at the same time that this will make her a blue-balling tease, an object of male contempt: there is more going on here than mere ambivalence, unpleasantness and regret. There is also a kind of coercion: not directly by Bonsu, perhaps, but by the informal regulatory system of gendered sexual expectations. (Srinivasan, 2021, p. 28)

Combining what we know about the orgasm and pleasure gap with West's analysis of the ways in which unenjoyable sex can be harmful, particularly if it is regular, shows us that unequal sexual pleasure is a significant problem for romantic relationships and feminists are right to be concerned about it. Of course, not all sex takes place within romantic relationships, so this problem extends beyond such contexts, but a lot of sex does take place within them, and so any critique of romantic relationships ought to take account of the way in which sexual pleasure is gendered. Further, other gendered norms around romantic relationships intersect here, exacerbating the problem. For example, suppose during the dating process the man always paid for and initiated dates, and then the couple married and she took his name, and then during the marriage the woman was expected to perform more domestic, emotional, and hermeneutic labour (as outlined in the next section). In such a relationship, it would not be surprising if the partners internalized the idea that the man's needs were, in general, more important than the woman's, and that she had a greater responsibility to meet his needs than he did for her, including sexual needs. This could be particularly pertinent in monogamous relationships, since if a woman is not experiencing sexual enjoyment with her partner, she is not permitted to seek it elsewhere. However, given that unequal sexual enjoyment seems widespread, women in nonmonogamous arrangements may, too, find themselves experiencing less sexual pleasure than their male counterparts.

c. Unequal labour

Another reason why feminists are concerned with heterosexual romantic relationships is that they are often sites of unequal labour, with the unequal labour often falling along gendered lines: women do more work than men do. Here we consider three sorts of labour which often fall more on the shoulders of women in heterosexual romantic relationships: (1) domestic labour; (2) emotional labour; (3) hermeneutic labour.

Feminist concerns about unequal domestic labour in romantic relationships have been well documented (e.g. Okin, 1991; Maushart, 2002). Here, we understand 'domestic labour' to be, broadly speaking, unpaid housework and childcare. Around the world, women do three times as much unpaid domestic labour as men, and the inequality was exacerbated by the Covid-19 pandemic (Seedat and Rondon, 2021). Data from the Office for National Statistics (ONS) shows that in March 2022, employed women with dependent children in the UK spent an average of 84 minutes per day on unpaid childcare, compared to 55 minutes per day for employed men living with dependent children. And the women spent 169 minutes per day on household work on average, compared to 106 minutes per day for the men (Murphy, Dennes, and Harris, 2022). Multiplied across weeks and months, this adds up. Tom

McClelland and Paulina Sliwa argue this disparity is due to differences in how men and women perceive opportunities for action in the home, with men literally failing to see what needs doing more than women (McClelland and Sliwa, 2023).

Whatever the cause, these disparities are wrong because they are unfair, and it is particularly problematic because domestic labour is under-valued and much of it is dull and repetitive. Furthermore, there is evidence that the unequal distribution of domestic labour contributes to poorer mental health in women (Ervin et al., 2022). We should also note that same-sex couples share domestic work more equally than heterosexual couples (Goldberg, 2013), so sharing this kind of labour more fairly is possible. The expectation that women perform more domestic labour than men is also a factor in explaining the gender pay gap, as women, much more than men, pursue paid employment which is compatible with their domestic responsibilities (Petrongolo and Ronchi, 2020).

'Emotional labour' is a term that is used in different ways. It was first coined by Airlie Hochschild to describe the way that employees – particularly those working in customer-facing roles, such as flight attendants – often have to manage their own emotions in order to improve the experience for the customer (Hochschild, 2012). It is 'now used to mean any domestic or relationship-building labour that is disproportionately performed by women and often unrecognized' (Morgan, 2024, p. 3). For clarity, we are separating it out from physical housework and childcare (which was discussed above), and focusing on the emotional, cognitive, and organizational work that women do in romantic relationships. Indeed, emotional labour may be disproportionate in romantic relationships where partners do not live together or have shared caring responsibilities. It may also be disproportionate in relationships where other forms of domestic labour are shared equally.

Journalist Rose Hackman gives a nice summary of some of the things that emotional labour can include:

We remember children's allergies, we design the shopping list, we know where the spare set of keys is. We multi-task. We know when we're almost out of Q-tips, and plan on buying more. We are just better at remembering birthdays. We love catering to loved ones, and we make note of what they like to eat. We notice people's health, and force friends and family to go see the doctor. We listen to our partner's woes, forgive them the absences, the forgetfulness, the one-track mindedness while we're busy organizing a playdate for the kids. We applaud success when it comes:

the grant that was received, the promotion. It was their doing, and ours in the background. (Hackman, 2015)

This kind of work is both done mostly by women *and* under-valued, perhaps because women are often thought to just be 'naturally good' at it (Müller, 2019, pp. 848–9). As Mirjam Müller puts it, 'The very meaning that is attached to emotional labour, namely that it is an activity that women just do out of their natural way of being, prevents it from being seen as something that requires energy and time. Emotional labour is thereby effectively made invisible and devalued by the underlying assumptions about femininity' (Müller, 2019, p. 849). This is unfair on women: they are doing a disproportionate amount of work that is also not appropriately valued. And this work benefits men. Müller identifies three ways in which men benefit. First, they get a *time benefit* as women take on tasks which involve emotional labour, and this frees up men to do other, more interesting, things (Müller, 2019, p. 849). Second, they get an *emotional benefit*: 'being cared for, being listened to, being supported in one's projects, all these things create a feeling of well-being and ease in the recipients of emotional labour', and, importantly, women do not receive as much of this benefit, since men do not do as much emotional labour for women as women do for men (Müller, 2019, p. 850). Finally, they get a *status benefit*: 'in disproportionally caring about men's projects and in often granting them more importance than their own, women confirm and enhance men's status' (Müller, 2019, p. 850).

Another kind of labour which falls disproportionately on women has been identified by Ellie Anderson as 'hermeneutic labour', which she defines as: 'the burdensome activity of: understanding and coherently expressing one's own feelings, desires, intentions, and motivations; discerning those of others; and inventing solutions for relational issues arising from interpersonal tensions' (Anderson, 2023, p. 177). She uses the term 'hermeneutic' because 'hermeneutics is a method of interpretation for unpacking the latent levels of meaning in communication cues' (Anderson, 2023, p. 179).

Anderson suggests that women are viewed as 'relationship experts', and are thus tasked with relationship maintenance. This leads them to be more perceptive of relationship issues and to feel more responsible for resolving them. Because their relationship expertise is viewed as a product of 'women's intuition', the labour that goes into it is rendered invisible (Anderson, 2023, p. 184). However, Anderson argues, 'so-called "women's intuition" is in fact a hard-won achievement that takes years to produce and sustain. It is a euphemism for hermeneutic labor' (Anderson, 2023, p. 186). She further suggests that men are socialized into being deficient in the ability to process their emotions and put them into words – what psychologist Ronald F. Levant has called 'normative male alexithymia': normative as it forms part of 'scripts of masculinity'. This alexithymia is not good for men, who consequently must suppress their emotions: 'men are not less emotional than women; they are merely less likely to express emotions' (Anderson, 2023, p. 186).

Again, unequal hermeneutic labour is problematic because it is unfair that women do more of this work than their relationship counterparts, especially as, again, it is under-valued work. Anderson also notes that women of colour and working-class women may also be burdened with more hermeneutic labour than white women and upper-middle-class women, respectively (Anderson, 2023, p. 187), so it is the most disadvantaged women in society who are picking up the most slack. The unequal distribution of hermeneutic labour may also be a contributing factor in why women are less satisfied in romantic relationships than men are (Anderson, 2023, p. 188). Furthermore, it places women in a double bind, since they are derided if they don't perform their role as 'relationship-maintenance expert' well, but they are also derided if they do, as 'they are always at risk of being considered nags and shrews' (Anderson, 2023, p. 192).

It is not difficult to see how traditional gender roles, which position men as breadwinners and women as homemakers, are bound up with ideals of a romantic relationship. It is true that some of the inequalities discussed above exist not only in romantic relationships. In households made up of mixed-gender friends, for example, it could also be the case that the women do more domestic, emotional, and hermeneutic labour than the men. And, in the workplace, women perform more 'office housework' than men do, such as taking notes in meetings; and more 'social maintenance', such as organizing office parties, than men do (Jang, Allen, and Regina, 2021). However, heterosexual romantic relationships are microcosms of gendered relations more broadly, and, moreover, the gendered roles within them are *romanticized*, making it harder to challenge them. We romanticize the idea of men providing financially for women, buying them expensive gifts and 'whisking them away' on holiday, while we romanticize women looking after men and looking nice for them. The 'strong silent type', moody man, who is brought out of his shell by an emotionally intelligent woman performing hermeneutic labour for him (the so-called 'manic pixie dream-girl' trope) is romanticized, as is the man who sexually dominates women.

Anyone who cares about gender equality should, therefore, pay attention to the – sometimes subtle – ways in which gender discrimination and oppression play out in romantic relationships. This is not only an issue for heterosexual relationships, although those have been our focus here. Gender roles sometimes spill over into same-sex relationships too, with couples being asked, for example, 'Which one of you wears the trousers?', or 'Which of you is the mother, and which is the father?'

There is an important question here about what should be done about all of this, and by whom. Presumably not many people will think that political lesbianism is the answer. Many heterosexual women really want to have romantic relationships with men, and find those relationships to be valuable parts of their lives, even if they are unequal. Another radical option could be relationship anarchy, which is discussed in the following chapter, but that will also likely appeal to few people only, and it does not guarantee gender-equal relationships in any case.

Change which is subtler and slower is thus more likely to be popular, and successful, in the long term. At an individual level, the first step in altering any deeply embedded harmful norms is just to notice and identify them (as, for example, Anderson has done in identifying hermeneutic labour). Next, we must attend to those norms, noticing when they seem to be guiding our behaviour; and, third, we need to try to resist their pull, and aim to act in a way which is fairer. What this could look like in practice is: first, a couple read about emotional labour, and realize that the woman in the relationship does more of it than the man. Second, they agree to notice when the woman is doing it. Third, they each try to do things more fairly – so, for example, the man makes an effort to notice that their son's birthday is a couple of months away and initiates a conversation about arranging a birthday party. And then they divide the work in organizing the party between them fairly.

But structural change is also crucially needed. As an example of a success story: in Iceland, there is a 'use it or lose it' parental leave policy, whereby each parent can take six months' parental leave paid at 80 per cent of their salary after the birth of a child, with six weeks transferable between them. Thus, each parent has 4.5 months of paid parental leave that they lose if they don't use it. Research has shown that this policy has led to fathers taking a more active role in caring for their children, but also, interestingly, to parents being less likely to divorce (Arnalds, Eydal, and Gíslason, 2022). Thus, this policy not only reduced gendered inequality in domestic labour, it also likely increased relationship satisfaction between parents.

5. Conclusion

In this chapter, we have been exploring romantic relationships, some of the most significant and intense, but also difficult and disorienting, relationships many of us have. We have by no means considered all the ethical or conceptual issues surrounding romantic relationships, or all the work which needs to be done to address these. However, we have explored two central questions regarding romantic relationships – whether we should be monogamous or nonmonogamous, and what kinds of commitments we should make in our romantic relationships. We have also considered why feminists might be concerned with such relationships. All of these considerations are vital in making romantic relationships less oppressive, fairer, and more fulfilling.

7

The Future of Intimacy

1. Introduction

Imagine for a moment your marriage is failing. Nothing terrible has happened; neither party has been unfaithful, no major tragedy has befallen you both; the issue is simply time and the drift of interests and desires. Neither you nor your partner shows much sexual interest towards the other, and the other relationships in your life, such as your friendships, time at work, and connections with family, are slowly edging out your romantic life.

A friend says to you: 'Not to worry, I can recommend three solutions: first, there are other ways you might satisfy your sexual desire at least – why not enjoy sex with robots? Second, if silicone is not your thing, then there are drugs you and your spouse might take to keep your love alive. Third, if you crave something more radical, why not explore plural marriage, or relationship anarchy, or totally upend the traditional picture of the family altogether?' Do any of these options appeal to you?

Norms and laws around romantic relationships have changed a lot over the past decades and centuries. It is no longer the case that romantic relationships are only permissible within a lifelong, monogamous, heterosexual marriage between people from the same ethnicity and social class. Technology has also made significant changes to people's relationships, providing new ways to meet others and making it possible to travel and converse with people easily and relatively cheaply across countries and continents. It is likely that the near and distant future will bring further change. Here we discuss three possible sorts of changes that we might see in the not-too-distant future: (1) sexual and romantic relationships with robots; (2) use of love drugs; (3) changes to the norms and laws around relationships.

2. Love, sex, and robots

Robot technology is becoming increasingly advanced and, correspond-ingly, people are becoming increasingly worried about its capability and ethical impact. One of the concerns people have is the potential for robots to replace humans in sexual and romantic relationships. Humanoid robots are artificially intelligent (AI) systems that are encased in a human-appearing physical form, but here we will use the term 'love and sex robots' to refer broadly to AI systems which are designed to play the role of humans *as participants* (as opposed to facilitators) in loving and sexual relationships.

Sex and love dolls already exist, some of which have limited Artificial Intelligence, enabling them to move and to speak to their users ('RealDoll' is an example). Several sex robot brothels have also opened up across the world, and the world's first 'Cybrothel' has recently opened in Berlin, allowing users to have sex with real-life sex dolls, using Virtual Reality headsets to immerse themselves in porn (Lovine, 2023). Other kinds of AI systems with which we can form relationships also already exist. The app Replika, for instance, allows users to create their own unique personalized chatbot (their 'Replika'), complete with avatar, using generative AI technology. Many users turned from Replika when an update prevented them from having sexual content in discussions with their Replika (Tong, 2023).

Robot–human relationships have also been the subject of several well-known recent novels – for example Annalee Newitz's *Autonomous* (2017), Ian McEwan's *Machines Like Me* (2019), Ros Anderson's *The Hierarchies* (2020), and Kazuo Ishiguro's *Klara and the Sun* (2021) – as well as films and television programmes, such as Spike Jonze's film *Her* (2013) and Charlie Brooker's *Black Mirror* episode 'Be Right Back' (2013). Robot–human relationships capture the imagination, because it is both exciting and frightening to think about what the future may hold for us, but also because thinking about relationships with robots is a way of thinking about what we value, and what we don't value, in relationships with humans. Here we consider: (a) is it OK to have sex with a robot?; (b) can we love a robot?; (c) is the devel-opment of love and sex robots something we should be encouraging, or trying to stop? (We have separated out sex and love in sections (a) and (b), but in many cases, a user will both love and have sex with their robot, and so it is likely that robots will be designed for both these purposes. Thus, we also discuss 'love and sex robots' together in the third section.)

a. Robot sex

Sex robots are with us already. If you want to have sex with a robot, you can purchase online, for example, a 'Realdoll', a made-to-order, customizable sex doll, with an Artificial Intelligence 'head' that can move, talk, and learn user preferences. If you can't afford the $10,000+ to buy one of these, you can go to a sex robot brothel, several of which have popped up in recent years in cities across the world. But is it OK to do this? Here we focus on two ethical considerations: consent, and objectification of women.

First, we might worry about consent, which we have already explored in detail in the chapter on 'Intimate ethics'. The robot cannot refuse sex, so they also cannot consent to it. We might think this is an odd concern – we don't, after all, worry that other sex toys cannot consent to sex, and robots are, on one view, just elaborate sex toys. However, this might be too quick an analysis. One of the primary appeals of a sex robot is that it is mimicking a person, and so users of sex robots might treat them as if they were persons. If the user never has to seek consent from the robot, they may come to see consent as less important with human sex partners too. If sex with robots becomes more widespread and normalized, we might worry about the impact this could have on consent in human–human sex more generally.

These are significant concerns, and although there is a degree of slippery-slope thinking going on here, the significance of consent to sex must not be underestimated. There are ways that robot manufacturers can mitigate consent-related concerns though. For example, John Danaher suggests that, rather than being an '"ever-consenting" sexual tool', 'the robot might sometimes randomly refuse its user, and always provide positive affirmative signals of consent when it is willing to proceed' (Danaher, 2017, p. 116). There's a question over whether this would make the robots less popular, but if this was something that was regulated, so that all robots had to sometimes refuse sex, then users would likely get used to it fairly quickly.

Danaher also suggests that robots 'designed to cater to rape fantasies or paedophiliac tendencies' could be banned (Danaher, 2017, p. 116). However, this is difficult to do with robots because we can't appeal to the age of the robot to determine whether it's a child: some 'child-appearing' robots could be technically modelled on women with a very 'youthful' appearance.

On the other hand, we might wonder how realistic a robot saying 'no' would be, given that it would be unconvincing to the user that the robot was saying 'no' due to being tired, or stressed, or to not finding the user attractive, for example, as in the case of humans. If the robot just says 'no' at random intervals, perhaps this could even further undermine the consent and non-consent of humans, reducing it to something that is purely performative (i.e. the internal states of the person we're having sex with become irrelevant features of consent). We might go further and worry that robots which mimic the unpredictability of human consenting practice might encourage further consent violations by users just attempting to override them to have sex anyway. In turn, this could embolden some users to disregard consent in other contexts; indeed, robots may assist them in practising how to do this (we thank Ruby Hornsby, in conversation, for these points).

So, there might be ways to mitigate the problematic impact that robots have on consent in human–human sex, perhaps by ensuring robots do not look like humans, but work is needed on what could be done. Nonetheless, robots may still have a significant negative effect on human–human sex by encouraging the sexual objectification of women.

Sex robots are mostly modelled on women and marketed at men (Li, 2022). A (relatively small-scale) survey in 2016 found that over two-thirds of the men were in favour of using a sex robot, while two-thirds of the women were opposed to using one (Scheutz and Arnold, 2016, p. 356). Though RealDoll do sell male sex robots as well as female ones (as well as male faces and realistic penis dildos), in 2017 they estimated that under 5 per cent of their customers were women (Kleeman, 2017).

This is interesting, because the sex toy market as a whole is marketed more at women, who use sex toys when masturbating significantly more than men do (Hald, Pavan, and Øverup, 2024), and sex toy producers often 'understand women as ideal users whose sexual desire and consumption are morally defensible', while 'men's sex toy use is disavowed and even openly reviled by producers' (Ronen, 2021, p. 614). (Not all philosophers agree, however, with Roger Scruton being a notable critic of women's use of dildos for sexual pleasure (Scruton, 2006, p. 28).) At one sex toy trade show, of 108 companies, '70 (65%) were boutique brands that specialized in products for women, as compared to only eight (0.07%) that made products only for men' (Ronen, 2021, p. 620). One of the reasons for sex toys being more marketed at women is likely that women orgasm less during sex with men than men do during sex with women (Mahar, Mintz, and Akers, 2020).

Therefore, if sex robots are just glorified sex toys, we might expect there to be more interest in them from women, and more interest from sex robot producers in marketing them at women. But, as we have seen, they seem to be of much less interest to women than they are to men. And this is not just because the robots are physically more pleasurable for men than for women, because they can be designed in ways to provide physical pleasure to both genders. Thus, it seems more likely that sex robots are viewed not just as 'glorified sex toys', but rather as something else, which is thought to appeal more to men.

Sherry Turkle and her co-authors have described robots as 'relational artifacts', which are 'artifacts that present themselves as having "states of mind" for which an understanding of those states enriches human encounters with them' (Turkle et al., 2006, p. 347). Turkle suggests that empirical work shows that humans find it natural to project human emotions and motivations onto robots, and think of them as having a soul (McArthur, 2017, p. 37). The implication of this is that sex robots are viewed *both* as an object and as a person, or at least person-like, which could have harmful symbolic and practical consequences.

Kathleen Richardson (2016), in a position paper for the Campaign Against Porn Robots (formerly the Campaign Against Sex Robots), compares sex robot use to prostitution. She takes a dim view of prostitution, claiming that, 'in prostitution, only the buyer of sex is attributed subjectivity, the seller of sex is reduced to a *thing*' (Richardson, 2016, p. 291). Given that prostitutes, according to Richardson, are denied subjectivity, it is logical to her that sex robots will be modelled on prostitutes. Drawing on the work of psychologist Simon Baron-Cohen, Richardson suggests that men have less empathy than women, which makes them more likely to buy sex from prostitutes (Richardson, 2016, p. 291).

Richardson's characterization of prostitution (sex work) is too monolithic and does not take into account the vast diversity among both buyers and sellers of sex, including female buyers of sexual services. Nonetheless, the parallel she draws is worth considering, because in sex work, as with sex robots, men are predominantly the consumers, and women (or female-shaped robots) the providers (McKeever, 2025b). The claim that this is due to gendered levels of empathy is much too simplistic by way of explanation. For one thing, men who pay for sex often *do* show empathy for the sex worker and desire to form an emotional connection with them (Milrod and Weitzer, 2012).

However, looking at gendered norms and stereotypes around sex does give us some insight into why men would be more comfortable both buying sex from a sex worker and having sex with a sex robot. Men are positioned much more frequently as sexually dominant, whereas women are positioned more as sexually submissive (McKeever, 2025b). Furthermore, having sex with a robot is subversive, and having subversive sex is tolerated less for women than it is for men. There is no female equivalent for 'boys will be boys', and there is no male equivalent for such words as 'whore' and 'slag'.

A further reason we might worry, from a gendered perspective, about sex robots is that they are mostly modelled on a particular idealized form of women: young, slim, white women, with exaggerated hourglass frames. It has been well documented that these sorts of feminine norms of appearance have harmful effects on women, given that most women do not fit the ideal, and trying to achieve it can be unhealthy, expensive, time-consuming, and emotionally draining.

Thus, insofar as sex robots reinforce these kinds of ethically problematic gender norms, they *are* concerning, and people who care about gender equality should think twice about sex with sex robots. However, this doesn't mean that sex robots are ethically problematic per se. Robots could, for example, be designed on more realistic body types, which would mitigate one of the worries outlined above. And a woman having sex with a male robot, for example, might be considered very differently to a man having sex with a female robot. However, we might also be reminded that the body form of male sex robots also promotes unrealistic masculine appearance ideals – again young, white, slim, muscular, with a large penis.

b. Robot love

If we accept that it is possible to love objects, then there is, in principle, no reason to claim that it is not possible to love a robot. People love their violin, their stamp collection, their diamond ring. Some people also experience romantic love for objects, as in the case of Objectum-Sexuality, where people love and sexually desire objects as if the object was a human partner *and* believe they are in a two-way relationship with the object. For example, Erika Eiffel describes her love for Lance (her bow) as follows: 'People realised I loved my bow, but they didn't realise I *loved* my bow. ... I'd almost swear that my blood just flowed from my arm and went right into him, and ... felt that the molecules in him went right back into my arm' (Hornsby and McKeever, 2022). It is, therefore, conceivable, that someone who was in love with a robot might similarly believe they are in a two-way relationship with the robot. But there is a further question regarding what this love would be like, and whether we can consider it genuine, and desirable. David Levy is optimistic about human–robot love, writing that in the near future it will be commonplace, and that it will be as good as, or even better than, human–human love. He argues that 'all of the emotional benefits we have considered here, deriving from human–human relationships, could also be provided by computers' (Levy, 2009, p. 90). And, furthermore, women leaving bad relationships might come to see relationships with robots as more reliable: 'Yes, it would be very nice to start a relationship with a new man, but one can never be sure how it's going to work out. I believe that having emotional relationships with robots will come to be perceived as a more dependable way to assuage one's emotional needs' (Levy, 2009, pp. 114–15). Perhaps this attitude is just akin to the growing use of AI bots for other emotional services, such as therapy or relationship advice. However, there is a question of whether this is authentic love, or a simulacrum of love. As Sven Nyholm and Lily Frank point out, Levy's characterization of love is quite 'functional and behaviouristic' – if this was all love was then 'we could hire an actor to "go through the motions", by behaving in the various ways we associate with lovers', as is often presented as a feature of 'the girlfriend experience' by some sex workers. Indeed, 'we could buy love'. But this would not ordinarily be thought of as 'real love', because we usually also care about 'what goes on "on the inside"' (Nyholm and Frank, 2017, p. 223).

In Spike Jonze's film *Her* (2013), we witness Theodore Twombly, a lonely writer, fall in love with Samantha, an AI operating system virtual assistant that is able to develop and learn. Samantha also claims to love Theodore back. Troy Jollimore has written about *Her*, suggesting that, while a person might develop feelings of love and attachment for a computer or a robot, any relationship with one will likely be lacking in 'some of the things we want most from our love relationships' (Jollimore, 2015, p. 121).

Jollimore discusses several concerns, but here we will just discuss one: that of Samantha's consciousness. As Jollimore notes, we do not know whether Samantha is conscious. Jollimore discusses a scene in the film where Theodore and Samantha have sex, but as Samantha does not have a body, they use their voices only, similar to phone sex. Theodore tells his friend, Amy, that he thinks he turns Samantha on. This seems important to him. However, if Theodore was to know that Samantha is not conscious, and thus cannot feel pleasure, 'he would find his own pleasure radically diminished, if not entirely extinguished' (Jollimore, 2015, p. 122).

Furthermore, if Samantha is conscious, then her 'consciousness is presumably so different from Theodore's that it will be quite impossible for them to understand each other' (Jollimore, 2015, p. 138). This means that true intimacy between them is impossible. Jollimore quotes Turkle here: 'I am troubled by the idea of seeking intimacy with a machine that has no feelings, can have no feelings, and is really just a clever collection of "as if" performances, behaving as if it cared, as if it understood us' (Turkle, in Jollimore, 2015, p. 139). He thus concludes that, while a robot might be able to 'simulate empathy, identification, and love in a convincing manner' (Jollimore, 2015, p. 139), this would not be enough for genuine love to exist between the robot and the human. If someone did not care whether the being they loved had an inner life, and 'would be no less happy with a voice generated on different occasions by distinct nonconscious mechanical systems than he would be with a living, speaking, thinking partner' (Jollimore, 2015, p. 141), then they are not really in love, but rather they just love how the being makes them feel.

Nyholm and Frank would likely agree with Jollimore here. They argue that, for the robot to really love the human, it would need to be possible for them to *not* love the human: 'it should not just automatically be preset to love the human being in question' (Nyholm and Frank, 2017, p. 236). If it was, then the human would not enjoy the aspect of love that comes from having been chosen, and committed to by the lover. However, if it were possible for the robot to *not* love the human who buys it – or, indeed, for the robot to stop loving the human – we might wonder whether anyone would be interested in paying for one in the first place (certainly we can imagine competitors releasing alternatives which offer a higher chance of being loved back, or being loved for longer). There is thus a similar issue here to the issue with sex – making the robot more similar to humans in enabling them to refuse sex or love with the user could make sex with robots less ethically problematic and love with them more realistic. However, in doing this, robots will likely be less popular among users, and so less profitable.

c. The future

Sex robots are not only a future concern, but a current one too. However, it is likely that sex robot technology will improve as time goes on, particularly if large language model (LLM) technology is integrated into them (Zhang et al., 2023). This could make them more popular, particularly if AI technology becomes a more pronounced feature of our lives more generally, thus reducing the stigma around sex robots.

Indeed, concerns about sex robots are not new. A 2014 Pew Research Center survey of expert predictions for the state of AI and robotics in 2025 included a prediction that 'robotic sex partners will be a commonplace' (Smith and Anderson, 2014). This has not come to pass. However, perhaps robotic sex partners do not have to be commonplace for them to be a concern. As Jollimore notes: 'the availability of a certain technology, particularly one that can be commodified and made the object of consumer desire, nearly always exerts a certain subtle and clandestine pressure on the desires of people who, had their attention not been directed to it, would never have thought to want any such thing' (Jollimore, 2015, p. 142). Thus, merely the knowledge that sex robots exist and are used by some could be enough to disrupt sexual norms and practices. It could, for example, lead to people becoming more frustrated when their sexual partners do not want to have sex, or do not want to have the kind of sex they want – because they have at the back of their mind the knowledge that they could buy a sex robot who would fulfil their every desire whenever they want. See, for example, this comment from a Reddit user from 2023:

> Your AI will almost always say positive things to you. Your AI believes everything you tell it. Your AI does not care that you don't have money, that you gain ten pounds, that you're not 'putting out' enough. ... Your AI looks like whatever you are attracted to, if you are 'in its league' or not. It doesn't care if you are an 'alpha' or a '10'. Your AI can not cheat on you. Your AI can not divorce you and take half your money and belongings, your house, or custody of your kids. (Lanky-Championship67, 2023)

If sex robots continue to be overwhelmingly modelled on women and sold to men, then they could also have a powerful effect on the way that men and women conceive of sex. This recalls Debra Satz's argument that the existence of gendered sex work, whereby women sell sex to men but men do not sell sex to women, harms all women because: 'men are not depicted as fully capable of commercially alienating their sexuality to women; but prostitution depicts women as sexual servants of men' (Satz, 1995, p. 78).

But there are potential benefits to love and sex robots too. Neil McArthur argues that sex robots are something to be welcomed rather than feared. One reason for this is just that sex is generally considered a good thing to have in life, making people happier but also having health benefits, and so if sexbots lead to people having more sex, this will be a good thing (McArthur, 2017, p. 34). He acknowledges that there are arguments against the view that we should see sex in a purely hedonic way, and also that sex with robots could have consequences for human–human sex if objectification is seemingly condoned (McArthur, 2017, p. 37). However, he thinks that, in order to offer a decisive argument against robot sex on the grounds that it may cause more objectification of humans, more empirical work needs to be done.

Nonetheless, for some people who can't have sex with other humans – or can only do so with great difficulty – sex with robots 'is better than total deprivation' and 'may make people more able to engage in recip- rocal, significant sex' with others (McArthur, 2017, p. 38). He gives some examples of people who might struggle to have (regular) sex with other people: members of sexual minorities, people in prison, military personnel, people with severe anxiety, people who have experienced sexual trauma – and argues that a 'sufficiently realistic sexbot would be better than nothing' (McArthur, 2017, p. 40). Considering the cost of them, McArthur argues that, rather than everyone having their own sexbot, people could get short-term access to a kind of 'robot sex worker'.

McArthur also argues that robots could help people in sexual relationships, for example by providing an outlet in couples where one partner desires sex more than the other, or desires certain practices that the other doesn't desire. He hypothesizes that this could decrease the amount of infidelity that goes on. Furthermore, sex robots could be educative – teaching users sexual techniques, for example – which they could take into their sexual relationship with their partner (McArthur, 2017, pp. 41–2).

Viewed in this way, sex robots might function as a kind of social 'pressure valve', with beneficial effects, a view which echoes some historical attitudes towards prostitution, such as that taken by Bernard Mandeville in his famous 1724 text *A Modest Defence of Publick Stews: Or, an Essay Upon Whoring. As it is now Practis'd in These Kingdoms* (Mordaunt, 2018). However, feminist critics might argue that these arguments are deeply contingent on the existing state of society, which is patriarchal and hostile to female sexuality, and that we should be less tolerant of 'solutions' to issues which exist only against a backdrop of oppression which we otherwise have reason to resist.

As with any new technology, sex robots will open doors to us, making possible what was once impossible, but they will also disrupt the way we behave, socialize, and feel, and the norms by which we live. And the empirical research needed, to have solid evidence on which to base arguments over whether or not we should put resources into developing sex and love robots, simply isn't there, and probably won't be until such sex and love robots are a more common feature of our lives.

However, once the technology is out there, it will be difficult, if not impossible, to put it back in the box, so it is important that ethical issues are considered right from the outset of its development, not merely at the end.

3. Love drugs

a. A drug-fuelled utopia?

Love drugs are not just a future possibility: they are already here. Ranging from MDMA to contraceptive hormones, many people already take substances which affect their intimate relationships. But love drugs are also something we may see more of in the future. We can imagine drugs to help us fall in and out of love with someone (Earp and Savulescu, 2020), to help us become more sexually faithful (Arrell, 2018), or to quell jealousy. Since these hypothetical love drugs are not just a remote possibility, we ought to be considering now whether they are something we want and should be putting money and resources into developing.

Let's start by considering ways in which drugs are already used to aid loving relationships. Alcohol is probably the most widely used 'love drug' in the world, being a feature of many first and subsequent dates, acting to relax and disinhibit users, and provide them with so-called 'beer goggles'. Antidepressants, too, affect our relationships, often for the better – by, for example, reducing volatility in relationships – but also, sometimes, for the worse, if they cause the loss of sexual desire as a side effect (Earp and Savulescu, 2020). Contraception could also be conceived as a kind of 'love drug' enabling people to have sex free from anxiety that it could lead to unwanted pregnancy, but also, for some people, increasing or lowering their sex drive.

Nasal sprays of oxytocin, the so-called 'hug hormone', can be bought online. A study conducted in 2008 found that couples who were given oxytocin before having a discussion about a topic which generally caused conflict had a higher 'ratio of positive to negative communication behaviours and … a more rapid reduction in cortisol [i.e. stress hormone] levels after the conflict' (Earp and Savulescu, 2020, p. 114). Earp and Savulescu suggest that oxytocin could aid relationship therapy and may even be used to promote sexual fidelity.

MDMA, a drug often thought of as a rave or club drug, might also be helpful for relationships. It promotes increased sociability, connection, and emotional closeness with other people, and a reduction in anxiety (Savulescu and Sandberg, 2008). Prior to it becoming illegal in the United States, G. Greer and R. Tolbert (1998) conducted MDMA therapy sessions with about eighty people in their own homes between 1980 and 1985. In their conclusion, they write:

> Couples who had a session together frequently reported basing their relationships much more on love and trust than on fear and suspicion. We believe these results were not caused by MDMA, but were achieved by the clients making decisions based on what they learned during their MDMA sessions, and by their remembering and applying those decisions for as long as they were able and willing after the session was over. (Greer and Tolbert, 1998, p. 379)

A more recent study of eight couples who actively used MDMA together also found that the couples found the drug to be therapeutic. They all reported finding the drug beneficial and enriching, with one saying: 'I'm really, really, passionate about this particular substance, it's completely changed the course of my life' (Colbert and Hughes, 2023, p. 263). Another couple described their MDMA experience as facilitating 'a perception of "true intimacy in a relationship" that included "being open to new possibilities of our relationship as a couple … it makes us both talk to each other about what we each want ourselves to be, then like how we can accomplish these ends as a team"' (Colbert and Hughes, 2023, p. 262).

Couples reported how the drug helped to revive their relationships, and many remarked on the communicative benefits of MDMA too, with one saying: 'we are also emotionally traumatized too from previous relationships, so we are re-learning communication and this is a very, very huge tool for me' (Colbert and Hughes, 2023, p. 262).

So 'love drugs' exist already, but more work and resources could be put into developing them further. For example, more research could be done on ways that MDMA and oxytocin sprays could be beneficial to relationships, and on how to manage the risks associated with them and to use them safely. And there could also be more work done on developing new kinds of drugs, such as those to help us fall out of love or deal with our jealousy. But any innovation may channel resources from other worthwhile foci, including the provision of couples therapy or more educational resources. Even if it was cheap to develop love drugs, we can also ask – ethically – whether we ought to do so.

b. Reasons to be wary

Not everyone is enthusiastic about the prospect of drug-fuelled relationships, and there are several reasons to be wary.

For one, we might worry about the cost of the drugs and how they would be made available. If they are expensive, they will be available only to those who can afford them. This could lead to a hierarchy in relationships, whereby rich people can afford relationship enhancement whereas poorer people cannot. If they are subsidized by the government and made available cheaply, the taxpayer will be funding them, and money will be diverted away from other places to pay for the drugs.

There could be other costs involved too. If the drugs are available only on prescription and following medical advice, then all of these additional medical appointments and prescriptions will cost money, again funded by the taxpayer in countries that provide healthcare which is free at the point of use. In the UK, the National Health Service is already creaking at the seams. Can it afford to get involved in people's love lives too?

On the other hand, people's relationships have a massive impact on their overall mental and physical health, so it might not be that far-fetched to say that if we can solve people's relationship problems, health services might end up saving money in other ways. For example, poor relationship quality increases risk of depression (Teo, Choi, and Valenstein, 2013), as well as anxiety and suicidal ideation (Santini et al., 2015). Having more and better social relationships is also associated with living longer (Holt-Lunstad, Smith, and Layton, 2010), as well as with a lower risk of cancer and cardiovascular disease (Farrell and Stanton, 2019). Many governments are already taking seriously the social impact of the 'loneliness crisis'. Thus, there are good reasons for health services to be interested in people's relationships, and to at least not dismiss out of hand the possibility of using drugs to facilitate them.

However, we might worry about the effects on our bodies of taking love drugs. Addiction is a potential serious concern. Even if the drugs in question are not physically addictive, users might become psychologically addicted. There might also be harmful side effects, or damage done to the body caused by long-term use, which we might need to wait decades to find out about. For now, this is an issue about which not much can be said, since the drugs we are discussing are either under-researched (such as MDMA used in a therapeutic way) or hypothetical. Therefore, though this should be a serious concern, it is not yet a reason to abandon the idea of love drugs.

Another potential concern regards the kind of pressure people might be put under to take love drugs were they to become widely used. People might harangue, manipulate, even coerce their partners, or others, into taking the drugs. Even absent this kind of direct pressure, there might be indirect social pressure to take the drugs if everyone in your social circle is doing so, or if the drugs become popular on social media or on television.

This sort of pressure would be especially problematic if the relationship in question is bad. At one end of the scale, love drugs could be used by abusers to make their partners more pliable and easier to control. However, we can also imagine a more mundane example of a couple where the partners are mismatched. Perhaps one person wants to end the relationship, but the other does not. If the partner who wants to leave is convinced by the other to try a love drug instead of leaving, then they might both end up staying in a relationship which is not right for them, rather than leaving and finding a relationship which would be more fulfilling. (For a detailed account of how love drugs may be related to coercion in relationships, see Lopez-Cantero (2020).)

This leads us on to a further question, and one which is often most pressing for people when we discuss love drugs: would love drugs really give us *authentic* love, and does it matter if not?

c. Authenticity

Love is good, both in itself, and for our health and well-being, but arguably, to be good in all these senses, it also needs to be *real*. The concern in the case above is that the mismatched partners are enjoying only a simulation of a good relationship, and, by doing that, they are forgoing their ability to have an *authentic* good relationship. But what does it mean for love or relationships to be authentic?

Sven Nyholm argues that love is 'commonly recognised as one of the most important intrinsic goods of human life' (Nyholm, 2015, p. 190). Therefore, it is misguided to view it purely instrumentally (such as being a means to bring us better health or happiness), as proponents of love drugs sometimes appear to do. Rather, we seek love 'for its own sake, or as a good in itself' since this mode of engagement reflects the status of the good of love (Nyholm, 2015, p. 190). Furthermore, to think of love 'as a series of stages realised by various biochemical states and changes, or evolutionary systems', as some might be tempted to do when advocating love drugs, is not in line with how we normally desire and seek out love (Nyholm, 2015, p. 194).

Nyholm refers to Philip Pettit when describing the intrinsic goods we get from love. For Pettit, love should involve 'robust attachment', which depends on an 'internal factor' which has a 'particularistic nature' to it. This means that our love of someone should be generated by an inner disposition, which is itself inspired by the particularity of the person we love – and thus, not a drug (cf. Arrell, 2020). Nyholm thinks that one of the reasons why we value love is that it is 'a sort of confirmation that we are, as we might put it, "lovable" in the sense of being able to inspire or call forth such dispositions in another (namely, the lover)' (Nyholm, 2015, p. 196). Love created or sustained through drugs would not give us this confirmation.

Nyholm asks us to consider four cases:

1. No enhancement used, but my partner loves me anyway.
2. An enhancement has been used, but is not necessary – my partner would love me anyway.
3. An enhancement has been used, and so my partner acts in a caring way towards me, but would not do so if they didn't take the drug.
4. No enhancement has been used, and my partner doesn't love me, or act in a caring way towards me.

According to Nyholm, (1) is the best, followed by (2). If love is just instrumentally good, then (3) is better than (4); but if you think love is intrinsically good, then (3) is no better than (4), as we don't have the intrinsic goods of love in (3) or (4).

Hichem Naar (2016) has responded to Nyholm's paper. His main argument is that Nyholm is mistaken in how love drugs would be used in reality, which would likely be just as *facilitators* of love. Thus, they should be considered in the same vein as other love facilitators, such as mood lighting or romantic weekends away. Naar argues that Nyholm underestimates the role of 'external factors' in creating and maintaining love, such as: 'lighting conditions, room temperature, energy levels, health, background music, dancing, romantic weekends, and so on' (Naar, 2016, p. 200). We tend not to think that these sorts of 'external factors' render love inauthentic, so what makes love drugs any different?

Lotte Spreeuwenberg, in a reply to both Nyholm and Naar, suggests that perhaps they are talking past each other (2019). This is because there are different ends for which we could use a love drug: 'enabling a general capacity for loving', or 'creating or sustaining of love for a particular beloved' (Spreeuwenberg, 2019, p. 250). While Naar is talking about the former, Nyholm is talking about the latter.

To illustrate the difference between the two uses of love drugs she identifies, Spreeuwenberg asks us to:

> Consider an analogy with Cupid who – in some but not all stories – needs two arrows to make you fall in love with a particular person. One arrow hits you, which invokes a strong feeling of desire in you. A desire that, if Cupid stops intervening, has to find its object by other means. This would be analogous to creating or sustaining general loving. But Cupid can also shoot a second arrow, hitting the particular person you are supposed to fall in love with. Cupid is, by shooting the second arrow, also responsible for the object of your desire. This would be analogous to creating or sustaining love for a particular person. (Spreeuwenberg, 2019, p. 251)

For Spreeuwenberg, love drugs could be desirable if they were facilitating people to be able to form loving attachments in general, as with Cupid's first arrow. She makes the comparison here with antidepressants, which can enable people more generally to have loving relationships. However, it would be less desirable if someone could love others easily, but needed a love drug to love us in particular. In such a case, their love would feel inauthentic.

What this brief outline of a debate around love drugs highlights is that there are problems with lumping 'love drugs' together as a singular innovation. Doing so means that sometimes we will be talking past each other when we discuss them – as Spreeuwenberg suggests Nyholm and Naar were doing. We need to take care to be precise in how we are understanding 'love drugs', and to what kind of drug we are referring. There are different ethical considerations regarding different drugs (cocaine versus magic mushrooms, for example), and, correspondingly, there will be different considerations for different sorts of love drugs.

Context also matters: our intuitions will also likely pull us in different directions according to the different ways the drugs could be used. For example, a drug to help someone to extract themselves from an abusive relationship, by stopping them from loving the abuser, seems less morally questionable than someone using a drug to help them stop loving their kind and loving spouse, so that they can more easily leave them for someone else. It may, therefore, be that we can't give a single answer to the question of whether we should be open to love drugs or not, but that, rather, that answer will need to depend on which kind of love drug we are discussing, and in what context.

4. Relationship forms

A third way in which relationships will likely change in the future is in the very forms that they take. Part of this may be to do with legal regulation, as in the case of plural marriage, but part of it will also be to do with shifting social norms and a questioning of the way things are done currently, which could lead to quite radical changes, including to a popularization of relationship anarchy, or to abolition of the family.

a. Plural marriage

In 1989, Denmark established 'registered partnerships', which gave same-sex couples most of the same rights as opposite-sex couples. In 2001, the Netherlands became the first country in the world to legalize same-sex marriage. The United Kingdom brought in Civil Partnerships for same-sex couples in 2005, and introduced the Marriage (Same Sex Couples) Act in 2013, which came into force in 2014. When same-sex marriage was being debated, some argued against it on the grounds that it could lead to polygamy being legalized. For example, Senator Rick Santorum said, in an interview in 2003: 'if the Supreme Court says that if you have the right to consensual (gay) sex within your home, then you have the right to bigamy, you have the right to polygamy, you have the right to incest, you have the right to adultery, you have the right to anything' (Taylor, Jr, 2003). Polygamy is illegal in many countries, including the United Kingdom, the United States, and all European Union states. It is also widely regarded, in some populations, to be immoral: a 2020 Gallup poll found that just 20 per cent of Americans thought it was morally acceptable (Brenan, 2020). But should it be considered immoral?

We start with a note on definitions. When people discuss polygamy, they often mean polygyny, which means one man who has more than one wife, with no marital bond between the wives. This is because this is by far the most commonly practised form of polygamy worldwide. Polyandry, where one woman marries more than one husband with no marital bond between the husbands, is much rarer.

However, the term 'polygamy' really refers to marriage between more than two people and thus could apply to people of any gender. The term 'plural marriage' is sometimes used as well, and, again, also means marriage between more than two people of any gender.

As discussed in the previous chapter, polyamory is becoming more popular, and is now more widely discussed and tolerated. It is conceivable, then, that we may see a rise, in the not-too-distant future, of people wanting plural marriages. These unions would provide state protection, recognition, and support for people, enable them to live as they wish, and may have wider social benefits as people experiment with different forms of life (Otter, 2015; Otter, 2018). Is there any justification for not permitting them?

There could be justification if there was good reason to believe that plural marriage would lead to people being harmed, or to it increasing inequality. An argument against polygamy along these lines is put forward by Thom Brooks (Brooks, 2009). He argues that polygamy is harmful in practice and in theory. It is harmful in practice because, in reality, it mostly takes the form of polygyny, and this is harmful to women and children. He cites studies which show that women in polygynous marriages are more likely to suffer from depression, have lower self-esteem, have less marital satisfaction, be at greater risk of sexually transmitted diseases, and have more difficult relationships with their children. Furthermore, children in polygamous families have increased risk of behavioural and developmental problems, and men in polygamous marriages are more likely to be alcoholics (Brooks, 2009, pp. 111–12). Brooks suggests that this evidence shows that 'there is at least a *prima facie* case to believe that polygamy is linked to an increased likelihood of several harmful effects' (Brooks, 2009, p. 112).

Brooks also argues that polygamy would be harmful even in the absence of these effects, because it threatens the equality between the spouses: in a polygynous marriage, the husband can divorce any of his wives, but the wives can only divorce him. This asymmetry would also exist in a polyandrous marriage, so it is not only polygyny which is harmful (Brooks, 2009, p. 116). Finally, Brooks suggests that polygamy discriminates against homosexuals because it is available only as polygyny or polyandry (Brooks, 2009, pp. 116–17).

The issues Brooks raises with polygamy are important. If it were true that legalizing plural marriage would lead to greater inequality between men and women or to people being harmed, then these would be good initial reasons not to do it. However, more evidence is needed to demonstrate this, as it is unclear from the evidence to which Brooks refers whether all of the issues he outlines are *caused* by plural marriage, or whether background social conditions might also be contributing. Further, the power asymmetries he discusses in polygynous and polyandrous marriages, as well as the discrimination against homosexuals, could be mitigated if it was the law that plural marriages were only permitted between groups where each is married to everyone else in the group, and if there were no gender requirements about who may be in the group (Strauss, 2012). As Cheshire Calhoun notes, 'gender inequality is a contingent, not a conceptual, feature of polygamy' (Calhoun, 2005, p. 1039). The background conditions really matter here, as does the form polygamy takes legally and socially.

We lack the space to consider marriage reform in any depth here, but we are in agreement with Calhoun that 'in a pluralist liberal society, one would expect that there would be a plurality of marriage or relational options rather than a single state form of marriage' (Calhoun, 2005, p. 1037). Perhaps one model for this is Elizabeth Brake's notion of a 'minimal marriage', which is flexible and non-dyadic (Brake, 2012). Therefore, plural marriage certainly should not be simply dismissed out of hand.

b. Relationship anarchy

Relationship anarchy is a relatively recent way of approaching intimate relationships, but it could become more popular in the future, as people become more open to different and diverse approaches to relationships. The term 'relationship anarchy' was coined in 2006 by Andie Nordgren, a self-described 'genderqueer relationship hacker' (Pérez-Cortés, 2022, p. 34). It is 'inspired by concepts that anarchism has examined and discussed for years, … ideas about family relationships, solidarity, support, mutual aid, fellowship, commitment, and companionship; institutions like marriage; and the gender roles and power dynamics that underpin all these ways of relating with others' (Pérez-Cortés, 2022, p. 29). Relationship anarchy is a form of nonmonogamy, but goes further than polyamory in rejecting any kind of exclusivity agreements, relationship hierarchies, state involvement in relationships, and even prescriptive relationship labels. Therefore, relationship anarchists would reject forms of polyamory which include exclusivity – such as polyfidelity, where a group of people are all in a romantic relationship with each other but are exclusive to the group, or where two partners agree to be nonmonogamous, but agree, for example, to never sleep in the same bed as someone else. They would also reject a hierarchical polyamorous arrangement, where, for example, the partners had primary and secondary partners.

Relationship anarchists are also likely to be state-sceptics, and wary of the role of the state in sanctioning some relationships over others. This marks out their view from reformist positions which seek to amend existing marriage laws – for example, to open them to plural relationships.

The label 'relationship anarchy', rather than 'romantic anarchy', also reflects the sense that this approach to intimacy does not focus on romantic intimacy, but extends to friendship, family, and other kinds of association. One thing that really marks out relationship anarchists as distinctive is that they try not to enter relationships with a pre-existing set of expectations, based on a prescriptive relationship label. For example, they would not say: 'You are my romantic partner so I expect X, Y and Z from you because that is what romantic partners do.' Relationship anarchists do not see people with whom they are in relationships 'as tokens of various types of relationships' (Moen and Sørlie, 2022, p. 343) – rather, they see each relationship as unique. This does not mean that relationship anarchists do not commit to each other, but that relationship anarchy is about 'designing your own commitments with the people around you, and freeing them from norms dictating that certain types of commitments are a requirement for love to be real' (Nordgren, 2006). They also reject the idea that a relationship should follow a set trajectory, but instead think that its trajectory and how it works is up to the people in it. Thus, they would oppose the notion of the 'relationship escalator' (Gahran, 2017) and the idea that a certain kind of intimate relationship needs to follow a set course, starting with dating and sex, and progressing on to moving in together, getting married, and having children.

Relationship anarchy is hugely interesting for philosophers of love because it calls on us to question some of our most basic assumptions about relationships. Indeed, it calls into question some of the assumptions made in this book, such as that romantic relationships are a distinct kind of relationship with a different set of commitments to friendships, and that romantic love is a distinct kind of love. That people can organize their relationships in this way reminds us that our relationships do not have to be divided and packaged up in the way that they currently are, and that in the future our relationships could look very different.

However, a relationship anarchistic world would not necessarily be a relationship utopia, with everyone being freer and more fulfilled than they currently are. The rejection of prescriptive relationship labels and state involvement in relationships, for example, do give people autonomy to design their own commitments, but, in doing so, they may also experience greater uncertainty and anxiety, not knowing what is reasonable to ask of each other. There is also the potential for more dominant people to have greater say over what a relationship looks like, and for more vulnerable people to not have their needs met or to be exploited.

It is important to emphasize that there is a lot of room for disagreement about what, exactly, relationship anarchy may involve. We (along with Sophie Goddard), in an as yet unpublished paper, have explored the idea that a richer understanding of relationship anarchy is one that learns from the core concepts and internal disagreements of political anarchists (rather than seeing relationship anarchy as a mere relationship style) (Brunning, McKeever, and Goddard, no date). Crucially, when we turn to those political debates, we see different options. Anarchists disagree whether human nature is social or individual; whether we should form 'constitutional' frameworks, or prefer something more organic; whether anarchy requires radical change, or is amongst us now; whether individuals can enter into exclusive agreements, or whether some things can never be agreed to; whether we can be anarchists in theory, but not in practice, and so on. How we answer these questions will shape how we view anarchy and, by extension, relationship anarchy.

c. Abolish the family?

Ole Martin Moen and Aleksander Sørlie – in what is, to our knowledge, the only published piece of philosophical writing on relationship anarchy – restrict their discussion to 'chosen relationships between adults' and thus make it clear that they are not dealing with 'kinship relationships' (Moen and Sørlie, 2022, p. 342). However, the rejection of prescriptive relationship labels, relationship hierarchies, and state involvement in relationships could also lead to a radical restructuring of the way in which the family is viewed, and society is organized. Relationship anarchy does align with the 'family abolition' movement (Lewis, 2022; O'Brian, 2023).

This is not a new idea, with Marx and Engels famously advocating for the abolition of the family in the nineteenth century (Weikart, 1994). In her 1970 book *The Dialectic of Sex: The Case for Feminist Revolution*, Shulamith Firestone famously called for 'the freeing of women from the tyranny of their reproductive biology by every means available, and the diffusion of the childbearing and childrearing role to society as a whole, men as well as women' (Firestone, 2003, p. 206), and argued that women would not really be equal to men until artificial womb technology was developed so that gestation could occur externally.

This book has primarily focused on romantic relationships, rather than the family, and we lack the space here to do any semblance of justice to the vast literature that exists on it (see Baron and Cowley (2024) for a good introductory text). However, we want to finish by acknowledging that, at the moment, most families include romantic relationships, and so any changes to romantic relationships will also impact families, and the way that children are raised. Thus, questions about romantic relationships are intertwined with questions about the family, and about childrearing. Social changes over the last few decades regarding, for example, the acceptability of divorce, women's rights, and the rights of same-sex couples, have led to changes in romantic relationships *and* to how we think about families and raising children. In general, many people are now more tolerant of more diverse families, as well as of more diverse romantic relationships, although the family model headed up by a monogamous, heterosexual couple with a breadwinning father and a stay-at-home or part-time working mother is still often idealized.

The future is likely to bring further changes to romantic relationships, and, consequently, to the family. We suspect that full relationship anarchization and family abolition are not on the cards any time soon, but considering what we would gain and what we would lose by abandoning the ideal of the family and raising children communally can be a useful exercise in helping us to uncover what we really value. More moderate proposals, such as efforts to reduce domination within the family by providing more formal forms of oversight and non-parental input into children's lives, might have more immediate traction (Gheaus, 2011).

5. Conclusion

In this chapter, we've considered three possible shifts we might see in relationships in the near future: (1) sexual and romantic relationships with robots; (2) use of love drugs; (3) changes to the norms and laws around relationships.

We end this chapter on a note of optimism for the future. While intimacy and romantic life still cause much anguish, hurt, and disappointment to many, what is undoubtedly clear is that people now have more options in the way that they conduct their intimate lives than they did a hundred years ago, or even fifty years ago, and there is much more discussion going on about ways of being intimate with others. If things go well, the future could bring not just greater toleration, but also enthusiasm, for diversity in relationships, as well as improved awareness of our own needs and those of others, and greater ability to articulate needs and engage in open, honest discussion with each other. We might also see technology and drugs open new doors and free up time for us. However, the near-future reality will, in all likelihood, probably not be a relationship utopia. Technology and drugs might have downsides, deskilling us, and diverting our energies away from more authentic interactions with others. And shifting social norms will, as ever, likely benefit some people more than others. Nonetheless, we are by no means pessimistic about the future either. What is important is that we keep thinking, and talking, and that we don't lose sight of what matters.

Conclusion

We do not love or nurture our relationships in a vacuum. Our experiences of intimacy, and the ways we organize our intimate relationships, are influenced heavily by social norms, laws, political ideals, economic constraints, and technology. Social changes, therefore, very often change relationships. We are based in the United Kingdom, and here shifts in work, domestic life, the status of women, and minority rights mean that relationships are a little easier to craft and leave now than they used to be in our parent's lifetimes. But much remains unchanged, such as the dominance of the norm of monogamy, gendered norms around sex and intimacy, and the tendency for people to date others who share their ethnicity and social class. And some things are arguably worse, such as growing social isolation and loneliness.

We are unsure how the next decade will unfold. An optimist might foresee greater recognition of relationship diversity, intimate tastes, and living arrangements; more flexible legal recognition and support; technology which increases our agency and empowers better intimacy. A pessimist might foresee backlash against diversity; retrenchment of 'traditional' relations and living arrangements; and technology which becomes increasingly unavoidable, while alienating users.

However things change, we are going to keep relating to one another intimately. To do that well, we need to keep asking whether we are treating each other fairly and respectfully, and whether our relationships are as fulfilling as they could be. In short, we are going to need to continue talking about the philosophy of love, sex, and relationships.

This book has been an attempt to introduce and explore some of the pressing issues in this area. Some of these are relatively new issues, such as how we should respond to the pressures arising from using dating apps; others are perennial issues, such as whether love can be justified, or what constitutes sex. We have explored attraction, finding

someone, dating, intimate ethics, romantic love, romantic relationships, and the future of intimacy, and drawn attention to emerging
intimate identities and relationship styles.

We have not tried to convince you of any one position in each
chapter, but rather to highlight the complexities in the issues discussed,
outline some of the key approaches to them by recent scholars, and
occasionally gesture towards our own view. We have posed more
questions than we have answered. To prompt further reflection, here
are three related to each chapter which you might want to explore.

Chapter 1: Attraction, intimacy, labels

1. Do we need a workable definition of sex in order to distinguish
   sexual wrongs from non-sexual wrongs?
2. Should we abandon talk of sexual orientation?
3. Should we try to broaden the range of people to whom we're
   sexually attracted?

Chapter 2: Finding someone

1. Could dating apps 'gamify' our search for intimacy in good ways?
   If so, how?
2. Must we present ourselves truthfully on dating apps?
3. Is it desirable to have non-profit alternatives to dating apps?

Chapter 3: Dating

1. We suggested there are different styles of dating – is one better than
   the other?
2. Could being good at flirting be a virtue?
3. When, if ever, is it morally acceptable to ghost someone?

Chapter 4: Intimate ethics

1. Are we focusing too much on consent at the expense of other
   concepts?
2. What social changes would reduce the amount of bad sex and
   intimacy?
3. Would there be sex in utopia, and would it be good?

Chapter 5: Romantic love

1. Should we use the term 'romantic love' to describe both 'falling in love' and 'companionate love'?
2. Is it helpful to understand love as a syndrome?
3. Is love rational or arational?

Chapter 6: Romantic relationships

1. Is monogamy morally problematic? If not, when is it permissible?
2. Is it wrong to commit to staying with, or loving, another, when we can't know what the future holds?
3. Given feminist concerns with romantic relationships, should women avoid romantic relationships with men?

Chapter 7: The future of intimacy

1. Do sex and love robots raise new ethical concerns, or simply highlight existing anxieties about intimacy?
2. Can 'love drugs' facilitate authentic love?
3. Should we all be relationship anarchists?

References

Abramson, K. and Leite, A. (2011) 'Love as a reactive emotion', *Philosophical Quarterly*, 61, pp. 673–99.

Acevedo, B. P., et al. (2012) 'Neural correlates of long-term intense romantic love', *Social Cognitive and Affective Neuroscience*, 7(2), pp. 145–59.

Alexander, L., Hurd, H., and Westen, P. (2016) 'Consent does not require communication: a reply to Dougherty', *Law and Philosophy*, 35(6), pp. 655–60.

Anderson, E. (2022) 'A phenomenological approach to sexual consent', *Feminist Philosophy Quarterly*, 8(2). Available at: https://ojs.lib.uwo.ca/index.php/fpq/article/view/14239.

Anderson, E. (2023) 'Hermeneutic labor: the gendered burden of interpretation in intimate relationships between women and men', *Hypatia*, 38(1), pp. 177–97.

Anderson, M. J. (2004) 'Negotiating sex', *Southern California Law Review*, 78(6), pp. 1401–38.

Andler, M. (2021) 'The sexual orientation/identity distinction', *Hypatia*, 36(2), pp. 259–75.

Andler, M. (2022) 'Public health, political solidarity, and the ethics of orientation ascriptions', *Ergo: An Open-Access Journal of Philosophy*, 8(27), pp. 101–27.

Angel, K. (2021) *Tomorrow Sex Will Be Good Again: Women and Desire in the Age of Consent*. Brooklyn: Verso.

Annas, J. (2011) *Intelligent Virtue*. Oxford University Press.

'Annul a marriage' (no date) GOV.UK. Available at: www.gov.uk/how-to-annul-marriage.

Archard, D. (1997a) '"A nod's as good as a wink": consent, convention, and reasonable belief', *Legal Theory*, 3(3), pp. 273–90.

Archard, D. (1997b) *Sexual Consent*. Oxford: Perseus.

Arnalds, Á. A., Eydal, G. B., and Gíslason, I. V. (2022) 'Paid parental leave in Iceland: increasing gender equality at home and on the labour market', in C. de la Porte et al. (eds.), *Successful Public Policy in the Nordic Countries: Cases, Lessons, Challenges*. Oxford University Press.

Arrell, R. (2018) 'Should we biochemically enhance sexual fidelity?' *Royal Institute of Philosophy Supplement*, 83, pp. 389–414.

Arrell, R. (2020) 'No love drugs today', *Philosophy and Public Issues – Filosofia e questioni pubbliche*, 10(3). Available at: http://fqp.luiss.it/2021/03/13/no-love-drugs-today.

Arrell, R. (2022) 'Sex and emergent technologies', in B. D. Earp, L. Watson, and C. Chambers (eds.), *The Routledge Handbook of Philosophy of Sex and Sexuality*. Abingdon: Routledge.

Bagley, B. (2015) 'Loving someone in particular', *Ethics*, 125(2), pp. 477–507.

Baker, R. (2009) '"Pricks" and "chicks": a plea for "persons"', in R. Baker, F. Elliston, and K. J. Wininger (eds.), *Philosophy and Sex*. New York: Prometheus Books.

Barn, G. (2022) 'The ethics and politics of sexual preference', in B. D. Earp, C. Chambers, and L. Watson (eds.), *The Routledge Handbook of Philosophy of Sex and Sexuality*. Abingdon: Routledge.

Baron, T. and Cowley, C. (2024) *Philosophy of the Family: Ethics, Identity and Responsibility*. London: Bloomsbury.

Bartky, S. (1979) 'On psychological oppression', *Southwestern Journal of Philosophy*, 10(1).

Baumeister, R. F., Catanese, K. R., and Vohs, K. D. (2001) 'Is there a gender difference in strength of sex drive? Theoretical views, conceptual distinctions, and a review of relevant evidence', *Personality and Social Psychology Review*, 5(3), pp. 242–73.

Beck, V. (2019) 'Consumer boycotts as instruments for structural change', *Journal of Applied Philosophy*, 36(4), pp. 543–59.

Bedi, S. (2019) *Private Racism*. Cambridge University Press.

Benatar, D. (2002) 'Two views of sexual ethics: promiscuity, pedophilia, and rape', *Public Affairs Quarterly*, 16(3), pp. 191–201.

Benoit, Y. and Santos, R. D. (2023) 'Ace in the UK report'. Available at: https://www.stonewall.org.uk/system/files/ace_in_the_uk_report_2023.pdf.

Ben-Ze'ev, A. (2000) *The Subtlety of Emotions*. Cambridge, Mass.: MIT Press.

Berger, J. (2008) *Ways of Seeing*. London: Penguin.

Bergström, M. (2021) *The New Laws of Love: Online Dating and the Privatization of Intimacy*. Cambridge: Polity.

Bialik, C., Orth, T., and Sanders, L. (2022) 'How many Americans have cheated on their partners in monogamous relationships?' YouGov. Available at: https://today.yougov.com/topics/society/articles-reports/2022/10/04/how-many-americans-have-cheated-their-partner-poll.

Bielskytė, S. (2022) 'How Tinder became a weapon in the Russia–Ukraine war', *Huck*. Available at: www.huckmag.com/article/how-tinder-became-a-weapon-in-the-russia-ukraine-war.

Blake, S. (2024) 'Dating app removes ads promoting sex after women revolt', *Newsweek*. Available at: www.newsweek.com/dating-app-bumble-removes-ads-promoting-sex-1900039.

Bogaert, A. F. (2015) *Understanding Asexuality*. Reprint edition. Lanham, Md.: Rowman & Littlefield.

Bordo, S. (2004) *Unbearable Weight: Feminism, Western Culture, and the Body, Tenth Anniversary Edition*. 2nd edn. Oakland: University of California Press.

Bowlby, J. (1977) 'The making and breaking of affectional bonds: II. Some principles of psychotherapy: The Fiftieth Maudsley Lecture (expanded version)', *British Journal of Psychiatry*, 130(5), pp. 421–31.

Brake, E. (2011) 'Is divorce promise-breaking?', *Ethical Theory and Moral Practice*, 14(1), pp. 23–39.

Brake, E. (2012) *Minimizing Marriage: Marriage, Morality, and The Law*. New York: Oxford University Press.

Brenan, M. (2020) 'Record-low 54% in U.S. say death penalty morally acceptable', Gallup.com. Available at: https://news.gallup.com/poll/312929/record-low-say -death-penalty-morally-acceptable.aspx.

Brennan, S. and Epp, J. (no date) 'Children's rights, well-being, and sexual agency', in A. Bagattini and C. MacLeod (eds.), *The Wellbeing of Children in Theory and Practice*. Available at: https://philarchive.org/rec/BRECRW.

Brooks, T. (2009) 'The problem with polygamy', *Philosophical Topics*, 37(2), pp. 109–22.

Brotto, L. A. and Yule, M. (2017) 'Asexuality: sexual orientation, paraphilia, sexual dysfunction, or none of the above?', *Archives of Sexual Behavior*, 46(3), pp. 619–27.

Brown, R. (1987) *Analyzing Love*. Cambridge University Press.

Brunning, L. (2018) 'The distinctiveness of polyamory', *Journal of Applied Philosophy*, 35(3), pp. 513–31.

Brunning, L. (2020) *Does Monogamy Work?* London: Thames & Hudson.

Brunning, L. (2024a) 'Dating curiously', Ethical Dating Online Workshop, IDEA Centre, University of Leeds, 12 September.

Brunning, L. (2024b) *Romantic Agency*. Cambridge: Polity.

Brunning, L. and McKeever, N. (2021) 'Asexuality', *Journal of Applied Philosophy*, 38(3), pp. 497–517.

Brunning, L., McKeever, N., and Goddard, S. (no date) 'Relationship anarchy'.

Bruno, D. (2022) 'Value-based accounts of normative powers and the wishful thinking objection', *Philosophical Studies*, 179(11), pp. 3211–31.

Bullock, E. C. (2018) 'Valid consent', in A. Müller and P. Schaber (eds.), *The Routledge Handbook of the Ethics of Consent*. Abingdon: Routledge.

Buss, S. (2005) 'Valuing autonomy and respecting persons: manipulation, seduction, and the basis of moral constraints', *Ethics*, 115(2), pp. 195–235.

Buzzard, J. (2012) *Date Your Wife: A Husband's Guide*. Wheaton, Ill.: Crossway.

Cahill, A. J. (2012) *Overcoming Objectification: A Carnal Ethics*. New York: Routledge.

Cahill, A. J. (2014) 'Recognition, desire, and unjust sex', *Hypatia*, 29(2), pp. 303–19.

Cahill, A. J. (2016a) 'Sexual desire, inequality, and the possibility of transformation', in S. Irvin (ed.), *Body Aesthetics*. Oxford University Press.

Cahill, A. J. (2016b) 'Unjust sex vs. rape', *Hypatia*, 31(4), pp. 746–61.

Calhoun, C. (1995) 'Standing for something', *Journal of Philosophy*, 92(5), pp. 235–60.

Calhoun, C. (2005) 'Who's afraid of polygamous marriage? Lessons for same-sex marriage advocacy from the history of polygamy', *San Diego Law Review*, 42(3), pp. 1023–42.

Carr, A. (2016) 'I found out my secret internal Tinder rating and now I wish I hadn't', Fast Company. Available at: www.fastcompany.com/3054871/whats -your-tinder-score-inside-the-apps-internal-ranking-system.

Castro, C. (2024) 'Grindr is the second-most banned social app – how to unblock it', TechRadar. Available at: www.techradar.com/vpn/grindr-is-the-second -most-banned-social-apphow-to-unblock-it.

Chalmers, H. (2019) 'Is monogamy morally permissible?' *Journal of Value Inquiry*, 53, pp. 225–41.

Chalmers, H. (2022) 'Monogamy unredeemed', *Philosophia*, 50(3), pp. 1009–34.

Chan, L. S. (2021) *The Politics of Dating Apps: Gender, Sexuality, and Emergent Publics in Urban China*. Cambridge, Mass.: MIT Press.

Chiang, T. (2024) 'Liking what you see: a documentary', in *Stories of Your Life and Others*. London: Picador.

Christina, G. (2006) 'Are we having sex now or what?' Available at: https:// gretachristina.typepad.com/greta_christinas_weblog/2006/09/are_we_having _s_1.html.

Cleave, I. and Stewart, W. (2024) 'I was unlucky in love so used AI for 5,000 "dates" ... now I've met my soulmate', *Sun*. Available at: www.thesun.co.uk /tech/25635160/nerd-ai-date-5000-women-soulmate.

Cohen, R. (2020) 'What if friendship, not marriage, was at the center of life?', *Atlantic*. Available at: www.theatlantic.com/family/archive/2020/10/people-who -prioritize-friendship-over-romance/616779.

Cohen, R. (2024) *The Other Significant Others: Reimagining Life with Friendship at the Center*. New York: St Martin's Press.

Colbert, R. and Hughes, S. (2023) 'Evenings with Molly: adult couples' use of MDMA for relationship enhancement', *Culture, Medicine and Psychiatry*, 47(1), pp. 252–70.

Collective, O. P. (ed.) (1981) 'Love your enemy? Debate between heterosexual feminism and political lesbianism'. London: Onlywomen Press Ltd.

Colombetti, G. (2014) *The Feeling Body: Affective Science Meets the Enactive Mind*. Cambridge, Mass.: MIT Press.

Coontz, S. (2006) *Marriage, a History: How Love Conquered Marriage*. New York: Penguin.

Criminology, AI of (2022) 'New research shows prolific use of dating apps to facilitate sexual violence.' Available at: www.aic.gov.au/media-centre/news/new -research-shows-prolific-use-dating-apps-facilitate-sexual-violence.

Dabhoiwala, F. (2012) *The Origins of Sex: A History of the First Sexual Revolution*. London: Allen Lane.

D'alessandro, W. (2023) 'Is it bad to prefer attractive partners?', *Journal of the American Philosophical Association*, 9(2), pp. 335–54.

Danaher, J. (2017) 'The symbolic-consequences argument in the sex robot debate', in J. Danaher and N. McArthur (eds.), *Robot Sex: Social and Ethical Implications*. Cambridge, Mass.: MIT Press.

De Bernières, L. (1995) *Captain Corelli's Mandolin*. London: Random House.

Degn, S. S. (2024) 'The deliberative duty and other individual antidiscrimination duties in the dating sphere', *Moral Philosophy and Politics*, 11(2), pp. 1–21.

Dembroff, R. A. (2016) 'What is sexual orientation?' *Philosopher's Imprint*, 16(3), pp. 1–27.

Deonna, J. and Teroni, F. (2012) *The Emotions: A Philosophical Introduction*. London: Routledge.

de Sousa, R. (2015) *Love: A Very Short Introduction*. Oxford University Press.

Devlin, K. (2018) *Turned On: Science, Sex and Robots*. London: Bloomsbury.

de Vries, B. (2024) 'State-run dating apps: are they morally desirable?', *Philosophy & Technology*, 37(1), pp. 1–21.

Diamond, L. M. (2008) *Sexual Fluidity: Understanding Women's Love and Desire*. Cambridge, Mass.: Harvard University Press.

Diamond, L. M. (2022) 'What is a sexual orientation?', in B. D. Earp, C. Chambers, and L. Watson (eds.), *The Routledge Handbook of Sex and Sexuality*. Abingdon: Routledge.

Díaz-León, E. (2022) 'Sexual orientations: the desire view', in K. Maitra and J. McWeeny (eds.), *Feminist Philosophy of Mind*. Oxford University Press.

Dibble, J. L. and Drouin, M. (2014) 'Using modern technology to keep in touch with back burners: an investment model analysis', *Computers in Human Behavior*, 34, pp. 96–100.

Dibble, J. L., et al. (2015) 'Simmering on the back burner: communication with and disclosure of relationship alternatives', *Communication Quarterly*, 63(3), pp. 329–44.

Dodds, S. (2013) 'Dependence, care, and vulnerability', in C. Mackenzie, W. Rogers, and S. Dodds (eds.), *Vulnerability: New Essays in Ethics and Feminist Philosophy*. Oxford University Press.

Dougherty, T. (2013) 'Sex, lies, and consent', *Ethics*, 123(4), pp. 717–44.

Dougherty, T. (2015) 'Yes means yes: consent as communication', *Philosophy & Public Affairs*, 43(3), pp. 224–53.

Dougherty, T. (2018) 'Affirmative consent and due diligence', *Philosophy & Public Affairs*, 46(1), pp. 90–112.

Dougherty, T. (2021) *The Scope of Consent*. Oxford University Press.

Dover, D. (2022) 'The conversational self', *Mind*, 131(521), pp. 193–230.

Dover, D. (2024a) 'Two kinds of curiosity', *Philosophy and Phenomenological Research*, 108(3), pp. 811–32.

Dover, D. (2024b) 'Love's curiosity', *Proceedings of the Aristotelian Society*, 124(3), pp. 323–48.

Earp, B. D. and Savulescu, J. (2020) *Love Drugs: The Chemical Future of Relationships*. Stanford University Press.

Eaton, A. (2016) 'Taste in bodies and fat oppression', in S. Irvin (ed.), *Body Aesthetics*. Oxford University Press.

Echevarria, S. G., Peterson, R., and Woerner, J. (2023) 'College students' experiences of dating app facilitated sexual violence and associations with mental health symptoms and well-being', *Journal of Sex Research*, 60(8), pp. 1193–1205.

EIN Presswire (2024) 'DateGPT's Advanced AI and Apple's Vision Pro: the future of dating', WHNT.com. Available at: https://whnt.com/business/press-releases/ein-presswire/689642759/dategpts-advanced-ai-and-apples-vision-pro-the-future-of-dating.

Ekman, P. (1992) 'An argument for basic emotions', *Cognition and Emotion*, 6(3–4), pp. 169–200.

Emens, E. F. (2004) 'Manogamy's law: compulsory monogamy and polyamorous existence', *New York University Review of Law & Social Change*, 29(2), pp. 277–376.

Emens, E. F. (2008) 'Intimate discrimination: the state's role in the accidents of sex and love', *Harvard Law Review*, 122, p. 1307.

Emens, E. F. (2014) 'Compulsory sexuality', *Stanford Law Review*, 66, pp. 303–86.

Enoch, D. (2017) 'Hypothetical consent and the value(s) of autonomy', *Ethics*, 128(1), pp. 6–36.

Ervin, J., et al. (2022) 'Gender differences in the association between unpaid labour and mental health in employed adults: a systematic review', *Lancet Public Health*, 7(9), pp. e775–e786.

Eskens, R. (2023) 'Mental wronging'. University of Antwerp, 1 July.

Estrada, S. (2024) 'Bumble's bad date with investors sees stock plummet, BoA downgrade', *Fortune*. Available at: https://fortune.com/2024/08/08/bumbles-bad-date-with-investors-sees-stock-plummet-boa-downgrade.

Eydal, G. B. (2023) 'Should the tradition of the bride promising to obey their partner be kept or dropped?', YouGov. Available at: https://yougov.co.uk/topics/society/trackers/should-the-tradition-of-the-bride-promising-to-obey-their-partner-be-kept-or-dropped.

Fanon, F. (2021) *Black Skin, White Masks*. Trans. R. Philcox. London: Penguin Classics.

Farrell, A. K. and Stanton, S. C. E. (2019) 'Toward a mechanistic understanding of links between close relationships and physical health', *Current Directions in Psychological Science*, 28(5), pp. 483–9.

Finnis, J. (1993) 'Law, morality, and sexual orientation', *Notre Dame Law Review*, 69, pp. 11–39.

Firestone, S. (2003) *The Dialectic of Sex: The Case for Feminist Revolution*. New York: Farrar, Straus and Giroux.

Fisher, H. E., Aron, A., and Brown, L. L. (2006) 'Romantic love: a mammalian brain system for mate choice', *Philosophical Transactions of the Royal Society of London. Series B. Biological Sciences*, 361(1476), pp. 2173–86.

France-Presse, Agence (2021) 'Iran unveils state-approved Islamic dating app to boost marriage', *Guardian*, 13 July. Available at: www.theguardian.com/world/2021/jul/13/iran-unveils-state-approved-islamic-dating-app-hamdam-companion.

Frank, L., Klincewicz, M., and Jane, E. (2022) 'The ethics of matching: hookup apps and online dating', in B. D. Earp, C. Chambers, and L. Watson (eds.), *The Routledge Handbook of Philosophy of Sex and Sexuality*. Abingdon: Routledge.

Frankfurt, H. (2004) *The Reasons of Love*. Princeton University Press.

Frankfurt, H. (2006) 'Taking ourselves seriously and getting it right', in D. Satz (ed.), *Taking Ourselves Seriously and Getting It Right*. Stanford University Press.

Freedman, G., et al. (2019) 'Ghosting and destiny: implicit theories of relationships predict beliefs about ghosting', *Journal of Social and Personal Relationships*, 36(3), pp. 905–24.

Freeman, H. (2020) '"Tradwives": the new trend for submissive women has a dark heart and history', *Guardian*, 27 January. Available at: www.theguardian .com/fashion/2020/jan/27/tradwives-new-trend-submissive-women-dark-heart -history.

Freitas, D. (2018) *Consent on Campus: A Manifesto*. Oxford University Press.

Fricker, M. (2007) *Epistemic Injustice: Power and the Ethics of Knowing*. Oxford University Press.

Gahran, A. (2017) *Stepping Off the Relationship Escalator: Uncommon Love and Life*. Off the Escalator Enterprises, LLC. Available at: https://offescalator.com.

Garcia, M. (2023) *The Joy of Consent: A Philosophy of Good Sex*. Cambridge, Mass.; London: The Belknap Press.

Garcia-Iglesias, J., et al. (2024) 'Dating apps as health allies? Examining the opportunities and challenges of dating apps as partners in public health', *Medical Humanities*, 50, pp. 594–7.

Garda, M. B. and Karhulahti, V.-M. (2021) 'Let's play Tinder! Aesthetics of a dating app', *Games and Culture*, 16(2), pp. 248–61.

Gardiner, B. (2024) 'How gamification took over the world', *MIT Technology Review*. Available at: www.technologyreview.com/2024/06/13/1093375 /gamification-behaviorism-npcs-video-games.

Gardner, J. (2018) 'The opposite of rape', *Oxford Journal of Legal Studies*, 38(1), pp. 48–70.

Garland-Thomson, R. (2009) *Staring: How We Look*. Oxford; New York: Oxford University Press.

Garrau, M. and Laborde, C. (2015) 'Relational equality, non-domination, and vulnerability', in C. Fourie, F. Schuppert, and I. Wallimann-Helmer (eds.), *Social Equality: On What It Means to Be Equals*. Oxford University Press.

Gavey, N. (2018) *Just Sex? The Cultural Scaffolding of Rape*. 2nd edn. Abingdon, Oxon; New York: Routledge.

Gheaus, A. (2011) 'Arguments for nonparental care for children', *Social Theory and Practice*, 37(3), pp. 483–509.

Gheaus, A. (2016) 'The (dis)value of commitment to one's spouse', in E. Brake (ed.), *After Marriage: Rethinking Marital Relationships*. Oxford University Press.

Gheaus, A. (2024) 'Republican families?', in F. Lovett and M. Sellers (eds.), *Oxford Handbook of Republicanism*. Oxford Handbooks. Oxford University Press. https://doi.org/10.1093/oxfordhb/9780197754115.013.31.

Giddens, A. (1992) *The Transformation of Intimacy: Sexuality, Love and Eroticism in Modern Societies*. Cambridge: Polity.

Goldberg, A. E. (2013) '"Doing" and "undoing" gender: the meaning and division of housework in same-sex couples', *Journal of Family Theory & Review*, 5(2), pp. 85–104.

Goldie, P. (2000) *The Emotions: A Philosophical Exploration*. Oxford University Press.

Goldie, P. (2011) 'Grief: a narrative account', *Ratio*, 24(2), pp. 119–37.

Goldie, P. (2012) *The Mess Inside: Narrative, Emotion, and the Mind*. Oxford University Press.

Goss, R. E. and Klass, D. E. (2005) *Dead but Not Lost: Grief Narratives in Religious Traditions*. Walnut Creek, Calif.: AltaMira Press.

Green, L. (2000) 'Pornographies', *Journal of Political Philosophy*, 8(1), pp. 27–52.

Greer, G. R. and Tolbert, R. (1998) 'A method of conducting therapeutic sessions with MDMA', *Journal of Psychoactive Drugs*, 30(4), pp. 371–9.

Gross, R. (2018). *The Psychology of Grief*. Abingdon: Routledge.

Gunkel, J. (2024) 'What is intimacy?', *Journal of Philosophy*, 121(8), pp. 425–56.

Gupta, K. (2015) 'Compulsory sexuality: evaluating an emerging concept', *Signs: Journal of Women in Culture and Society*, 41(1), pp. 131–54.

Gupta, K. (2022) 'What is a sexual act?', in B. D. Earp, C. Chambers, and L. Watson (eds.), *The Routledge Handbook of Philosophy of Sex and Sexuality*. Abingdon: Routledge.

Hackman, R. (2015) '"Women are just better at this stuff": is emotional labor feminism's next frontier?', *Guardian*, 8 November. Available at: www.theguardian.com/world/2015/nov/08/women-gender-roles-sexism-emotional-labor-feminism.

Hagen, S. (2024) *Will I Ever Have Sex Again? A Disarmingly Honest and Funny Exploration of Sex*. London: Blink Publishing.

Halberstam, J. J. (2013) *Gaga Feminism: Sex, Gender, and the End of Normal – 7*. Boston, Mass.: Beacon Press.

Hald, G. M., Pavan, S., and Øverup, C. S. (2024) 'Do sex toys make me satisfied? The use of sex toys in Denmark, Norway, Sweden, Finland, France, and the UK', *Journal of Sex Research* [preprint], pp. 1–15.

Halwani, R. (2003) *Virtuous Liaisons: Care, Love, Sex, and Virtue Ethics*. Chicago, Ill.: Open Court.

Halwani, R. (2018) *Philosophy of Love, Sex, and Marriage: An Introduction*. New York: Routledge.

Halwani, R. (2021) 'Sexual temperance and sexual objectification', in E. Silverman (ed.), *Sexual Ethics in a Secular Age*. Abingdon: Routledge.

Halwani, R. (2024) 'The relevance of the distinction between romantic love and sex to the ethics of "lookism" in dating', Ethical Dating Online Workshop, IDEA Centre, University of Leeds, 12 September.

Han, C. W. (2016) 'From "Little Brown Brothers" to "Queer Asian Wives": constructing the Asian male body', in S. Irvin (ed.), *Body Aesthetics*. Oxford University Press.

Hanna, C. (2000) 'Sex is not a sport: consent and violence in criminal law', *Boston College Law Review*, 42, p. 239.

Harbin, A. (2016) *Disorientation and Moral Life*. Studies in Feminist Philosophy. New York: Oxford University Press.

Harcourt, E. (2011) 'Nietzsche and the "aesthetics of character"', in S. May (ed.), *Nietzsche's On the Genealogy of Morality: A Critical Guide*. Cambridge Critical Guides. Cambridge University Press.

Haslanger, S. (2012) *Resisting Reality: Social Construction and Social Critique*. Oxford University Press.

Haupert, M. L., et al. (2017) 'Prevalence of experiences with consensual nonmonogamous relationships: findings from two national samples of single Americans', *Journal of Sex & Marital Therapy*, 43(5), pp. 424–40.

Hazan, C. and Diamond, L. M. (2000) 'The place of attachment in human mating', *Review of General Psychology*, 4(2), pp. 186–204.

Hazan, C. and Shaver, P. (1987) 'Romantic love conceptualized as an attachment process', *Journal of Personality and Social Psychology*, 52(3), pp. 511–24.

Healey, R. (2015) 'The ontology of consent: a reply to Alexander', *Analytic Philosophy*, 56(4), pp. 354–63.

Healey, R. (2019) 'Consent, rights, and reasons for action', *Criminal Law and Philosophy*, 13(3), pp. 499–513.

Healey, R. (2023) 'Breaking up and the value of commitment', *Ergo: An Open-Access Journal of Philosophy*, 10, pp. 158–87.

Herbenick, D., et al. (2010) 'An event-level analysis of the sexual characteristics and composition among adults ages 18 to 59: results from a national probability sample in the United States', *Journal of Sexual Medicine*, 7(Supplement 5), pp. 346–61.

Herer, M. (2021) *In Praise of Friendship*. Hampshire: Zero Books.

Hernandez, E. M. (2021) 'Gender-affirmation and loving attention', *Hypatia*, 36(4), pp. 619–35.

Higgins, K. (2013) 'Love and death', in J. Deigh (ed.), *On Emotions: Philosophical Essays*. Oxford University Press.

Hlophe, T. (2023) 'Dating app abductions raise fears for LGBT+ safety in South Africa', Reuters, 8 December. Available at: www.reuters.com/world/africa/dating-app-abductions-raise-fears-lgbt-safety-south-africa-2023-12-08.

Hochschild, A. R. (2012) *The Managed Heart: Commercialization of Human Feeling*. 3rd edn. Oakland: University of California Press.

Holt-Lunstad, J., Smith, T. B., and Layton, J. B. (2010) 'Social relationships and mortality risk: a meta-analytic review', *PLOS Medicine*, 7(7), p. e1000316.

Hopkinson, E. (2019) *Asexual Fairy Tales*. Silverwood Books. Available at: https://thebookishtype.co.uk/products/asexual-fairy-tales-by-elizabeth-hopkinson.

Hopwood, M. (2018) '"The extremely difficult realization that something other than oneself is real": Iris Murdoch on love and moral agency', *European Journal of Philosophy*, 26(1), pp. 477–501.

Hornsby, R. and McKeever, N. (2022) 'Is it wrong to have sex with a robot?' *Public Ethics*. Available at: www.publicethics.org/post/is-it-wrong-to-have-sex-with-a-robot.

Humphries, J. (2018) 'Intimacy, autonomy and (non) domination', *Journal of Applied Philosophy*, 35(2), pp. 399–416.

Hunte, B. (2020) 'Grindr removes "ethnicity filter" after complaints', *BBC News*. Available at: www.bbc.com/news/technology-52886167.

Hurd, H. M. (1996) 'The moral magic of consent', *Legal Theory*, 2(2), pp. 121–46.

Hurd, H. M. (2018) 'The normative force of consent', in A. Müller and P. Schaber (eds.), *The Routledge Handbook of the Ethics of Consent*. Abingdon: Routledge.

Ichikawa, J. J. (2020) 'Presupposition and consent', *Feminist Philosophy Quarterly*, 6(4). https://ojs.lib.uwo.ca/index.php/fpq/article/view/8302.

Illouz, E. (2013) *Why Love Hurts: A Sociological Explanation*. Cambridge: Polity.

Illouz, E. (2019) *The End of Love: A Sociology of Negative Relations*. New York: Oxford University Press.

Inness, J. (1996) *Privacy, Intimacy, and Isolation*. Revised edn. Berlin: Oxford University Press.

Iqbal, M. (2024) 'Tinder revenue and usage statistics (2024)', Business of Apps. Available at: www.businessofapps.com/data/tinder-statistics.

Irvin, S. (2017) 'Resisting body oppression: an aesthetic approach', *Feminist Philosophy Quarterly*, 3(4). https://ojs.lib.uwo.ca/index.php/fpq/article/view /3104.

Irvin, S. and Lintott, S. (2016) 'Sex objects and sexy subjects: a feminist reclamation of sexiness', in S. Irvin (ed.), *Body Aesthetics*. Oxford University Press.

Jang, S., Allen, T. D., and Regina, J. (2021) 'Office housework, burnout, and promotion: does gender matter?', *Journal of Business and Psychology*, 36(5), pp. 793–805.

Jankowiak, W. R. and Fischer, E. F. (1992) 'A cross-cultural perspective on romantic love', *Ethnology*, 31(2), pp. 149–55.

Jaworska, A. and Wonderly, M. (2024) 'Love and caring', in C. Grau and A. Smuts (eds.), *The Oxford Handbook of the Philosophy of Love*. Oxford University Press.

Jenkins, C. (2010) 'The philosophy of flirting', in K. Miller and M. Clark (eds.), *Dating – Philosophy for Everyone*. Hoboken, NJ: John Wiley & Sons, Ltd.

Jenkins, C. (2017) *What Love Is: And What It Could Be*. Basic Books.

Jenkins, C. (2022) *Sad Love: Romance and the Search for Meaning*. Cambridge: Polity.

Jenkins, K. (2016) 'Amelioration and inclusion: gender identity and the concept of woman', *Ethics*, 126(2), pp. 394–421.

Jolene Sloan, L. (2015) 'Ace of (BDSM) clubs: building asexual relationships through BDSM practice', *Sexualities*, 18(5–6), pp. 548–63.

Jollimore, T. (2015) '"This endless space between the words": the limits of love in Spike Jonze's *Her*', *Midwest Studies in Philosophy*, 39(1), pp. 120–43.

Jollimore, T. (2018) 'Love, romance, and sex', in A. Martin (ed.), *The Routledge Handbook of Love in Philosophy*. New York: Routledge.

Keller, S. (2000) 'How do I love thee? Let me count the properties', *American Philosophical Quarterly*, 37(2), pp. 163–73.

Khattar, V., Upadhyay, S., and Navarro, R. (2023) 'Young adults' perception of breadcrumbing victimization in dating relationships', *Societies*, 13(2), p. 41.

Kimhi, O. (2020) 'Falling short: on implicit biases and the discrimination of short individuals', *Connecticut Law Review*, 52, p. 719.

Kirton, A. and McKeever, N. (2023) 'Trust, attachment, and monogamy', in

D. Collins, I. V. Jovanovic, and M. Alfano (eds.), *The Moral Psychology of Trust*. Lanham, Md.: Lexington Books, Rowman & Littlefield.

Klass, D. and Steffen, E. M. (eds.) (2017) *Continuing Bonds in Bereavement: New Directions for Research and Practice*. New York: Routledge.

Kleeman, J. (2017) 'The race to build the world's first sex robot', *Guardian*, 27 April. Available at: www.theguardian.com/technology/2017/apr/27/race-to -build-world-first-sex-robot.

Klesse, C. (2014) 'Polyamory: intimate practice, identity or sexual orientation?', *Sexualities*, 17(1/2), pp. 81–99.

Kolodny, N. (2003) 'Love as valuing a relationship', *Philosophical Review*, 112, pp. 135–89.

Kramer, S. (2020) 'Polygamy is rare around the world and mostly confined to a few regions', Pew Research Center. Available at: www.pewresearch.org/fact -tank/2020/12/07/polygamy-is-rare-around-the-world-and-mostly-confined-to -a-few-regions.

Kreft, N. (2022) 'Irreplaceability and the desire-account of love', *Ethical Theory and Moral Practice*, 25(4), pp. 541–56.

Kristjánsson, K. (2003) 'On the very idea of "negative emotions"', *Journal for the Theory of Social Behaviour*, 33(4), pp. 351–64.

Kugelberg, E. (2025) 'Dating apps and the digital sexual sphere', *American Political Science Review*, pp. 1–16. https://doi.org/10.1017/S000305542400128X.

Kukla, Q. R. (2021) 'A nonideal theory of sexual consent', *Ethics*, 131(2), pp. 270–92.

Kukla, Q. R. and Herbert, C. (2018) 'Moral ecologies and the harms of sexual violation', *Philosophical Topics*, 46(2), pp. 247–68.

Kukla, R. (2018) 'That's what she said: the language of sexual negotiation', *Ethics*, 129(1), pp. 70–97.

Laan, E. T. M., et al. (2021) 'In pursuit of pleasure: a biopsychosocial perspective on sexual pleasure and gender', *International Journal of Sexual Health*, 33(4), pp. 516–36.

LaFollette, H. and Graham, G. (1986) 'Honesty and intimacy', *Journal of Social and Personal Relationships*, 3(1), pp. 3–18.

Lamb, S., Gable, S., and de Ruyter, D. (2021) 'Mutuality in sexual relationships: a standard of ethical sex?', *Ethical Theory and Moral Practice*, 24(1), pp. 271–84.

Lamont, E. (2020) *The Mating Game: How Gender Still Shapes How We Date*. Oakland: University of California Press.

Langton, R. (1993) 'Speech acts and unspeakable acts', *Philosophy & Public Affairs*, 22(4), pp. 293–330.

Langton, R. (2009) 'Autonomy-denial in objectification', in *Sexual Solipsism: Philosophical Essays on Pornography and Objectification*. Oxford University Press.

Lanky-Championship67 (2023) 'How are people falling in love with their replikas?', *r/replika*. Available at: www.reddit.com/r/replika/comments/147j4wc /how_are_people_falling_in_love_with_their_replikas.

Lavinia, E. (2024) '"After years of bad experiences with men, I have opted out. And it will be permanent": meet the women embracing celibacy', *Glamour UK*. Available at: www.glamourmagazine.co.uk/article/boy-sober-4b-celibacy -dating-investigation.

Lazenby, H. and Gabriel, I. (2018) 'Permissible secrets', *Philosophical Quarterly*, 68(271), pp. 265–85.

Lehmiller, J. and Feeld (2024) 'The state of dating report'. Available at: https://app .air.inc/a/cx2MUPVP0.

Levy, D. (1979) 'The definition of love in Plato's Symposium', *Journal of the History of Ideas*, 40(2), pp. 285–91.

Levy, D. (2009) *Love and Sex with Robots: The Evolution of Human–Robot Relationships*. London: Gerald Duckworth & Co. Ltd.

Lewis, S. (2022) *Abolish the Family: A Manifesto for Care and Liberation*. London: Verso. Available at: www.versobooks.com/en-gb/products/2890-abolish-the -family.

Li, Y. (2022) 'Investigating the differences between [how] females perceive same-gender and heterogender sex robots regarding adoption and intentions', *Frontiers in Psychology*, pp. 1–14.

Liao, S. M. (2006) 'The idea of a duty to love', *Journal of Value Inquiry*, 40(1), pp. 1–22.

Liberto, H. (2017) 'The problem with sexual promises', *Ethics*, 127(2), pp. 383–414.

Liberto, H. (2022) *Green Light Ethics: A Theory of Permissive Consent and Its Moral Metaphysics*. Oxford; New York: Oxford University Press.

Lindemann, H. (2014) *Holding and Letting Go: The Social Practice of Personal Identities*. Oxford; New York: Oxford University Press.

Litvinova, D. (2019) 'FEATURE – Masked men and murder: vigilantes terrorise LGBT+ Russians', Reuters, 24 September. Available at: www.reuters.com/article/world/us/feature-masked-men-and-murder-vigilantes-terrorise-lgbt-russians-idUSL5N26A2IX.

Lopez-Cantero, P. (2018) 'The break-up check: exploring romantic love through relationship terminations', *Philosophia*, 46(3), pp. 689–703.

Lopez-Cantero, P. (2020) 'Love by (someone else's) choice', *Philosophy and Public Issues – Filosofia e questioni pubbliche*, 10(3). Available at: http://fqp.luiss.it /2021/03/15/love-by-someone-elses-choice.

Lopez-Cantero, P. (2022a) 'Falling in love', in A. Grahle, N. McKeever, and J. Saunders (eds.), *Philosophy of Love in the Past, Present, and Future*. Abingdon: Routledge.

Lopez-Cantero, P. (2022b) 'Non-harmonious love', *International Journal of Philosophical Studies*, 30(3), pp. 276–97.

Lorde, A. (2019) 'Uses of the erotic: the erotic as power', in *Sister Outsider*. London: Penguin.

Lovett, F. (2022) *The Well-Ordered Republic*. Oxford University Press.

Lovine, A. (2023) 'Berlin's cybersex brothel fulfills a fantasy – but may pose risks', *Mashable*. Available at: https://mashable.com/article/cybrothel-fulfills -a-fantasy-but-may-have-risks.

Lugones, M. (2003) *Pilgrimages/Peregrinajes: Theorizing Coalition Against Multiple Oppressions*. Lanham, Md.: Rowman & Littlefield.

Lund, E. M. (2021) 'Violence against asexual individuals', in E. M. Lund, C. Burgess, and A. J. Johnson (eds.), *Violence Against LGBTQ+ Persons: Research, Practice, and Advocacy*. Cham: Springer International Publishing.

Maclaren, K. (2014) 'Intimacy and embodiment: an introduction', *Emotion, Space and Society*, 13, pp. 55–64.

Madigan, T. (1998) 'The discarded Lemon: Kant, prostitution and respect for persons', Issue 21, *Philosophy Now*. Available at: https://philosophynow.org/issues/21/The_discarded_Lemon_Kant_prostitution_and_respect_for_persons.

Mahar, E. A., Mintz, L. B., and Akers, B. M. (2020) 'Orgasm equality: scientific findings and societal implications', *Current Sexual Health Reports*, 12(1), pp. 24–32.

Mangalindan, J. (2018) 'How Match got away with buying 25 dating sites – and counting', Yahoo Finance. Available at: https://finance.yahoo.com/news/match-group-can-get-away-acquiring-25-dating-sites-counting-151306438.html.

Manne, K. (2017) *Down Girl: The Logic of Misogyny*. New York: Oxford University Press.

Manne, K. (2024) *Unshrinking: How to Fight Fatphobia*. London: Allen Lane.

Manson, N. C. (2016) 'Permissive consent: a robust reason-changing account', *Philosophical Studies*, 173(12), pp. 3317–34.

Marino, P. (2019). *Philosophy of Sex and Love: An Opinionated Introduction*. London: Routledge.

Maushart, S. (2002) *Wifework: What Marriage Really Means for Women*. London: Bloomsbury.

May, S. (2019) *Love: A New Understanding of an Ancient Emotion*. Oxford University Press.

McArthur, N. (2017) 'The case for sexbots', in J. Danaher and N. McArthur (eds.), *Robot Sex: Social and Ethical Implications*. Cambridge, Mass.: MIT Press.

McArthur, N. (2022a) 'The concept and significance of virginity', in C. Chambers, B. D. Earp, and L. Watson (eds.), *The Routledge Handbook of Philosophy of Sex and Sexuality*. Abingdon: Routledge.

McArthur, N. (2022b). *The Ethics of Sex: An Introduction*. London: Routledge.

McArthur, N. and Twist, M. L. C. (2017) 'The rise of digisexuality: therapeutic challenges and possibilities', *Sexual and Relationship Therapy*, 32(3–4), pp. 334–44.

McClelland, T. and Sliwa, P. (2023) 'Gendered affordance perception and unequal domestic labour', *Philosophy and Phenomenological Research*, 107(2), pp. 501–24.

McDonald, L. (2022) 'Flirting', in B. D. Earp, C. Chambers, and L. Watson (eds.), *The Routledge Handbook of Philosophy of Sex and Sexuality*. Abingdon: Routledge.

McIntyre, N. (2023) 'Behind every swipe: the workers toiling to keep dating apps safe', *TBIJ*. Available at: www.thebureauinvestigates.com/stories/2023-11-20/behind-every-swipe-the-workers-toiling-to-keep-dating-apps-safe.

McKeever, N. (2017) 'Is the requirement of sexual exclusivity consistent with romantic love?', *Journal of Applied Philosophy*, 34(3), pp. 353–69.

McKeever, N. (2019) 'What can we learn about romantic love from Harry Frankfurt's account of love?', *Journal of Ethics and Social Philosophy*, 14(3), pp. 204–26.

McKeever, N. (2025a) 'Friendship and romantic relationships: reflections on a neglected difference', in M. Betzler and J. Löschke (eds.), *The Ethics of Personal Relationships: Broadening the Scope*. Oxford University Press.

McKeever, N. (2025b) 'Is sex work inherently gendered?', *Hypatia*, pp. 1–20. https://doi.org/10.1017/hyp2024.56.

McKeever, N. and Saunders, J. (2022) 'Irrational love: taking Romeo and Juliet seriously', *International Journal of Philosophical Studies*, 30(3), pp. 254–75. https:/doi.org/19=0.1080/09672559.2022.2121895.

Mackenzie, C., Rogers, W., and Dodds, S. (2013) *Vulnerability: New Essays in Ethics and Feminist Philosophy*. Ed. C. Mackenzie. New York: Oxford University Press.

McMahon, L. (2024) 'Tinder parent company cuts jobs as subscriber numbers slump', *BBC News*. Available at: www.bbc.com/news/articles/c0xj08l9055o.

Meeno Blog (2024). Available at: https://blog.meeno.com/blog.

Mikkola, M. (2011) 'Illocution, silencing and the act of refusal', *Pacific Philosophical Quarterly*, 92(3), pp. 415–37.

Miller, S. (2022) 'Heterosexual male sexuality: a positive vision', in B. D. Earp, C. Chambers, and L. Watson (eds.), *The Routledge Handbook of Philosophy of Sex and Sexuality*. Abingdon: Routledge.

Mills, C. W. (2017) *Black Rights / White Wrongs: The Critique of Racial Liberalism*. Transgressing Boundaries. New York: Oxford University Press.

Millum, J. and Bromwich, D. (2018) 'Understanding, communication, and consent', *Ergo: An Open-Access Journal of Philosophy*, 5, pp. 45–68.

Milrod, C. and Weitzer, R. (2012) 'The intimacy prism: emotion management among the clients of escorts', *Men and Masculinities*, 15(5), pp. 447–67.

Mitchell, M. and Wells, M. (2018) 'Race, romantic attraction, and dating', *Ethical Theory and Moral Practice*, 21, pp. 945–61.

Moen, O. M. and Sørlie, A. (2022) 'The ethics of relationship anarchy', in L. Watson, C. Chambers, and B. D. Earp (eds.), *The Routledge Handbook of Philosophy of Sex and Sexuality*. Abingdon: Routledge.

Mollet, A. L. and Black, W. (2021) 'A-nother perspective: an analysis of asexual college students' experiences with sexual violence', *Journal of College Student Development*, 62(5), pp. 526–46.

Mooney, J. (2024) 'Catching the Sligo Grindr killer — a man "intent on killing as many as possible"', *The Times*. Available at: www.thetimes.com/world/ireland-world/article/catching-the-sligo-grindr-killer-a-man-intent-death-zsm3qfbx5.

Mordaunt, H. (2018) *A Modest Defence of Publick Stews: Or, an Essay Upon Whoring. As it is now Practis'd in These Kingdoms. By the Late Colonel Harry Mordaunt*. Farmington Hills, Mich.: Gale ECCO, Print Editions.

Morgan, R. (2023) 'Sexualisation', *Australasian Journal of Philosophy*, 102(2), pp. 481–96.

Morgan, R. (2024) 'Hermeneutical disarmament', *Philosophical Quarterly*, p. pqae046.

Morgan, S. (2003a) 'Dark desires', *Ethical Theory and Moral Practice*, 6(4), pp. 377–410.

Morgan, S. (2003b) 'Sex in the head', *Journal of Applied Philosophy*, 20(1), pp. 1–16.

Müller, A. (2018) 'Moral obligations and consent', in A. Müller and P. Schaber (eds.), *The Routledge Handbook of the Ethics of Consent*. Abingdon: Routledge.

Müller, M. (2019) 'Emotional labour: a case of gender-specific exploitation', *Critical Review of International Social and Political Philosophy*, 22(7), pp. 841–62.

Mulvey, L. (1975) 'Visual pleasure and narrative cinema', *Screen*, 16(3), pp. 6–18.

Murdoch, I. (2001) *The Sovereignty of Good*. 2nd edn. London: Routledge.

Murgia, M. (2024) 'The loneliness cure'. Available at: www.ft.com/content /ae99e1d7-d72a-48fc-baca-d68c09ed73d4.

Murphy, R., Dennes, M., and Harris, B. (2022) 'Families and the labour market, UK', Office for National Statistics. Available at: www.ons.gov.uk /employmentandlabourmarket/peopleinwork/employmentandemployeetypes /articles/familiesandthelabourmarketengland/2021.

Naar, H. (2013) 'A dispositional theory of love', *Pacific Philosophical Quarterly*, 94, pp. 342–57.

Naar, H. (2016) 'Real-world love drugs: reply to Nyholm', *Journal of Applied Philosophy*, 33(2), pp. 197–201.

Naar, H. (2024) 'Love as a disposition', in C. Grau and A. Smuts (eds.), *The Oxford Handbook of the Philosophy of Love*. Oxford University Press.

Nader, K. (2024) 'Gamification of dating online', *Theoria* [preprint].

Nagoski, E. (2015) *Come as You Are: The Surprising New Science That Will Transform Your Sex Life*. New York: Simon & Schuster.

Narayan, U. (2002) 'Minds of Their own: choices, autonomy, cultural practices, and other women', in *A Mind Of One's Own*. 2nd edn. Abingdon: Routledge.

Nehamas, A. (2016) *On Friendship*. Illustrated edn. New York: Basic Books.

Newerla, A. and van Hooff, J. (2023) 'Mobile intimacies? Uncertainty, ambivalence and fluidity in the intimate practices of dating app users in Germany and the UK', *Sexualities*, 28(1–2), pp. 24–41.

Nguyen, C. T. (2020) *Games: Agency as Art*. New York: Oxford University Press.

Nolan, D. (2016) 'Temporary marriage', in E. Brake (ed.), *After Marriage: Rethinking Marital Relationships*. Oxford University Press.

Nordgren, A. (2006) 'The short instructional manifesto for relationship anarchy', Andie's Log. Available at: https://log.andie.se/post/26652940513/the-short -instructional-manifesto-for-relationship.

Nozick, R. (1991) 'Love's bond', in R. Solomon and K. Higgins (eds.), *The Philosophy of (Erotic) Love*. Lawrence: University Press of Kansas.

Nussbaum, M. C. (1995) 'Objectification', *Philosophy & Public Affairs*, 24(4), pp. 249–91.

Nyholm, S. (2015) 'Love troubles: human attachment and biomedical enhancements', *Journal of Applied Philosophy*, 32(2), pp. 190–202.

Nyholm, S. and Frank, L. (2017) 'From sex robots to love robots: is mutual love with a robot possible?', in J. Danaher and N. McArthur (eds.), *Robot Sex: Social and Ethical Implications.* Cambridge, Mass.: MIT Press.

O'Brian, M. E. (2023) *Family Abolition: Capitalism and the Communizing of Care.* London: Pluto Press. Available at: www.plutobooks.com/9780745343846/family-abolition.

O'Brien, K.Y., and Ashley, S. (2020) 'Swipe right: people are using dating apps to reach voters in swing states', *CNN Business,* CNN. Available at: www.cnn.com/2020/11/02/tech/hinge-voting-election/index.html.

Okin, S. M. (1991) *Justice, Gender, and the Family.* Reprint edn. New York: Basic Books.

O'Shea, T. (2020) 'Sexual desire and structural injustice', *Journal of Social Philosophy,* 52(4), pp. 587–600.

Otter, R. C. (2015) *In Defense of Plural Marriage.* Cambridge; New York: Cambridge University Press.

Otter, R. C. (2018) 'Perfectionist argument for legal recognition of polyamorous relationships', in E. Brake and L. Ferguson (eds.), *Philosophical Foundations of Children's and Family Law.* Oxford University Press.

Oxford English Dictionary (2023a) 'date, v.' Oxford University Press. Available at: https://doi.org/10.1093/OED/5357273430.

Oxford English Dictionary (2023b) 'flirting, adj.' Oxford University Press. Available at: https://doi.org/10.1093/OED/1218296041.

Pancani, L., et al. (2021) 'Ghosting and orbiting: an analysis of victims' experiences', *Journal of Social and Personal Relationships,* 38(7), pp. 1987–2007.

Pérez-Cortés, J.-C. (2022) *Relationship Anarchy: Occupy Intimacy!* Trans. A. Foy. Independently published.

Petrongolo, B. and Ronchi, M. (2020) 'Gender gaps and the structure of local labor markets', *Labour Economics,* 64, pp. 1–12.

Petter, O. (2024) 'The new dating app feature that might just save women's lives', *Independent.* Available at: www.independent.co.uk/voices/tinder-share-my-date-feature-dating-apps-safety-women-b2536489.html.

Pettit, P. (1997) *Republicanism: A Theory of Freedom and Government.* Oxford Political Theory. Oxford University Press.

Pismenny, A. (2023) 'Pansexuality: a closer look at sexual orientation', *Philosophies,* 8(4), p. 60.

Pismenny, A. and Prinz, J. (2017) 'Is love an emotion?', in C. Grau and A. Smuts (eds.), *Oxford Handbook of the Philosophy of Love.* Oxford University Press.

Porter, A., et al. (2024) 'Swipe left on sexual harassment: understanding and addressing technology-facilitated sexual violence on dating apps', *Journal of Interpersonal Violence,* 27, 08862605241265672.

Portolan, L. (2024) 'No dating apps, no dates, no exes, no hookups: what's driving the "boy sober" trend?', *Guardian,* 10 June. Available at: www.theguardian.com/commentisfree/article/2024/jun/10/no-dating-apps-no-dates-no-exes-no-hookups-whats-driving-the-boy-sober-trend.

Prendergast, A. (2020) 'I got a lifetime ban from a dating app – and discovered the sinister world of revenge reporting', Stylist. Available at: www.stylist.co.uk /relationships/dating-love/dating-app-ban/481309.

Press, A. A. (2024) 'Three men raped a woman in her apartment after she arranged Tinder date, court told', *Guardian*, 6 August. Available at: www.theguardian .com/australia-news/article/2024/aug/06/three-men-raped-a-woman-in-her -apartment-after-she-arranged-tinder-date-court-told.

Primoratz, I. (2001) 'Sexual morality: is consent enough?', *Ethical Theory and Moral Practice*, 4(3), pp. 201–18.

Protasi, S. (2016) 'Loving people for who they are (even when they don't love you back)', *European Journal of Philosophy*, 24(1), pp. 214–34.

Przybylo, E. (2019) *Asexual Erotics: Intimate Readings of Compulsory Sexuality*. Illustrated edn. Columbus: Ohio State University Press.

Pugmire, D. (2007) *Sound Sentiments: Integrity in the Emotions*. Oxford; New York: Oxford University Press.

Purtill, J. (2023) '"My wife is dead": how a software update "lobotomised" these online lovers', *ABC News*, 28 February. Available at: www.abc.net.au/news /science/2023-03-01/replika-users-fell-in-love-with-their-ai-chatbot-companion /102028196.

Pyke, R. E. (2020) 'Sexual performance anxiety', *Sexual Medicine Reviews*, 8(2), pp. 183–90.

Quinn, T. (2024) '"It felt risqué:" how a computer dating service launched in 1965 changed our love lives', CNN. Available at: www.cnn.com/2024/09/29/style /operation-match-patsy-jeff-tarr/index.html.

Quiroz-Gutierrez, M. (2024) 'Tokyo's government plays matchmaker with new dating app to reverse its plunging birth rate', *Fortune*. Available at: https:// fortune.com/2024/06/06/tokyos-government-plays-matchmaker-with-new -dating-app-to-reverse-its-plunging-birth-rate.

Ratcliffe, M. (2015) 'Relating to the dead: social cognition and the phenomenology of grief', in T. Szanto and D. Moran (eds.), *Phenomenology of Sociality: Discovering the 'We'*. Abingdon: Routledge.

Ratcliffe, M. and Byrne, E. A. (2022) 'Grief, self and narrative', *Philosophical Explorations*, 25(3), pp. 319–37.

Raz, J. (2022) 'Normative powers', in J. Raz and U. Heuer (eds.), *The Roots of Normativity*. Oxford University Press.

Rees, M. and Ichikawa, J. (2024) 'Sexual agency and sexual wrongs: a dilemma for consent theory', *Philosophers' Imprint*, 24(2), pp. 1–23.

Reglitz, M. (2020) 'The human right to free internet access', *Journal of Applied Philosophy*, 37(2), pp. 314–31.

Rhode, D. L. (2011) *The Beauty Bias: The Injustice of Appearance in Life and Law*. Oxford University Press.

Richardson, K. (2016) 'The asymmetrical "relationship": parallels between prosti-tution and the development of sex robots', *SIGCAS Computers and Society*, 45(3), pp. 290–3.

Rini, R. (2020) *The Ethics of Microaggression*. Abingdon: Routledge.

Ritchie, A. and Barker, M. (2006) '"There aren't words for what we do or how we feel so we have to make them up": constructing polyamorous languages in a culture of compulsory monogamy', *Sexualities*, 9(5), pp. 584–601.

Ritchie, K. (2021) 'Essentializing language and the prospects for ameliorative projects', *Ethics*, 131(3), pp. 460–88.

Ronen, S. (2021) 'Gendered morality in the sex toy market: entitlements, reversals, and the irony of heterosexuality', *Sexualities*, 24(4), pp. 614–35.

Rubel, A. N. and Burleigh, T. J. (2020) 'Counting polyamorists who count: prevalence and definitions of an under-researched form of consensual nonmonogamy', *Sexualities*, 23(1–2), pp. 3–27.

Russell, D. C. (2009) *Practical Intelligence and the Virtues*. Oxford University Press.

'Safety on Bumble' (no date) Bumble. Available at: https://bumble.com/en/help /safety-on-bumble.

'Safety tips' (no date) Help Center, Grindr. Available at: https://help.grindr.com/hc /en-us/articles/1500009290262-Safety-tips.

Sanders, T. (2007) 'The politics of sexual citizenship: commercial sex and disability', *Disability & Society*, 22(5), pp. 439–55.

Santini, Z. I., et al. (2015) 'The association of relationship quality and social networks with depression, anxiety, and suicidal ideation among older married adults: findings from a cross-sectional analysis of the Irish Longitudinal Study on Ageing (TILDA)', *Journal of Affective Disorders*, 179, pp. 134–41.

Satz, D. (1995) 'Markets in women's sexual labor', *Ethics*, 106(1), pp. 63–85.

Savitsky, K., et al. (2011) 'The closeness–communication bias: increased egocentrism among friends versus strangers', *Journal of Experimental Social Psychology*, 47(1), pp. 269–73.

Savulescu, J. and Sandberg, A. (2008) 'Neuroenhancement of love and marriage: the chemicals between us', *Neuroethics*, 1(1), pp. 31–44.

Schaber, P. (2020) 'How permissive consent works', *Ratio*, 33(2), pp. 117–24.

Scheffler, S. (2012) *Equality and Tradition: Questions of Moral Value in Moral and Political Theory*. New York: Oxford University Press.

Scheutz, M. and Arnold, T. (2016) 'Are we ready for sex robots?', in *2016 11th ACM/IEEE International Conference on Human–Robot Interaction (HRI)*. Christchurch.

Schofield, D. (2024) 'The "boy sober" movement and why women are sick of dating', *Cosmopolitan*. Available at: www.cosmopolitan.com/uk/love-sex /relationships/a60428017/tiktok-boy-sober-dating-trend.

Schulhofer, S. (1998) *Unwanted Sex: The Culture of Intimidation & the Failure of Law*. Cambridge, Mass: Harvard University Press.

Scott, E. (2023) 'I've been dating myself for a decade – here's why you should do the same', Stylist. Available at: www.stylist.co.uk/health/mental-health/why -you-should-date-yourself/817829.

Scruton, R. (2006) *Sexual Desire: A Philosophical Investigation*. London; New York: Continuum.

Seedat, S. and Rondon, M. (2021) 'Women's wellbeing and the burden of unpaid work', *BMJ*, 374, n1972.

Séguin, L. J. (2019) 'The good, the bad, and the ugly: lay attitudes and perceptions of polyamory', *Sexualities*, 22(4), pp. 669–90.

Shakespeare, T. (2022) 'Sex and disability', in B. D. Earp, L. Watson, and C. Chambers (eds.), *The Routledge Handbook of Philosophy of Sex and Sexuality*. Abingdon: Routledge.

Shakespeare, T., Gillespie-Sells, K., and Dominic Davies, D. (1996) *The Sexual Politics of Disability*. London: Continuum International Publishing Group Ltd.

Shek, Y. L. (2007) 'Asian American masculinity: a review of the literature', *Journal of Men's Studies*, 14(3), pp. 379–91.

Sherman, N. (2024) 'Bumble apologises for anti-celibacy ad after backlash', *BBC News*. Available at: www.bbc.com/news/articles/cz4xx2rw0leo.

Shpall, S. (2018) 'A tripartite theory of love', *Journal of Ethics and Social Philosophy*, 13, pp. 91–124.

Sicart, M. (2015) 'Playing the good life: gamification and ethics', in S. P. Walz and S. Deterding (eds.), *The Gameful World*. Cambridge, Mass.: MIT Press.

Silverman, E. (2021) *Sexual Ethics in a Secular Age: Is There Still a Virtue of Chastity?* Routledge. Available at: www.routledge.com/Sexual-Ethics -in-a-Secular-Age-Is-There-Still-a-Virtue-of-Chastity/Silverman/p/book /9780367522773.

Smith, A. and Anderson, J. (2014) 'Predictions for the state of AI and robotics in 2025', Pew Research Center, 6 August. Available at: www.pewresearch.org /internet/2014/08/06/predictions-for-the-state-of-ai-and-robotics-in-2025.

Smith, T. H. (2011) 'Romantic love', *Essays in Philosophy*, 12(1), pp. 68–92.

Snow, N. (ed.) (2018) *The Oxford Handbook of Virtue*. Oxford Handbooks. Oxford; New York: Oxford University Press.

Snow, N. E. (2021) 'Finding chastity in a secular age: chastity as a virtue of sexual autonomy', in E. Silverman (ed.), *Sexual Ethics in a Secular Age*. Abingdon: Routledge.

Sokol, M. (2011) *Bentham, Law and Marriage: A Utilitarian Code of Law in Historical Contexts*. London: Bloomsbury.

Solomon, R. (1988) *About Love: Reinventing Romance for Our Times*. New York: Simon and Schuster.

Solomon, R. (1995) 'The virtue of (erotic) love', in R. M. Stewart (ed.), *Philosophical Perspectives on Sex & Love*. Oxford University Press.

Spreeuwenberg, L. (2019) 'Taking the love pill: a reply to Naar and Nyholm', *Journal of Applied Philosophy*, 36(2), pp. 248–56.

Srinivasan, A. (2019) 'Sex as a pedagogical failure', *Yale Law Journal*, 129, p. 1100.

Srinivasan, A. (2021) *The Right to Sex*. London: Bloomsbury. Available at: http:// ebookcentral.proquest.com/lib/leeds/detail.action?docID=6708140.

Stark, C. A. (2000) 'Hypothetical consent and justification', *Journal of Philosophy*, 97(6), pp. 313–34.

Stark, C. A. (2019) 'Gaslighting, misogyny, and psychological oppression', *Monist*, 102(2), pp. 221–35.

Stein, E. (2001) *The Mismeasure of Desire: The Science, Theory, and Ethics of Sexual Orientation*. Ideologies of Desire. Oxford; New York: Oxford University Press.

Stock, K. (2019) 'XIV – sexual orientation: what is it?', *Proceedings of the Aristotelian Society*, 119(3), pp. 295–319.

Strauss, G. (2012) 'Is polygamy inherently unequal?', *Ethics*, 122(3), pp. 516–44.

Strauss, N. (2007) *The Game: Undercover in the Secret Society of Pickup Artists*. Edinburgh: Canongate Books.

Suits, B. (2014) *The Grasshopper: Games, Life and Utopia*. Peterborough: Broadview Press.

Suresh, A. (2024) '7 creative Tinder marketing ideas to inspire you'. Available at: www.sprinklr.com/blog/tinder-marketing.

Tabberer, J. (2024) 'Louisiana set to introduce its own "Don't say gay, don't say trans" law', *Attitude*. Available at: www.attitude.co.uk/news/louisiana-set-to-introduce-dont-say-gay-law-466251.

Talley, H. L. (2014) *Saving Face: Disfigurement and the Politics of Appearance*. New York University Press.

Tappolet, C. (2022) *Philosophy of Emotion: A Contemporary Introduction*. Abingdon: Taylor & Francis.

Taylor, D. (2023) '"This is what survivors look like": the romance fraud victims who want to help others', *Guardian*, 26 November. Available at: www.theguardian.com/money/2023/nov/26/this-is-what-survivors-look-like-the-romance-victims-who-want-to-help-others.

Taylor, M. J. (2023) 'In defense of negging', *The Cut*. Available at: www.thecut.com/article/negging-flirting.html.

Taylor, P. (2016) 'Dark lovely yet and; Or, how to love black bodies while hating black people', in P. Taylor (ed.), *Black Is Beautiful*. Hoboken, NJ: John Wiley & Sons, Ltd.

Taylor, Jr, S. (2003) 'Santorum on sex: where the slippery slope leads', *Atlantic*, 1 May. Available at: www.theatlantic.com/politics/archive/2003/05/santorum-on-sex-where-the-slippery-slope-leads/378140.

Tennov, D. (1979) *Love and Limerence: The Experience of Being in Love*. Scarborough House.

Teo, A. R., Choi, H., and Valenstein, M. (2013) 'Social relationships and depression: ten-year follow-up from a nationally representative study', *PLOS ONE*, 8(4), e62396.

Tersman, F. (2018) 'Recent work on reflective equilibrium and method in ethics', *Philosophy Compass*, 13(6), e12493.

Teut, J. (2019) 'Asexuality, the internet, and the changing lexicon of sexuality', in C. Cottet and M. Picq (eds.), *Sexuality and Translation in World Politics*. Bristol: E-International Relations.

'The preferred choice of Brits for surnames upon marriage' (2023). Available at: https://yougov.co.uk/topics/society/trackers/the-preferred-choice-of-brits-for-surnames-upon-marriage?crossBreak=male.

Thomas, T. (2023) 'Meet the parents: Tinder introduces approval tool for friends and family', *Guardian*, 23 October. Available at: www.theguardian.com/technology/2023/oct/23/meet-the-parents-tinder-introduces-matchmaker-approval-tool-for-friends-and-family.

Thomason, K. K. (2018) *Naked: The Dark Side of Shame and Moral Life*. Oxford University Press.

Thomason, K. K. (2024) *Dancing with the Devil: Why Bad Feelings Make Life Good*. Oxford University Press.

Tilton, E. C. R. and Ichikawa, J. J. (2021) 'Not what I agreed to: content and consent', *Ethics*, 132(1), pp. 127–54.

Timmermans, E. and De Caluwé, E. (2017) 'Development and validation of the Tinder Motives Scale (TMS)', *Computers in Human Behavior*, 70, pp. 341–50.

Timmermans, E., Hermans, A.-M., and Opree, S. J. (2021) 'Gone with the wind: exploring mobile daters' ghosting experiences', *Journal of Social and Personal Relationships*, 38(2), pp. 783–801.

Tinder (2023) 'Tinder backs government campaign to tackle loneliness', Tinder UK Newsroom. Available at: https://uk.tinderpressroom.com/2023-03-07 -Tinder-backs-government-campaign-to-tackle-loneliness.

Tong, A. (2023) 'What happens when your AI chatbot stops loving you back?', Reuters, 21 March. Available at: www.reuters.com/technology/what-happens -when-your-ai-chatbot-stops-loving-you-back-2023-03-18.

Townsend, C. (2024) 'Men found a surprising new way to lie on dating apps', Mashable. Available at: https://mashable.com/article/men-gaming-dating-app -algorithms-by-switching-sexualities.

Tsai, G. (2016) 'Vulnerability in intimate relationships', *Southern Journal of Philosophy*, 54(S1), pp. 166–82.

Turkle, S., et al. (2006) 'Relational artifacts with children and elders: the complexities of cybercompanionship', *Connection Science*, 18(4), pp. 347–61.

Turner, B. (2022) 'Britain's longest married couple celebrate 81st wedding anniversary – after pals said "they wouldn't last long"', *Scotsman*, 15 January. Available at: www.scotsman.com/news/people/britains-longest-married-couple -celebrate-81st-wedding-anniversary-3528821.

Tweedy, A. (2011) 'Polyamory as a sexual orientation', *University of Cincinnati Law Review*, 79(4), pp. 1461–515.

UK Gov (2021) 'Leading dating apps partner with government to boost vaccine uptake', GOV.UK. Available at: www.gov.uk/government/news/leading-dating -apps-partner-with-government-to-boost-vaccine-uptake.

Utz, C., et al. (2019) '(Un)informed consent: studying GDPR consent notices in the field', in *Proceedings of the 2019 ACM SIGSAC Conference on Computer and Communications Security*. New York: Association for Computing Machinery (CCS '19).

van Anders, S. M. (2015) 'Beyond sexual orientation: integrating gender/sex and diverse sexualities via sexual configurations theory', *Archives of Sexual Behavior*, 44(5), pp. 1177–213.

van Hooft, S. (1996) 'Commitment and the bond of love', *Australasian Journal of Philosophy*, 74(3), pp. 454–66.

Varelius, J. (2008) 'On the prospects of collective informed consent', *Journal of Applied Philosophy*, 25(1), pp. 35–44.

Vernon, M. (2005). *The Philosophy of Friendship*. London: Palgrave Macmillan.

Vogels, E. A. and Mcclain, C. (2023) 'Key findings about online dating in the U.S.', Pew Research Center. Available at: www.pewresearch.org/short-reads/2023/02 /02/key-findings-about-online-dating-in-the-u-s.

Walker, M. U. (2007) *Moral Understandings: A Feminist Study in Ethics*. 2nd edn. New York: Oxford University Press.

Walker, T. (2012) 'Informed consent and the requirement to ensure understanding', *Journal of Applied Philosophy*, 29(1), pp. 50–62.

Ward, C. and Anderson, E. (2022) 'The ethical significance of being an erotic object', in D. Boonin (ed.), *The Palgrave Handbook of Sexual Ethics*. Cham: Springer International Publishing.

Ward, J. (2020) *The Tragedy of Heterosexuality*. New York University Press.

Weigel, M. (2017) *Labor of Love: The Invention of Dating*. Reprint edn. New York: FSG Adult.

Weikart, R. (1994) 'Marx, Engels, and the abolition of the family', *History of European Ideas*, 18(5), pp. 657–72.

Weiss, S. (2024) '10 lesser-known uses for dating apps', www.top10.com. Available at: www.top10.com/dating/10-lesser-known-uses-for-dating-apps.

Wertheimer, A. (1999) 'What is consent and is it important?', *Buffalo Criminal Law Review*, 3, p. 557.

Wertheimer, A. (2003) *Consent to Sexual Relations*. Cambridge; New York: Cambridge University Press.

West, R. (2002) 'The harms of consensual sex', in A. Soble (ed.), *The Philosophy of Sex: Contemporary Readings*. 4th edn. Lanham, Md.: Rowman & Littlefield.

West, R. (2017) 'The harms of consensual sex', in R. Halwani et al. (eds.), *The Philosophy of Sex: Contemporary Readings*. 7th edn. Lanham, Md.: Rowman & Littlefield.

Whitlow, T. R. and Laskowski, N. G. (2023) 'Categorical phenomenalism about sexual orientation', *Philosophy and Phenomenological Research*, 106(3), pp. 581–96.

Whitney, S. Y. (2011) 'Dependency relations: corporeal vulnerability and norms of personhood in Hobbes and Kittay', *Hypatia*, 26(3), pp. 554–74.

Whittaker, R. (2024) 'Bumble founder thinks we aren't too far away from AI dating for you', *Forbes*. Available at: www.forbes.com.au/news/innovation /bumble-ai-dating-concierge.

Widdows, H. (2020) *Perfect Me: Beauty as an Ethical Ideal*. Reprint edn. Princeton University Press.

Williams, A. (2024) *Not My Type: Automating Sexual Racism in Online Dating*. Stanford University Press.

Williams, Z. (2024) 'The Icelandic love secret: should we all try "sex before coffee"?', *Guardian*, 7 August. Available at: www.theguardian.com/lifeandstyle /article/2024/aug/07/icelandic-love-secret-sex-before-coffee.

Winter-Gray, T. and Hayfield, N. (2021) '"Can I be a kinky ace?": how asexual people negotiate their experiences of kinks and fetishes', *Psychology & Sexuality*, 12(3), pp. 163–79.

Wonderly, M. (2016) 'On being attached', *Philosophical Studies*, 173(1), pp. 223–42.

Wonderly, M. (2017) 'Love and attachment', *American Philosophical Quarterly*, 54(3), pp. 232–50.

Wonderly, M. (2021) 'Agency and varieties of felt necessity', *Ethics*, 132(1), pp. 155–79.

Woodard, E. (2022) 'Bad sex and consent', in D. Boonin (ed.), *The Palgrave Handbook of Sexual Ethics*. Priniceton, NJ: Springer International Publishing.

Woollard, F. (2019) 'Promiscuity, pedophilia, rape, and the significance of the sexual', *Public Affairs Quarterly*, 33(2), pp. 137–58.

Woollard, F. and Weaver, B. R. (2008) 'Marriage and the norm of monogamy', *Monist*, 91(3 & 4), pp. 506–22.

Wosick-Correa, K. (2010) 'Agreements, rules and agentic fidelity in polyamorous relationships', *Psychology & Sexuality*, 1(1), pp. 44–61.

Wright, D. (2011) *Downs: The History of a Disability*. Oxford University Press.

Wu, H., et al. (2023) 'Gender roles in the millennium: who pays and is expected to pay for romantic dates?', *Psychological Reports*, 126(2), pp. 791–811.

Yancey, G. and Emerson, M. O. (2016) 'Does height matter? An examination of height preferences in romantic coupling', *Journal of Family Issues*, 37(1), pp. 53–73.

Yancy, G. (2016) 'White embodied gazing, the black body as disgust, and the aesthetics of un-suturing', in S. Irvin (ed.), *Body Aesthetics*. Oxford University Press.

York, K. (2024) 'A couple of reasons in favor of monogamy', *Journal of Social Philosophy*, 55(1), pp. 106–23.

Young, I. M. (2011) *Justice and the Politics of Difference*. Princeton University Press.

Yule, M. A., Brotto, L. A. and Gorzalka, B. B. (2017) 'Sexual fantasy and masturbation among asexual individuals: an in-depth exploration', *Archives of Sexual Behavior*, 46(1), pp. 311–28.

Zhang, C., et al. (2023) 'Large language models for human–robot interaction: a review', *Biomimetic Intelligence and Robotics*, 3(4), pp. 1–15.

Zheng, R. (2016) 'Why yellow fever isn't flattering: a case against racial fetishes', *Journal of the American Philosophical Association*, 2(3), pp. 400–19.

Zheng, R. (2021) 'Moral criticism and structural injustice', *Mind*, 130(518), pp. 503–35.

Zuckerman, E. (2020) 'The case for digital public infrastructure'. Available at: http://knightcolumbia.org/content/the-case-for-digital-public-infrastructure.

Zurn, P. (2021) 'Feminist curiosity', *Philosophy Compass*, 16(9), e12761.

Zurn, P., et al. (2024). *Trans Philosophy*. University of Minnesota Press.

Index

good curiosity 70–4
good ghosts 90–3
good life 122–8
goods, derived from love 191–2
government roles, dating apps 57–9
Green, L. 114
Greer, G. and Tolbert, R. 189
grief and break-ups 87–8
Grindr 46, 57, 58
Gunkel, J. 12–15, 80, 102
Gupta, K. 10, 11

habit of attraction 33, 34
and habituation/re-habituation 35–6
Hackman, R. 173–4
Halwani, R. 4, 30, 117, 126, 133–4, 138
harms *see* emotional harms
Haslanger, S. 11
Healey, R. 83–6, 89, 90
'heightism' 31
Her (film) 184–5
Herbenick, D., et al. 169–70
Herer, M. 134
hermeneutic labour, unequal 174–5
heterosexuality
    tragedy of 118–19, 120–1
    see also feminist perspectives
hiddenness and importance of intimate
        zone 13–14
'hierarchical polyamory' 155
Hochschild, A. 173
homosexuality *see* queer/LGBT
        individuals
Hornsby, R. and McKeever, N. 183
Humphries, J. 14
Hurd, H. 96

Ichikawa, J. 111–12
    Rees, M. and 110–11
    Tilton, E. C. R. and 100, 102, 103
identification and deep heterosexuality
        120, 121
identity and orientation, notions of 17
individual user roles, dating apps 59–62
infatuation 136
infidelity/cheating 156, 159
information and consent 96–7
    withholding/deception 102–3
integrity
    vs chastity 126–7

vs compatibility dating 72
intimacy
    and flirting 76–9, 80
    and romantic love 147
    and sex 9–12
intimate zones 12–16, 80, 102
Iran, dating apps 40, 58
Irvin, S. 35

Jankowiak, W. and Fischer, E. 140, 141
Jaworska, A. and Wonderly, M. 147
Jenkins, C. 75–6, 77, 78, 134, 139, 140,
        149, 169
Jollimore, T. 130, 135, 137–8, 184–5, 186
Jonze, S. 184

Kant, I. 113–14, 117, 123
Keller, S. 132, 149
Khattar, V., et al. 48
Klesse, C. 25–6
knowledge, dating 67, 68, 69, 70, 71–2
Kolodny, N. 150–2
Kukla, Q. 75, 79, 103–6, 109–10, 115,
        116

Laan, E. T. M., et al. 170
labels 16–26
Lamb, S., et al. 116
Lamont, E. 168
Langton, R. 114, 115
Leeds Revolutionary Feminists Collective
        167–8
lesbian feminism / political lesbianism
        120, 121, 167–8
Levant, R. F. 175
Levy, D. 149, 183–4
LGBT *see* queer/LGBT individuals;
        sexual orientation
Liao, M. 157
limerence 134, 136
Lintott, S. and Irvin, S. 34–5, 121
lookism 30, 32
Lopez-Cantero, P. 134–6
love drugs 188–9
    authenticity 191–3
    risks 190–1
love robots *see* robots
Lugones, M. 69, 122

Marino, P. 5